"*Cultural Identity and the Purposes of G* [...]
I have read in recent years on the subjec[t ...]
purposes for cultural identity. Bryan's in[...]
passages reveals new understandings be[...]
Revelation, including the account of the [...] ...ation of Israel,
events in the Gospels, conflicts in the early church, and the visions in Revelation. These biblical insights, combined with commentary on today's issues, illuminate pervasive blind spots, demystify certain passages (such as the apparent genocide of Canaan), and equip us to act on principles that align with God's call to spread the gospel in ways that both destabilize and renew cultures. I recommend this book to all mission workers and all believers who seek greater self-awareness about their own cultural identity and the dynamics of culture. I recommend it to all who desire to act with greater clarity, compassion, and redemptive impact in contexts where we face unprecedented cultural, ethnic, national, and racial conflicts."

Joshua Bogunjoko, International Director, SIM

"This book does not provide simple answers, based on a few proof texts, to the complex issues surrounding ethnicity, nationality, and race. Instead, Bryan harvests the rich biblical theology behind the portrayal of diversity in the Bible and provides teaching that is vitally needed for our confused generation."

Ajith Fernando, Teaching Director, Youth for Christ, Sri Lanka; author, *Discipling in a Multicultural World*

"Among the heated arguments and rancorous debates that characterize much Western conversation, expressions such as *culture, ethnicity, race, cultural identity, assimilation, individualism,* and *diversity* are dropped into live discussions like grenades. It takes a few minutes to grasp how these words mean different things to different people, and are often deployed with more zeal than insight—the purpose being to score points, not win arguments. What a pleasure it is, then, to read Steven Bryan's learned and evenhanded book and to listen in on presentations that are mature, reasoned, and convincing. Better yet, the stances Dr. Bryan adopts are grounded in careful exegesis and wonderfully refreshing biblical theology. It could have been written only by a faithful and competent biblical scholar who has spent many years in fresh study of Scripture while being immersed in more than one culture. This is not a book to skim, it is a book to ponder."

D. A. Carson, Cofounder and Theologian-at-Large, The Gospel Coalition

"In this book, Steven Bryan helps us to see culture holistically and redemptively by weaving biblical theology into this all-important study. We travel together, surveying cultural identity in the beauty of creation, the tragic results of the fall, and the hope reignited in the winding path of redemption and the new creation. This fresh approach leaves us appreciating the differences in the variety of cultures and how God's plan will finally make us one people, with Christ being our ultimate identity. This tour de force is worth putting your teeth into. It will certainly mature and enrich you!"

Conrad Mbewe, Pastor, Kabwata Baptist Church, Lusaka, Zambia; Founding Chancellor, African Christian University

Cultural Identity and
the Purposes of God

Cultural Identity and the Purposes of God

A Biblical Theology of Ethnicity, Nationality, and Race

Steven M. Bryan

WHEATON, ILLINOIS

Library of Congress Cataloging-in-Publication Data

Names: Bryan, Steven M., author.
Title: Cultural identity and the purposes of God : a biblical theology of ethnicity, nationality, and race / Steven M. Bryan.
Description: Wheaton, Illinois : Crossway, 2022. | Includes bibliographical references and index.
Identifiers: LCCN 2021044913 (print) | LCCN 2021044914 (ebook) | ISBN 9781433569739 (trade paperback) | ISBN 9781433569746 (pdf) | ISBN 9781433569753 (mobipocket) | ISBN 9781433569760 (epub)
Subjects: LCSH: Christianity and culture. | Multiculturalism—Religious Aspects—Christianity. | Cultural pluralism—Religious Aspects—Christianity. | Ethnicity—Religious aspects—Christianity.
Classification: LCC BR115.C8 B78 2022 (print) | LCC BR115.C8 (ebook) | DDC 261—dc23
LC record available at https://lccn.loc.gov/2021044913
LC ebook record available at https://lccn.loc.gov/2021044914

Crossway is a publishing ministry of Good News Publishers.

BP		30	29	28	27	26	25	24	23	22
14	13	12	11	10	9	8	7	6	5	4	3	2	1

To Dawn

Contents

Preface

THOUGH INTENDED BY GOD to be a rich source of blessing, differences in collective identity have instead become one of humanity's greatest sources of conflict, suspicion, alienation, and violence. The animosity engendered by cultural difference has also cut deep chasms within the church. No less than others, Christians have struggled to understand and respond to the many ways in which our sense of belonging to a group shapes our experience of life and our perceptions of those who belong to other groups. As a result, these differences in collective identity and the cultural expressions that mark them out easily become a source of distrust and division.

Scripture, however, casts a vision for the recovery of cultural identity as a means of blessing for all peoples. The aim of this book is to enable Christians to see and experience the restoration of this blessing.

A New Testament scholar by training, I have spent most of my adult life teaching outside of my passport country. In doing so, I have come to appreciate the profound importance of biblical theology to the life of God's people around the world. I have witnessed the maturity and faith that come as Christians grasp the way in which the various parts of Scripture work together to tell a unified story of God's purposes. These experiences and convictions come together in the pages that follow.

The origins of this book may be traced to a seminar on ethnicity that I helped lead several years ago at the Ethiopian Graduate School of Theology. It was in that seminar that I began to grasp something of the centrality of cultural identity to the purposes of God. Over the course of more than two decades of living and teaching in Ethiopia, I experienced a growing appreciation of the power and importance of cultural identity as a fundamental feature of human existence. But I could also see the profound struggle within most nations to hold cultural multiplicity within themselves. As I finished writing the book, ethnic tensions that had long simmered in Ethiopia erupted in civil war. In one sense, the war is news, but in another, it is part of an age-old story.

That story is told and retold wherever culturally distinct groups come together within a larger whole, from ancient empires to modern states. To be sure, the way the story is told varies with the particularities of the cultural groups involved and of the contexts in which they interact with one another. Thus, after returning to the United States, I was quickly reminded that the fault lines here are more regularly marked out in other ways. Ethnicity plays a part, but more often cultural identity is defined in racial or national terms.

However cultural identity is conceived, the tensions that arise when cultures collide have led many to think that cultural difference is itself a problem. Many have succumbed to the temptation of thinking that cultural multiplicity within a society is ultimately unworkable and must somehow be prevented, banished, or reduced. Many who identify as Christians have found themselves implicated in a global resurgence of ethnonationalism—the belief that a nation should be culturally singular. Others have supported regimes of cultural dominance or insularity. However, to take such views is to suppose that cultural multiplicity plays no part within the purposes of God or is itself a problem to overcome.

The vulnerability of Christians to such temptations increases dramatically when they take a limited view of what Scripture is about. For many Christians, the Bible is fundamentally about the relationship between God and the individual. In important ways, this is true. But it is far from the whole story. The aim of this book is to explore what Scripture has to say about God's purposes not only for people but also for peoples. As we shall see, the Bible situates individuals within families and families within peoples. Further, the relationship between peoples turns out to be a crucial, if often overlooked, feature of the biblical story. Only by understanding God's intentions for peoples can we live in the world as God intended and live in hope of the world to come.

I owe a great debt to a generation of Ethiopian students who graciously engaged my attempts to set my not fully formed understanding of God's purposes into a not fully formed understanding of Ethiopian cultural and ecclesial realities. My hope is that many of them will benefit from this book as a more developed form of ideas that began to take shape in those years together. I am especially grateful to much-cherished Ethiopian colleagues from several intersecting spheres of life and ministry. Three of them—Worku Haile-Mariam, Donek Tesfaye, and Bekele Deboch—read all or part of this manuscript amid the pressures of a pandemic and the tragedy of war. If there is balm in these pages for the wounds of a nation, it will be applied by men and women like these.

When the manuscript was still rough, Nydiaris Hernández-Santos organized a group of students from Trinity Evangelical Divinity School, where I now teach, to meet by Zoom to read and discuss each chapter. The members of the group came from a variety of cultures from around the world. I am told that the discussions were reliably lively! Nydiaris's weekly distillation of comments from the group led to many substantive improvements. Judging from the experience of the group, I think the greatest value of the book may well come as it is read and discussed in culturally diverse groups like this one. Many of the questions posed to the group by Nydiaris have found their way into the discussion questions posed for each chapter. I am deeply grateful to George Aidoo, Caroline Thao, Kazusa Okaya, Eliezer Brayley, Alan Lee, Miranda George, Jinsook Kim, and especially Nydiaris.

My untiring graduate assistant, Olle Larson, undertook the enormous task of tidying and trimming the manuscript, squeezing it into a busy summer of ministry. In the course of doing so, he asked a number of questions that sharpened—and shortened!—the argument. My sister, Shawna Loyd, read the whole manuscript and chipped away considerable dross. Each of my three sons—Jack, Cooper, and Cy—read all or parts of the book on short notice, leaving me to marvel at how I came to have such clear-thinking and well-read offspring. In addition to providing excellent company, they served up editorial acumen, cultural insight, and gentle critique that made the final stages of the writing process fun. Our beloved daughter-in-law Hannah has brought much joy into our family, not least for her uncommon warmth and straightforward openness. Our backyard conversations about a host of things, including this book, were a summerlong delight.

The last of my in-house editors to read the manuscript was my mother. When I was convinced that there were no more infelicities left to find, she found plenty. Her late-stage editorial work was but one of the many ways that she and Dad have supported me over many years. I can only hope that I will approach eighty with as much acuity, grace, and love for God and family as she has.

I dedicate the book to my wife, Dawn. I cannot imagine a more well-informed, engaged, and encouraging partner in thought for the ideas of this book. I may have put them onto paper, but she puts them into practice every day with consummate wisdom and skill.

1

Ethnicity, Nationality, and Race

The Problem of Cultural Identity

I have a dream.

MARTIN LUTHER KING JR. (AUGUST 28, 1963)

I had a dream.

NEBUCHADNEZZAR (DAN. 2:3)

LONG BEFORE MARTIN LUTHER KING JR. shared his dream on a warm August day in 1963, another leader of another sort had a very different dream. Unlike MLK, Nebuchadnezzar, king of Babylon, refused to share his dream. He had no idea what it meant, and he was afraid of it. When a young Hebrew exile deciphered its meaning, this nation-conquering king may have been unsurprised to learn that he had dreamed of empires. But his dream augured ill not only for his empire but for all that would follow.

In his dream, the king had seen an enormous four-part statue in human form. "The head of this image was of fine gold, its chest and arms of silver, its middle and thighs of bronze, its legs of iron, its feet partly of iron and partly of clay" (Dan. 2:32–33). Nebuchadnezzar was doubtless happy to learn that he and his empire were the head of gold, though less happy to hear that his empire would be followed by three more. Scholars still debate the identities of the four empires, but the more salient point may be that there were four. One of the most frequent keys to the interpretation of biblical dreams is numbers,[1] and the number four frequently symbolizes the earth in its totality.[2] Both individually and together, the four empires represented human dominion over the whole earth and its peoples.

However, there was a weakness in the feet of the statue, rendering the whole of human dominion unstable and fragile. The feet, we are told, were formed from a mixture of iron and clay. The iron, of course, was the material of the final empire (the legs), but the weakness of the feet undermined the strength of the whole. Though empires claim to enfold the peoples of their domain into a unified whole, the rhetoric of unity never quite matches the reality. As the young Hebrew explained it, the mixture of materials represented a mixing of peoples who "will not remain united, any more than iron mixes with clay" (Dan. 2:43 NIV).[3] As a result, every empire stands on feet of clay.

A weakness of human dominion in virtually every form arises from the challenge of incorporating peoples who differ from one another into one people. Is it even possible to forge one people from many? The waking dream of Martin Luther King Jr. was a response to one tragi-

---

1   John Joseph Collins and Adela Yarbro Collins, *Daniel: A Commentary on the Book of Daniel*, Hermeneia (Minneapolis: Fortress, 1993), 166.

2   Moisés Silva, ed., *New International Dictionary of New Testament Theology and Exegesis* (Grand Rapids, MI: Zondervan, 2014), 4:486.

3   Translations of Daniel 2:43 vary, reflecting a difference of opinion among commentators regarding the meaning of the Hebrew idiom "mixing of seed." Commentators who regard the fourth kingdom as Greece take this as a reference to an unsuccessful attempt to forge unity between the Seleucid and Ptolemaic dynasties through intermarriage, perhaps in the hope of recovering a unified Greek empire. Conservative commentators tend to regard the fourth kingdom as Rome and understand the verse as a reference to the attempt to forge unity between the various peoples that comprised the empire: "As diversity of languages split up the Tower of Babel, so the inability of cultures within this empire to live in peace dismantles this behemoth of destruction. [Cultural multiplicity] would become tribalism and the social and political fabric of the empire would not hold." Eugene Carpenter, "Daniel," in *Cornerstone Biblical Commentary: Ezekiel & Daniel* (Carol Stream, IL: Tyndale House, 2010), 346.

cally common "solution" to the problem—for one people to subjugate all others. Against this, King called for a renewed focus on individuals. The best ideals of America—the ideals of equality, freedom, and justice—were rooted in the biblical notion that every individual is made in the image of God and equally endowed with dignity and worth. As a result, King longed for the day when his children would "not be judged by the color of their skin but by the content of their character."[4]

Some have supposed that these well-known words reflect an aspiration for a nation no longer comprised of *peoples* but of *individuals*. To be sure, King's vision placed the individual squarely into focus, but he was addressing a nation accustomed to thinking about not just individuals but also groups. In that context, King reasoned that if all individuals are equal, the fact that they belong to different groups should not and must not change that fact.

King certainly knew that groups also matter, even if group membership has no bearing on the dignity and worth of the individual. But how do they matter? How should we think about the relationship between the groups that make up a society? Is the multiplicity of groups within a society even *good?* Or should the only group be the nation as a whole? These questions, in turn, point us to more fundamental questions. What does it mean for a nation to be a nation? Is a nation a collection of individuals or of peoples? Can a nation have many cultures or must it have only one? If a nation has many peoples, each with its own identity, what is the nature of their national identity? Can they even have one? Can a nation contain within it many peoples or will such a mixing of peoples always lead to weakness, division, and, ultimately, dissolution?

Individuals and Cultures: The Question of Identity

To ask these questions reflects the fact that a fundamental dimension of human existence, well attested in both experience and Scripture, is that humans are social, relational beings. That fact inexorably

4   Martin Luther King Jr., "I Have a Dream," American Rhetoric, https://www.american rhetoric.com/.

results in the formation of groups—a process described early in Scripture and assumed throughout its pages. This does not mean that the groups to which we belong gather together and function in an intentionally coordinated way—only that human social inter-actions invariably result in a sense of belonging, derived from an awareness of similarity with some and difference from others.[5] As we shall see, there are different types of groups. Some people think of their groups in ethnic terms; others think in national terms; still others identify themselves in racial terms. These are not the only possibilities. Scripture, for instance, speaks of "tribes" and "clans"—forms of social organization that remain important in some parts of the world today. There are important differences between these forms of collective identity, and we will need to understand them if we are to make sense of the biblical witness regarding the nature of groups. However, though the forms of collective identity vary, the phenomenon itself is universal.

Not only is the phenomenon of group identity universal, it is often multiple: it is possible for people to sense that they belong to more than one group. This can happen with a child who has parents who come from different groups, for example. It can also happen because people identify with more than one kind of group. An Ethiopian friend from some years ago won a lottery for the US State Department's Diversity Visa program. Shortly after arriving in the United States, he joined the US Army, served in Iraq, and eventually became a US citizen. For those reasons (and others), he thought of himself as an American. However,

---

5   Certain theorists have criticized the application of the term *group* to social categories of people; so especially, Rogers Brubaker, *Ethnicity without Groups* (Cambridge: Harvard University Press, 2004). However, in using the term *group*, I am not suggesting that the "groups" to which people belong are actual groups, conceived as relatively homogenous, bounded, socially organized sets of people whose actions are coordinated. Rather a group to which we apply terms such as *ethnicity* may be only a loose collectivity, "the members of which recognize its existence and their membership in it." So Richard Jenkins, *Rethinking Ethnicity* (London: Sage, 2008), 26. As Jenkins notes, even if there is no actual group, we feel that we are members of a group. Our perception of membership refers to the subjective sense of belonging that emerges from social interactions that produce an awareness of similarity with some and difference from others.

he also still thought of himself as an Ethiopian. When he was with other Ethiopians, he sometimes identified as an Amhara—one of Ethiopia's many ethnic groups. As these examples imply, there are not only different kinds of groups, but different ways of belonging to groups. A person might identify with one group in certain circumstances and with another group in other situations.

Our sense of belonging to a group or groups is shaped in part by the fact that we intuitively recognize similarity. That recognition creates a feeling of affinity. That sense of affinity or kinship influences the way we think and act, often in ways we might not realize. Our sense of belonging to a group is also shaped by our awareness of other groups. Thus, when we see others as belonging to a different group, we intuitively respond in ways that reflect that fact—for good and for ill. This instinctive response to "otherness" need not be oppositional. Often, however, it is.

To recognize group identity is not to deny the obvious fact of variation between individuals who belong to the same group. Thus, it is possible to distinguish between personal identity and collective identity.[6] Still, groups, as such, do not have an identity in the way that individuals do. In fact, we may think of collective identity as a dimension of personal identity.[7] Whereas personal identity focuses on my sense of self that I share with no one else, collective identity focuses on the sense of self that I share with others—the recognition that I share ways of thinking, speaking, and acting with others whom I believe to be like me. We may account for *why* we share these commonalities in different ways. But all individuals form a sense of personal identity, in part, through the experience of belonging to a group.

6   For recent discussions of personal identity from a Christian perspective, see Klyne Snodgrass, *Who God Says You Are: A Christian Understanding of Identity* (Grand Rapids, MI: Eerdmans, 2018) and Brian S. Rosner, *Known by God: A Biblical Theology of Personal Identity* (Grand Rapids, MI: Zondervan, 2017).

7   Jenkins draws on the anthropologist Clifford Geertz's well-known definition of ethnicity as "socially ratified personal identity" and concludes that it is "collective and individual, externalized in social interaction and the categorization of others, and internalized in personal self-identification." *Rethinking Ethnicity*, 13–14.

To this point, I have primarily used the term "collective identity," but much of what I have said thus far has to do with a particular form of collective identity—that is, cultural identity. We could imagine other kinds of collectives—"all students" or "all children," for example—and even speak meaningfully about common features of such groups. But we would soon discover that the dissimilarities between individuals within those groups outweigh the traits they share. The similarities within these broad collectives do not constitute a whole pattern of life within which members make sense of the world. By contrast, in speaking of "culture," we are talking about a constellation of similarities in the ways that the members of a group think, speak, and act. Those similarities coalesce into a kind of playbook that guides our actions and interactions. That playbook not only contains implicit rules for how we play the game, but constantly evolves as the rules evolve and plays are added, changed, or struck from the playbook. Individuals choose how they want to play the game, but they choose their plays from the playbook.

Though notoriously difficult to define, the word *culture* remains widely used and useful. The term suffers somewhat from being used in widely different ways, but is commonly used to describe the sense that we belong to a people. Thus, when we speak of cultural identity, we are speaking of "peoplehood." Business leaders often speak of their "corporate culture." I teach at a university where we sometimes refer to the "campus culture." Although these "cultures" shape our sense of self in some ways, it would be odd to describe the environment of the company or school where I work as a meaningful part of my "cultural identity." At a workplace or on a campus, there may be a shared "language" and a way of doing things that people share while there. But that is not *my* culture. I get this not so much from places with people, but from a people who have a place that they think of as their own. Cultural identity, then, is the sense that I belong to a people and make sense of the world in relation to the constellation of norms and values, beliefs and practices associated with that people.

Nations, Cultures, and Individuals:
Modern States and an Ancient Problem

If individuals have a cultural identity by virtue of belonging to a people, how does this shape what it means for a nation to be a nation? Or, to ask the question differently, what is the relationship between cultural identity and nationality? Can a nation comprise more than one people and, if so, how?

To consider these questions in a modern context means that we must think about "states." The term *state* refers to internationally recognized political sovereignty over a territory with defined borders, together with the institutions and order that preserve and maintain that sovereignty.[8] Though the two terms are sometimes used interchangeably, *state* and *nation* can be distinguished. Whereas a state is a government, a nation is a people. Often we think of a nation as the people governed by a state, and nationality as a form of identity that comes from a sense of belonging to that nation. But if the nation is a people, what about cultural groups inside a nation?

At the heart of debates about political systems are conflicting conceptions of the relationship between individuals, groups, nations, and states. The deepest divisions in these debates have to do with the nature of the relationship between the varying cultural identities of the peoples governed by the state and the national identity fostered by the state.

---

8   A state in this sense should be distinguished from the use of the term to refer to the internal states (plural) that come under the authority of the state (singular). So, for example, the states of the United States or India have only limited sovereignty. Nigeria and Australia are also examples of states that have internal states. Other states have internal entities of other names and types, such as provinces (e.g., Saskatchewan in Canada), territories (e.g., Puerto Rico in the United States), countries (e.g., England, Scotland, Wales, and Northern Ireland in the UK), and even nations (e.g., the Cherokee Nation within the United States). A single state can have multiple forms of internal entities, some of which reflect the diversity of peoples under its sovereignty. The cultural identity derived by a sense of belonging to these internal entities can vary widely. Though confusing to some, it is sensible to many Cherokees to have both Cherokee and American nationality, just as it is sensible to many to be both English and British. In some countries, official internal entities often mean rather less from the perspective of cultural identity than internal regions, e.g., "the South" in the United States.

As we see in the following brief survey of the various approaches that states take to the challenge of containing peoples of different cultural identities within one nation, no approach fully resolves Nebuchadnez-zar's dilemma.

1. *Civic Nationalism and the Creation of a National Culture: Individuals Make States, States Make National Identity.* In the years preceding the American and French Revolutions, there emerged a new way of thinking about what it means to be a nation. In the ancient conception, a nation was a people bound by kinship and custom (i.e. ethnicity). But with the Enlightenment, that began to change. The French philosopher Jean-Jacques Rousseau argued that a nation should be formed by "a social contract" between individuals who come together around a set of universal truths about individuals. The social contract, it was held, would bind individuals together within a system of laws and governance designed to protect the "universal," "natural," or "inalienable" rights of individuals.

In this new way of thinking, a nation was formed by individuals whose commonality was a shared set of ideas about the primacy of the individual. This has sometimes been called a "civic nation" as opposed to an "ethnic nation."[9] The cultural identity of a "civic nation" is not the *basis* of nationhood but its by-product. As such, the formation and fostering of national identity—a cultural identity that takes the form of nationality—becomes an ongoing project of the state.[10] Thus, when

9   For the distinction, see especially Anthony Smith, *National Identity* (London: Penguin, 1991), 11–13.

10   Though the term *nation* refers to a people, the nature of that people is disputed. By some accounts, a nation differs very little from an ethnic group. By other accounts, a nation is any group of individuals bound together by the desire to share a common political life. This has given rise to discussions of two types of nations, "ethnic" and "civic." An attempt to mediate between the two regards a nation as a cultural group bound by civic ties, whether or not the culture of that group is that of a single ethnicity. See Nenad Miscevic, "Nationalism," *The Stanford Encyclopedia of Philosophy* (Fall 2020 Edition), https://plato .stanford.edu/, citing Michel Seymour, "On Redefining the Nation," in *Nationalism and Ethnic Conflict: Philosophical Perspectives*, ed. Nenad Miscevic (Chicago: Open Court, 2000), 25–56.

the American founders came together to form a nation, they were self-consciously creating a new kind of nation—one based on certain universally valid affirmations about individuals. In theory, at least, the nation is first an idea about individuals and then a people with a national identity derived from that idea.

The individualism that characterizes many Western societies reflects this fundamental assessment of the individual as properly prior to any conception of the group.[11] Often referred to as "liberalism" or "classical liberalism," its basic assumptions are held not only by "liberals" but also by people who identify as "libertarians," "conservatives," and more. In other words, assumptions about the priority of the individual give rise to a range of political views because of differences over human nature and over the meaning of liberty, equality, and justice. However, the shared assumption remains that the nation begins not with the cultural identity of a group but with universal truths about individuals. In countries such as France, the focus on individuals is so strong that

---

The distinction between ethnic and civic forms of nationality remains useful, not least in grappling with the difference between modern nations (which are often closer to the civic type) and ancient ones (which are closer to the ethnic type), including the various nations to which Scripture refers. What is clearly modern and not ancient is the concept of the state, predicated on principles of international recognition and fixed borders. The influential view of Anthony Smith is that modern nations have their origin in ancient ethnic groups, which he calls *ethnie* (a French word for "ethnic communities"). Thus, Smith both distinguishes ancient nations and modern nations and also sees continuity between them. Partly for this reason, Smith distinguishes between the states of "civic nations" and "nation-states." While nations of both types may have ethnic origins, the term *nation-states* refers only to the small number of countries in which a single ethnic group comprises most or all of the population. See Smith, *The Ethnic Origins of Nations* (Oxford: Blackwell, 1986).

Like ethnic groups, nations of both types are "imagined communities"—an expression coined by Benedict Anderson to express the idea that nations exist as a sociological phenomenon in which the members imagine themselves as a group because of a shared sense of history, language, ethnicity, culture, religion, or ideology. See Benedict Anderson, *Imagined Communities: Reflections on the Origin and Spread of Nationalism*, rev. ed. (London: Verso, 1991).

11   The origins of individualism remain hotly debated. One common idea is that individualism is an outcome of the Reformation, but this idea has met strong resistance. See, for example, Malcolm B. Yarnell, III, *Royal Priesthood in the English Reformation* (Oxford: Oxford University Press, 2013), 1–9.

any discussion of the racial or ethnic identity of groups can easily give offense. In such contexts, the pressure for minority cultures to assimilate to the national culture can be considerable.

2. *Globalization and the Creation of a Global Culture: Individuals Make States, So Who Needs Nations?* If certain truths about individuals are both primary and universal, many have supposed that they are as applicable in Baghdad as they are in Boise. For many, it has been a short step from this notion to the idea that nations can and perhaps should cede all or part of their sovereignty to regional federations or superstates, or perhaps even a global superstate. If states are formed by the consent of individuals to the universal values and norms of an implicit social contract, why not superstates?

In the heady days of the early 1990s, the Soviet Union was flying apart and a "new world order" seemed tantalizingly near. The fall of the iron curtain led many to expect the imminent emergence of a stable social order founded on internationalism, liberal values, and individual human rights. As Francis Fukuyama famously theorized, "What we may be witnessing is not just the end of the Cold War, or the passing of a particular period of post-war history, but the end of history as such . . . the end point of mankind's ideological evolution and the universalization of Western liberal democracy as the final form of human government."[12] Many who shared that view believed that they could see an emerging global order in which nations would either cease to exist or surrender much of their sovereignty to global or international institutions.

The political order anticipated by Fukuyama never materialized, and the concept now appears naive. Still, a kind of global order did emerge with borderless free trade, a free flow of information, and, for some at least, free immigration across increasingly open borders. This global order, often described as "globalization," has a kind of cultural identity associated with it, especially among urban youth for whom

---

12   Francis Fukuyama, "The End of History?," *The National Interest* 16 (1989): 5.

social media and the internet became a powerful medium for a global cultural identity centered in pop culture. I recall stepping into a public minibus on the outskirts of Nairobi a few years ago—packed with people and pulsing with American rap music. Later, when I spoke of it with a friend, he said that he thought that youth in African cities such as Nairobi or Lagos were culturally more similar to youth in Los Angeles than to their own parents. The impact of a globalized culture has been more concentrated not only among youth but also in cities, where access to media facilitates the diffusion of a kind of globalized cultural identity.

While the phenomenon was celebrated by some, others regarded it as destructive. Many of the latter readily embraced calls to "protect" local cultures and traditions against the sameness of a globalized culture. Some of these calls have had a decided ethnonationalist cast.

3. *Ethnonationalism and the Preservation of National Culture: Cultures Are Nations, Each of Which Should Have Its Own State.* Perhaps the most concrete political achievement inspired by a vision for a world of attenuated national identity was the formation of the European Union in the early 1990s. But even as the details of the Maastricht Treaty of 1993 that formed the EU were being worked out, ancient ethnonationalist animosities erupted in the heart of Europe. Scarcely half a century had passed since the Holocaust, and once more "ethnic cleansing" and "genocide" dominated the headlines from Europe with the outbreak of armed conflict in Bosnia. The horrors of the Rwandan genocide soon followed and further highlighted the belief that every ethnic group, every people, and every cultural identity should have its own state, and that the state is properly the manifestation of a single cultural identity. On this understanding, every people is a nation with its own culture. In order to ensure the preservation of that culture, every nation should have its own state.[13]

---

13 Cf. Ernst Gellner's definition of nationalism: "a theory of political legitimacy which requires that ethnic boundaries should not cut across political ones." Gellner, *Nations and Nationalism* (Oxford: Blackwell, 1983), 1. For a Christian critique of nationalism,

The impulses of ethnonationalism that led to two world wars in the twentieth century have by no means disappeared, as Fukuyama had hoped and others had dreamed. Instead, they have morphed. The rise of militant Islam in the late twentieth century gave this old idea a new form. Against the Western dream of a globalized liberal order, the radical vision of Al Qaeda and the Islamic State was for a single Arabized culture centered on a "pure" form of Islam as the basis for a single state.

Ethnonationalist ideologies like these are often deeply opposed to democracy, but they also take root inside of democracies. Among the newer forms of nationalism, we could count "illiberal democracy"— an expression coined by the Hungarian prime minister Victor Orbán to defend the curtailment of a free press and independent judiciary on grounds that liberal institutions oppose the right of the people to preserve the integrity of their national identity and land. Similar nationalist impulses have fueled reactions to a tide of immigration and the growth of minority groups in many of the democracies of North America and Europe on grounds that, without strict limits, cultural outsiders alter the culture of the nation. Common to all such impulses is the notion that a nation should have but one people with one culture—an identity properly expressed in the form of the state and properly protected by the power of the state.

4. *Collectivism and the Protection of a Common Culture: States Are Guardians of a Nation's Culture.* The principles that undergird most Western liberal democracies have little influence in places such as China, Russia, or Iran. In China, for instance, discussion of rights does not focus on the individual alone but on the collective good for which

---

see especially the recent analysis of the thought of Karl Barth in Carys Moseley, *Nations and Nationalism in the Theology of Karl Barth* (Oxford: Oxford University Press, 2013). Moseley traces the development of Barth's repudiation of "the nationalist dogma that every nation must have its own state" and places his thinking about nationalism both within the context of his developing theology of nationality and his experience as a Swiss theologian teaching in Germany until his employment was terminated by the Nazis. Moseley, *Nations and Nationalism*, 13.

the sovereignty of the state is foundational and the interests of the state primary. As the inverse of liberalism, collectivism regards the state as philosophically prior to the individual. But the interests of minority peoples are also suborned to the good of the state. In China, the primary right of the individual is not to liberty but to economic well-being, and this depends on the security and sovereignty of the state.[14] Thus, discussions of the rights of ethnic groups or minority "nationalities" within China begin with the presumption not of individual freedom but of the common good on which individual well-being depends. To the extent that the perception of the common good is tied to a common culture guarded and promoted by the state, the encouragement of cultural diversity within the whole is limited at best. At worst, those whose way of life varies too much from accepted norms and values may be subject to cultural "re-education."

To the extent that people are viewed through the lens of economic class, the desire to reduce economic difference in order to subsume all people within a single class further attenuates the significance of cultural difference in the eyes of the state. However, religion and ethnicity can also generate a political impulse to regard all who come under the authority of the state as an undifferentiated whole, the integrity of which the state seeks to preserve in the interests of national unity and stability.

5. *Ethnic Federalism and the Disappearance of National Identity: States Are Guardians of Multiple Cultures.* The approaches surveyed above have a common focus on the cultivation of a singular national identity, often at the expense of the concerns of constituent cultures— particularly minority cultures. One might say that the pursuit of unity comes at the cost of diversity. But what if the opposite were the case? What if the state focused not on a single national identity but on the identities of its constituent cultures?

---

14 Roland Boer, "The State and Minority Nationalities (Ethnic Groups) in China," in *The Palgrave Handbook of Ethnicity*, ed. Steven Ratuva (Singapore: Palgrave Macmillan, 2019), 93–107.

In 1994, Ethiopia adopted a new constitution and, with it, a new form of government that many regarded as novel, even experimental. If there was anything new under the sun, this seemed to be it. The new form of government was dubbed "Ethnic Federalism" because the constitution made explicit and primary the country's commitment to the "nations, nationalities and peoples" within its borders. Of course, most countries have multiple groups within their borders. A few even acknowledge this plurality in their constitutions, but no country had gone as far in making ethnic diversity "a principle of political organization."[15]

This principle was evident from the opening line of the new constitution. As many have observed, the preamble did not open with "We, the people . . ." but with "We, the nations, nationalities and *peoples* . . ." The point was clear. The nation would be a democracy in some sense but not a Western-style *liberal* democracy premised on the inalienable rights of individuals and held together by a single national culture. Neither would the nation be an empire under the domination of one people, as it had been during the country's long imperial history. And neither would it be a centralized state with a singular cultural identity mediated and guarded by the state, as it had been under seventeen years of communist rule. Instead, it would be a country of peoples, with a state designed to ensure the rights of every ethnic group.

If the novel arrangement secured the rights of each ethnic group, it was less clear whether and how some eighty different peoples could remain unified around a common sense of national identity. The constitution had made Ethiopia a country of peoples, but could it be a people of peoples? The commitment to remain as one unified people was strictly conditional: each group was granted the right to secede from the whole. More importantly, the constitution did not, and per-

---

15   As the noted political philosopher Will Kymlicka put it, Ethiopia was unique in "the explicitness, at the constitutional level, of its affirmation of national [i.e., ethnic] self-determination and the logical consistency with which it attempts to institutionalize that principle." Kymlicka, "Emerging Western Models of Multination Federalism: Are They Relevant for Africa?" in *Ethnic Federalism: The Ethiopian Experience in Comparative Perspective*, ed. David Turton (Oxford: James Currey, 2006), 51–52.

haps could not, ensure that any one people would pursue the good of every other people along with its own.[16]

Before long, it was clear that one ethnic group had become dominant in its control of the nation's power and resources. As suspicion between the various ethnic groups of the country grew and divisions between them became more intense, many wondered whether the unity of the nation could hold. As I write, ethnic conflict tears at the seams of a country in which ethnic identity has become for many the only identity that matters.

6. *Multiculturalism, Identity Politics, and the Attenuation of National Identity: The Secular State as a Response to Diversity.* As we have observed, nearly every country today must deal with the challenge of multiple cultures within their borders—a reality often described with the term *multicultural.* However, as a political philosophy, "multiculturalism" has had a major impact on liberal democracies, which have sought to accommodate the recognition of minority groups within a liberal order predicated on the primacy of the individual.

Initially, the impact of multiculturalism was felt particularly in debates over education. Advocates sought greater recognition of the presence and importance of minority cultures in school curricula as a form of resistance to the assimilationist tendencies of an education wholly shaped by the dominant culture in the name of national unity.

Two leading theorists of multiculturalism have been the Canadian philosophers Will Kymlicka and Charles Taylor. Kymlicka's work has focused in particular on the "group-differentiated rights" of minorities. He initially held that recognition of the rights of constituent cultures did not subvert the liberal focus on the individual because culture provides a necessary context for individuals to exercise their freedom. If liberalism presumes the freedom of individuals to choose, cultures pose the choices. In this view, nationality was little more than a political

16 A point well made by Jack Bryan, "From Rule to Responsibility: A Path Forward for Ethiopia," *Ethiopia Insight,* October 27, 2020, https://www.ethiopia-insight.com/.

identity; the cultural identity of the nation was simply the sum of its constituent cultures. On this understanding, a unified sense of national identity is sublimated to the interests and cultures contained within a country. Or, to put it another way, national identity *is* multicultural. More recently, Kymlicka has stressed the need for liberal democracies to cultivate a common "societal culture" that makes a degree of assimilation of minority cultures unavoidable.[17]

Though Taylor is better known for his work on secularism, his earlier work focused on the problem of diversity within nations.[18] Indeed, he considers the two issues together. Thus, he writes, "We [mistakenly] think that secularism . . . has to do with the relation of the state and religion, whereas in fact it has to do with the (correct) response of the democratic state to diversity."[19] That response should not be to form an antireligious culture, as many suppose, but to form a "political identity" around a common commitment to the basic premises of liberalism—democracy (the consent of individuals to be governed), the rights and freedoms of individuals, and equality—and shared historical, linguistic, or religious traditions.[20] Taylor here clearly means to say that a country needs a collective political identity to make democracy possible, but he carefully avoids saying that it needs a common *cultural* or national identity. Down that road lie the dangers of nationalism.

Criticism of multiculturalism as an attempt to account for multiple cultures within the framework of liberalism has often come from defenders of liberalism in its original form.[21] One important reason for

17 See the summary of Kymlicka's thought in Sarah Song, "Multiculturalism," *The Stanford Encyclopedia of Philosophy* (Fall 2020 Edition), https://plato.stanford.edu/.

18 Charles Taylor, "The Politics of Recognition," in *Multiculturalism: Examining the Politics of Recognition*, ed. Amy Gutmann (Princeton: Princeton University Press, 1994), 25–74.

19 Charles Taylor, "The Meaning of Secularism," *Hedgehog Review* 12 (2010): 25.

20 Taylor, "Meaning," 31.

21 Taylor's fellow Canadian, Jordan Peterson, is well-known for his reassertion of liberalism's focus on the individual: "Your group identity is not your cardinal feature. That's the great discovery of the west. That's why the west is right. And I mean that unconditionally. The west is the only place in the world that has ever figured out that the individual is sovereign. And that's an impossible thing to figure out. It's amazing that we managed it. And it's the key to everything that we've ever done right." Cited in Tim Lott, "Interview:

this has been the fact that the multiculturalist goal of providing greater recognition and rights for minority cultures has been broadened to include a wide variety of groups, including some that come under the umbrella of LGBTQ. As a result, critics are now more likely to decry the rise of "identity politics" and see its focus on group identities of all sorts as corrosive of a national unity predicated on the liberal focus on the individual.

A People of Peoples

The differences between these various approaches to the question of the relationship between nationality on the one hand and ethnicity and race on the other are obviously immense. Yet, no system has proven particularly adept at dealing with the reality of cultural multiplicity within a society. To be sure, though liberalism does not account for groups within a society, it has resources for addressing issues that arise from differences between groups that others do not. Within such a society, Martin Luther King Jr. could appeal to the fundamental value of all individuals, whatever their skin color. But the fact that he had to make that appeal within a supposedly liberal society demonstrates the persistence of Nebuchadnezzar's dilemma—the mixing of peoples within a single polity always seems to make it brittle. Is there another way?

Nebuchadnezzar's dream did not end with an image of an idol with brittle feet. That image gives way to the image of a stone that crushes the idol. This stone strikes at every form of human pretense to dominion over the peoples of the earth, erupting beneath the fragile feet of all earthly power like a newly forming mountain that fills the earth (Dan. 2:34–35). This is the rule of God. Nebuchadnezzar did not see the nature of God's rule over all peoples. He only saw the end of human

Jordan Peterson: "The Pursuit of Happiness Is a Pointless Goal,'" *The Guardian*, January 21, 2018, https://www.theguardian.com/. By contrast, other popular voices come close to saying that liberalism without multiculturalism is racist. This, for instance, is the stance of Robin DiAngelo with respect to the American discourse on race: "To say that whiteness is a standpoint is to say that a significant aspect of white identity is to see oneself as an individual, outside or innocent of race—'just human.'" DiAngelo, *White Fragility: Why It's So Hard for White People to Talk About Racism* (Boston: Beacon, 2018), 29.

dominion brought by the advent of God's rule. He could not see how God's kingdom would address the weakness that marks all human dominion and every political system.

But we can. The mystery of God's purpose for the summing up of all things and all peoples into one has been disclosed (cf. Eph. 1:10). Although many have thought of Scripture as the story of God's purposes for individuals, that is only part of the story. It also reveals the purposes of God for peoples. It casts a vision for the profound significance of cultural identity as a source of blessing within the renewed and unified humanity of the new creation. In doing so, it never loses sight of individuals. Rather, it announces the good news that God in Christ has justified individuals and made that justification the basis for the fulfillment of his purpose to form a people of peoples. In contexts riven with ethnic and racial hatreds, it shows his people how to live in hope of the full and final fulfillment of his purposes for all peoples within one people.

2

The Divine Vision

God's Intention for a World
Teeming with Peoples

*But what are nations? What are these groups which are so
familiar to us, and yet, if we stop to think, so strange . . . ?*

WALTER BAGEHOT, IN *PHYSICS AND POLITICS* (1872)

GROWING UP, I never thought much about culture. I never had to.
Culture is something you may not know you have until you meet someone who has a different one or have the unpleasant experience of being
treated as different. I didn't have that experience growing up. Rather
ironically, the small southwest Kansas town where I spent my early years
was called "Liberal," and the people I knew were all pretty much like me.

Occasionally, missionaries would come to our small Baptist church
with stories of faraway peoples. Their customs seemed odd, and it was
easy to assume that the American way of doing things was better. In
my culturally monolithic hometown, I would have been shocked to
learn of the extraordinary variety of cultures within America even then.

Years later, I went back to Liberal and was startled by how much
the town had changed. Several agricultural industries had come into

the area, attracting migrant workers and a number of immigrant communities, including a large population of Somalis. More than half the population spoke a language other than English. A recent public health campaign for the area had gone out in ten different languages in videos posted to a YouTube channel called "It's a Beautiful Day in Our Neighborhood."

Compared to my early years in Liberal, it was a new day. But not everyone thought it was beautiful. Some took steps to recover the cultural monolith of the past. Three area residents hatched a plan to bomb a predominantly Somali apartment complex in the nearby town of Garden City. They were caught before they could carry out their plan and given lengthy prison sentences. Still, not so many Somalis live in Liberal these days.

The increase of diversity in the town took place long after I left, but sooner or later, we all meet someone whose experience of life, way of life, or way of looking at the world differs from our own. The differences between us are not just those of age and personality—differences that distinguish any individual from another. They are the differences that distinguish groups of people. These differences define our world and often divide it. Where do these differences come from? How should we think about them? And what do we do with them when we meet them? To answer those questions, we need an origin story.

Created for Cultural Identity

In the beginning, there were two kinds of nothing—the earth was "formless" and "empty" (Gen. 1:2 NIV). Both descriptors are significant. The uncreated world had nothing to fill the forms it did not have; there was nothing to fill and nothing with which to fill it. God's creative act addressed both kinds of nothingness. The heavens and earth lacked structure and purpose. So, God imbued the cosmos with both. On the first three days, form and structure emerge as the divine word "separates" light from darkness, sea from sky, and land from water. Then, with the varied forms now fit for habitation, God fills them. On day four, the light and darkness are populated with the heavenly bodies that govern them—the sun to rule the day and the moon and stars to rule the night. On day five, the sea teems with aquatic life, and the sky teems with avian life. Then, on day six, the land similarly teems with life.

The creation of living things on the sixth day proceeds as before, with the earth bringing forth living creatures "according to their kinds" (Gen. 1:25), just as the sea and sky brought forth the creatures of the sea and the birds of the air on day five. But God's creative action on day six differs from that of days four and five in three important ways.

First, at the culmination of his creative activity, he creates people "in his own image" (Gen. 1:27). The parallel creation account of Genesis 2 indicates that God fashions humans from the dust of the earth, but the earth does not bring them forth according to their kind as with other living creatures. Similarly, like the other creatures, they are told to multiply, but not according to their kind. Rather, they multiply in the likeness of God. Human offspring resemble their parents, of course, but they ultimately resemble their parents' resemblance of God. Like the parents, the offspring bear the divine image (Gen. 5:3). Genesis does not immediately indicate what it means for humans to be made in God's image, preferring to fill out that picture over the ensuing chapters. However, it is clear from the outset that no human is more human than any other: all alike bear God's image.

Second, the man and woman were to share in God's governance of his creation. The expression "image of god" was used widely in the ancient Near East to describe a king as one who singularly represented the rule of a god over a people.[1] Genesis, however, confers the divine image not on royalty but on humanity, assigning the royal task of governing God's creation to every human. Thus, every human is endowed with equal dignity and worth.

Third, God tells the humans that in carrying out their commission to govern creation on his behalf, they are to "fill the earth" (Gen. 1:28). God had similarly appointed the birds to "multiply on the earth" and the creatures that swim to "fill the waters" (1:22), but only the humans

---

1   David J. A. Clines, "The Image of God in Man," *Tyndale Bulletin* 19 (1968): 53–103.

are called to "fill the earth." This suggests that the extent to which the nonhuman land creatures fill the earth is a matter of human stewardship of the land they occupy together. Even if the charge to "fill the earth" is given only to the humans among the creatures of the land, God clearly prizes variety here as well. If the goodness pronounced over each element of creation consists in its fitness and suitability for the intended purpose, that goodness consists as well in the teeming diversity God intends for each sphere. It is with that diversity that each sphere is to be filled.

From the beginning, the sea and sky "teem" (Gen. 1:20 NIV) with diversity, but diversity does not seem to mark humanity at the outset. God creates humanity in his image, and in doing so, he creates both male and female. They differ from one another. Even so, there are only two. As yet, they are of one kind. The difference in sex alone does not constitute the diversity with which God intends for humanity to fill the earth. However, as the ensuing narrative demonstrates, sexual difference forms the basis of that diversity.

That God makes humanity both male and female underscores the fact that they bear God's image not only in the charge to govern the world on his behalf but also in the relationality that characterizes God's own being. These two aspects of the divine image—what theologians call the functional and relational aspects of the image of God—work together to achieve the divine intention that humanity fill the earth. How does this take place?

Although they are told to fill the earth, they are placed in the limited domain of a garden. In both art and popular imagination, the garden appears as a kind of bucolic paradise with unbidden abundance that the first humans simply receive. Had they not rebelled, we assume, they would simply have stayed put, enjoying the largesse of the God-planted garden in perpetual leisure. It is thus easy to forget that the command to fill the earth predates the fall. Here, perhaps, our imagination needs reformation.

Given that God places the humans in a garden that he tells them to tend and situates the garden on the earth that he tells them to fill, the command to fill the earth is not a summons to *leave* the garden but to *expand* it. The contrast is not between paradise within and the barren waste beyond, but between the cultivated and not-yet-cultivated portions of creation, the whole of which God pronounces "good." The garden is formed by God and given to humans as a model for their creative cultivation of the whole.

The fact that the humans are called not only to cultivate the garden but also to expand it is fundamental to a theology of work. However, it is important for another reason as well. The term *cultivate* is slightly misleading, as it tends to suggest a purely agrarian shape to the divine mandate. Not so. As the humans multiply, they begin to interact with the created world in a variety of ways. They farm, but they also hunt and herd. Some lead settled lives, while others, such as Abel and Abraham, are described as pastoralists, living in tents and moving as rainfall and grass conditions required. At the same time, those who settle are not all farmers. Some build cities. Others begin to work with metal. Still others become poets or musicians.

However rudimentary, these varied pursuits and patterns of life represent the emergence of cultures. Nothing in the text suggests that these alternative ways of life are a consequence of the fall.[2] To be sure, these cultural expressions are readily bent to rebellious ends. Nevertheless, the creativity ascribed to humans mirrors the creativity of God in the opening chapter, enriching our understanding of what it means to be made in the image of God and filling out our understanding of what it means to fill the earth.[3] Work is central to God's intention for humanity, but *how* we work and how we value various kinds of work are part of what we mean by "culture." As humans, we fulfill our calling to "fill the

2 Some have suggested that these early forms of culture represent the varied forms of rebellion that take humanity away from the divine intent that humans till the earth. Only with the fall are animals killed for clothing, food, and sacrifice. Prior to the fall, humans are given seeds and fruits to eat, but not animals. But the point of the Genesis narrative is not that humans are not to make use of the animal world—only the fruit from the tree of the knowledge of good and evil is forbidden. Rather, the point is that the day three preparation of the land for habitation includes vegetation capable of sustaining both parts of the day six creation—forage for animals and edible seeds for humans.
3 Only God is the subject of the Hebrew verb translated as "create."

earth" in the myriad of ways in which we steward God's creation—that is, in imaging God through our creative engagement with his creation.

Constructed or Inherent?

But there is more. Though we must not lose sight of individuals and individual innovation, culture is fundamentally a collective undertaking—something we do and produce in relation to particular groups of people. Thus, as distinct patterns of life emerge through human interaction with creation, Genesis also indicates that these patterns emerge through human interaction with one another. Humanity does not fill the earth simply by procreating but also by forming groups. People not only form families but also wider kinship groups.

The importance of this relational outworking of the divine image can be grasped by thinking about the widely varied ways in which different groups carry out similar actions. Differing patterns and practices emerge over time as expressions of shared values and ways of life. Just as many foreigners are baffled by the protracted outpouring of communal grief after someone dies in Ethiopia, I expect Ethiopians are equally mystified by the restrained, contemplative culture of mourning in America. It would be easy to multiply examples of cultural difference across a vast range of human experience. Whether or not anyone can explain why they do things as they do, the practices develop over time as members of a group interact with the world, each other, and with members of other groups. Individuals may innovate new ways of doing things; groups make them normal. In this way, cultures not only emerge but also change over time.

Those who read Genesis under the influence of individualism might assume too quickly that the early indications of cultural identity are attributes of individuals. To be sure, many cultural traits are associated with individuals. However, many of these traits are found in genealogical material, where emerging cultural forms are tied to particular individuals and the groups associated with them. Thus, Genesis 4 ties certain cultural practices not only to Lamech's three sons but to their descendants as well:

And Lamech took two wives. The name of the one was Adah, and
the name of the other Zillah. Adah bore Jabal; he was the father of
those who dwell in tents and have livestock. His brother's name was
Jubal; he was the father of all those who play the lyre and pipe. Zillah
also bore Tubal-cain; he was the forger of all instruments of bronze
and iron. (Gen. 4:19–22)

The point here is not that anyone who played a musical instrument
was connected by that talent to Jubal, but that the nation or people who
descended from Jubal were remembered for their musical ability. Just
as we think of the Scottish as those who wear kilts or associate tulip
production with the Dutch, Lamech's three sons became the eponymous
heads of peoples who were known for particular cultural characteristics.
Thus, the divine commission to "fill the earth" is fulfilled not simply by
populating the earth with people. Rather, the divine intention plays out
as humanity fills the earth with culturally distinct *peoples.*

The so-called Table of Nations in Genesis 10 makes this point with
particular force. Here we find the "families" of the earth delineated in
an expansive genealogy that differentiates seventy nations. The table
reflects what Richard Bauckham calls "representative geography."[4] The
point is not to claim that there were (or would only ever be) precisely
seventy human families. Rather, seventy symbolizes the full number of
the peoples though whom the divine purpose that humanity "fill the
earth" came to fulfillment. It is a genealogical picture of the earth filled
with diverse families with diverse cultures in diverse places. The Table
of Nations depicts what Paul asserts before the Areopagus: "From one
man [God] made all the nations, that they should inhabit the whole
earth" (Acts 17:26 NIV).

Two very important implications follow from this discussion. First,
the emergence of diverse peoples who fill the earth with a rich variety
of cultures is central to the divine vision for humanity. We shall return

---

4   Richard Bauckham, *Bible and Mission: Christian Witness in a Postmodern World* (Grand
     Rapids, MI: Baker, 2003), 63.

to this point in our discussion of the incident at Babel, but long before Babel, the divine intent was clear.

Second, the fact that humanity is charged with the task of filling the earth by filling it with culturally distinct peoples tells us that *God created human beings for, rather than with, cultural identity.* Misunderstanding of this point has plagued the study of ethnicity, nationality, and race.

Until relatively recently, anthropologists and sociologists subscribed to what has been called a "primordial" understanding of ethnicity and the related concepts of nationality and race. On this view, cultural identity was understood as a given, something you were born with and thus an inherent and fixed essence of human existence, an unchanging and unchangeable biological reality.

If few anthropologists and sociologists still hold this view, many ordinary people do. To be sure, collective identity can *feel* inherent and given, especially when members of a group believe there is a bio-logical dimension that forms the basis of their "groupness." But the notion that collective identities are rooted in the distant past and are fixed and unchanging has been the source of untold evils, including strongly held beliefs, even laws, that ethnic groups and races ought not mix or intermarry. This is not to deny the reality of physical descent, but Genesis does not portray the formation of peoples as a matter of preserving pure and unmixed bloodlines. Later on, Scripture warns against intermarriage between the people who worship God and those who worship idols (e.g., Deut. 7:3). However, Scripture is also replete with examples of sanctioned marriage between individuals from dif-ferent peoples (e.g., Ruth).

The rejection of the primordial view in the social sciences has given rise to a "constructivist" view that resembles what we have seen in the early chapters of Genesis. To be sure, many have read a primordial understanding of ethnicity, nationality, and race back into the biblical text, but it is both important and right to insist that collective identity is not given to peoples but constructed by them. However much it may *feel* that our cultural identity originated in the mists of the distant past, the reality is that culture is always under construction—not least through the complex interactions between peoples in marriage, commerce, and adaptation of innovation.

Building Blocks for Cultural Identity

If the creation of cultures is central to God's purposes for humanity, what are the key building blocks in the construction of cultural identity? What factors guide how we think about what it means to be "us?" We can begin with an adaptation of a widely used list of characteristics of ethnicity and then move in the next section to consider other forms of cultural identity in both Scripture and in our world.

The building blocks of ethnic identity are (1) a shared name, (2) a shared sense of place, (3) a shared sense of the past, (4) a shared sense of belonging or kinship, and (5) a widely shared set of beliefs and values that give rise to a shared set of practices and norms.[5] This fifth building block comprises the things that we often think of as a people's culture and that were central to our definition of *culture* in chapter 1. These may include such things as religious beliefs and practices, language, cultural conventions, and customs, as well as cultural "products" such as literature, music, architecture, and art.[6]

---

5 Adapted from James C. Miller, "Ethnicity and the Hebrew Bible: Problems and Prospects," *Currents in Research* 6, no. 2 (2008): 174. For these building blocks, Miller draws on ethnic characteristics formulated by John Hutchinson and Anthony D. Smith, "Introduction," in *Ethnicity*, ed. John Hutchinson and Anthony D. Smith (Oxford: Oxford University Press, 1996), 6–7. Miller, along with others, considers nationality and race as forms of ethnicity.

6 Although they adopt a similar definition of ethnicity to that of Hutchinson and Smith, Stephen E. Cornell and Douglas Hartmann critique the common notion that ethnicity is "shared culture." The characteristics listed by Hutchinson and Smith show that there is more to ethnicity than culture. However, the primary concern of Cornell and Hartmann is that some groups maintain a sense of ethnic identity even when cultural distinctiveness has declined, as, for instance, when a group of immigrants assimilates to the surrounding culture while maintaining a sense of ethnic identity. However, such a situation simply reflects the reality of cultural multiplicity. Cornell and Hartmann's own definition of ethnicity retains a clear cultural component. They follow Richard Schermerhorn in suggesting that ethnic identity includes "a cultural focus on one or more symbolic elements defined as the epitome of their peoplehood." Cornell and Hartmann, *Ethnicity and Race: Making Identities in a Changing World* (Thousand Oaks, CA: Pine Forge, 2007), 19. Schermerhorn's definition is cited from *Comparative Ethnic Relations: A Framework for Theory and Research* (Chicago: University of Chicago Press, 1978), 12.

We see many of these five features of cultural identity begin to emerge in the opening chapters of Genesis. The Table of Nations in Genesis 10 associates the various peoples with the individuals from whom they derived their names and with their "territories." Thus, the genealogy is divided between the three sons of Noah who survived the flood, and each section concludes with a summary statement such as the one we find in verse 5, which speaks of several peoples descended from Japheth who "spread out into their territories by their clans within their nations, each with its own language" (NIV).

Here we see that peoples began to distinguish themselves from one another, forming identities rooted in a shared name, a shared sense of place, and a sense of kinship. There are also hints within the material of variations in way of life. Among the descendants of Japheth, for example, are several groups who adopted a seagoing way of life. Among the descendants of Ham, Nimrod is described as a builder of cities (Gen. 10:8–12).

We shall return to these building blocks, but one block calls for particular comment—the role of history. The shared sense of the past that contributes to a sense of group identity is sometimes called a "myth." To call it a myth is not to dispute its truth, but to indicate that the history of a people has a social function. It is a shared story that tells us something of who we are as a people. Whether rooted in actual history or not, the myth is how a people collectively remembers the past.

To consider the way in which a people's history functions as myth helps us understand why we feel threatened or angry when someone tells the story of his or her group in a way that seems to conflict with the way that we think about history. This is why the adoption of a new history curriculum becomes a flashpoint for political debate or conflict at a school board meeting. The issue can certainly arise when someone seeks to retell the history of a people, but it is perhaps most acute when groups that share the same space record their histories in different ways. History is often perceived as a dull affair, but when it touches on central elements of our cultural identity, the effects can be volatile. Turks and Armenians remain bitterly divided over whether to characterize the deaths of up to 1.5 million Armenians at the hands of the Turks beginning in 1915 as genocide.[7] There is much at stake in how the story is told, not least the identities of these neighboring peoples. Such an example highlights the importance of ensuring that our cultural myths be true. It also demonstrates the importance of thinking carefully about the way in which history sometimes elevates one group at the expense of others.

A shared sense of the past is just one of the building blocks of cultural identity. It is important that we think through all of them to understand not only our own cultural identity but also how that identity shapes the way we relate to those whose cultural identity differs from our own.

Forms of Collective Identity

One of the features of the Genesis narrative that carries through the rest of Scripture is the diversity of terms associated with peoplehood. This is particularly evident in the genealogical material of Genesis 10, where the various peoples descended from Noah's three sons are described with reference to their "lands," "languages," "clans," and "nations" (10:5, 20, 31, 32). As Derek Kidner puts it, the varied terms "take into account the shifting and mingling to which human groups are subject."[8] But the terms also account for the various factors that contribute to a particular people's self-conception. The plurality of terms is itself instructive, implying the variety of ways in which people think about the groups to which they belong.

Scripture uses other terms as well, including, for instance, the designation of a people by the name of its most prominent city. The aim here is not to catalog all the ways in which peoples are identified in Scripture, but rather to highlight the variability in the forms of peoplehood attested in Scripture.

7   The Turkish statement of the number of Armenians who died is only one-fifth as much.
8   Derek J. Kidner, *Genesis: An Introduction and Commentary*, Tyndale Old Testament Commentaries (Downers Grove, IL: InterVarsity Press, 1967) 114.

We see a similar variability in the forms of cultural identity used today. Three prominent forms are ethnicity, nationality, and race. Many consider the latter two to be variations of ethnicity. Nationality and race make use of the same building blocks of cultural identity listed above for ethnicity. They differ from ethnicity only with respect to how the building blocks are conceptualized. Those who have an ethnic identity stress shared ancestry in their understanding of kinship and belonging in a way that is not typically the case for those whose identity is national or racial.[9] For those whose identity is national, the accent falls on the territory over which an acknowledged authority rules. For those whose identity is racial, the focus falls on phenotypical traits.

We can consider these different forms of peoplehood by setting them alongside one another and assessing the degree to which they have precursors in Scripture. We can then explore several implications of these forms of cultural identity. We begin with the form most evident in Scripture.

1. *Nationality*. The terms typically translated as "nation" in Scripture do not precisely correspond to modern usage of the term.[10] In contemporary geopolitics, virtually everyone has a "passport country." The habitable parts of the earth have been divided into nations with defined, if sometimes disputed, borders. This was often not the case in the ancient world. As a result, some have suggested that the notion of nationality did not exist in the ancient world.[11] It is certainly true that the whole of the ancient world was not divided into states that exercised sovereignty over their own affairs within internationally recognized borders. Still, nations did exist in the ancient world, defined by a sense of belonging to a people in

---

9   Miller, "Ethnicity," 175.

10 For a discussion of the relationship between "nation" and "state" in the modern sense, see chap. 1.

11 See especially Steven Grosby, *Biblical Ideas of Nationality: Ancient and Modern* (Winona Lake, IN: Eisenbrauns, 2002), 13.

a particular land with common religious commitments, political organization, and leadership. However, the boundaries of those lands were in more or less constant flux, shifting with the ebb and flow of power.[12]

Sometimes nations could serve as hosts for other forms of collective identity, as when conquest or displacement brought a recognizably "foreign" people under another people's territorial domain. In the ancient world, the foreignness of that people was frequently religious in nature, but doubtless it had other features as well. Other forms of collective identity did not involve the perception of foreignness at all, but functioned as constituent elements within a wider whole. Thus, within Israel, the various tribes are granted territorial allotments and, in turn, were constituted by smaller units of extended families or clans. For the Levites, tribal identity was primarily ancestral and religious, notably lacking any territorial dimension. In certain contexts, tribal identity within a people had more salience than the cultural identity of the whole. To be a Danite or Benjamite, for instance, had distinct cultural content, but that cultural content also had meaning within the culture of Israel as a whole.

2. *Ethnicity.* Even when a sense of nationality was not present, a sense of peoplehood could still exist. Prior to the emergence of the Greek Empire, Greece existed less as a nation than as a number of cities, each ruled by its own king. Nevertheless, those who lived in these cities had a sense of kinship to one another that existed in the absence of any political expression. This sense of peoplehood did not derive from the perception of kinship alone, but also from a way of thinking about the world. Well before the emergence of the Greek Empire or anything resembling a Greek nation, the Athenian rhetorician Isocrates famously associated Greek identity with the cultural outlook formed by a proper Greek education. Thus, he claimed that "the name 'Hellenes' suggests no longer a people but an intelligence, and . . . the title 'Hellenes' is

12 Grosby, *Biblical Ideas of Nationality*, 14–39.

applied rather to those who share our culture than to those who share a common blood."[13]

Another form of nonnational collective identity in the ancient world resulted from national dissolution following political fragmentation or the mass deportation and dispersal of entire populations. The Old Testament portrays the exile of Israel as the death of a nation—albeit a death in two parts—as first the northern nation of Israel and then the southern nation of Judah not only lost their independent rule over the land but also suffered the removal of significant portions of their populations from the land as well. Even after Israel was split into two nations—Judah and Israel—a sense of kinship created by a shared language and history remained. It is sensible, in that context, to think of someone with Benjamite tribal identity as having Judahite national identity and Israelite ethnic identity.[14] Later, after the exile of both nations, a sustained sense of kinship persisted, even when the realities of dispersion meant the loss of a common language among those identifying themselves as descendants of Abraham.

These nonnational forms of collective or cultural identity resemble what we often refer to today as ethnicity. Central to most contemporary definitions of ethnicity is the perception of kinship by its members. I shall fill this out in chapter 4, but for now I simply note that ethnicity is a form of peoplehood derived from a shared sense of ancestry.[15]

3. *Race.* But what about race? As a modern social category, race is rather different from nationality and ethnicity in that it does not have

---

13 Isocrates, *Panegyricus* 50, cited in F. W. Walbank, "The Problem of Greek Nationality," *Phoenix* 5 (1951): 45–46. The intent of Isocrates's statement is disputed, but Isocrates was probably not opening up Greek cultural identity to any and all who imbibed Greek language and learning. Rather, he was suggesting that Greek blood *alone* was an inadequate basis for "Greekness."

14 After the secession of the ten northern tribes, the nation formed by that secession was most frequently called "Israel," or, less frequently, "Ephraim." Perhaps because of the use of "Israel" for the northern nation without Judah and Benjamin, the eponym "Jacob" became a common way of referring to the unified nation in memory or expectation.

15 Hutchinson and Smith, "Introduction," 6–7. Hutchinson and Smith refer to the "myth" of common ancestry, in part, because no group is, in fact, biologically isolated from all others.

a clear biblical precedent.[16] This, in itself, does not make the category unbiblical, though it is sometimes thought of as such.[17] It is easy to see why. The history of the concept is deeply problematic, and its use is laden with oppression. The concept of race originated in the pseudo-science of "scientific racism" that assigned people to broad categories based on observable traits. It was assumed rather than proven that such traits reliably map back to unseen qualities such as intellect, rationality, and emotional disposition. This, then, was made the basis for the claim that differences in skin color corresponded to a natural social hierarchy that justified systems of oppression, discrimination, and enslavement.

The horrific history of race as a concept and the fact that the concept has no basis in biological reality have led many to avoid the term *race* altogether, preferring to constrain all or most forms of cultural identity under the umbrella of ethnicity.[18] Indeed, there are compelling reasons to wish that the concept had never been created. It is certainly possible to imagine that a society might move away from the racialization of identities as a way of rejecting the oppressions of the past.[19] Alternatively, we can also imagine a society in which the concept of race has

16   The term *race* appears in some English translations of the Bible in texts such as 1 Peter 2:9, where "race" translates the Greek term *genos* in the ESV, NRSV, NET, and other translations. The NIV and NLT opt for "people." "Race" is also used in some translations of Ezra 9:2; Acts 7:19; and Rom. 9:5. The primary problem with translations that render the term as "race" is that *genos* is a broad term specifying a "kind" or "social category" of people with no indication of the basis for the categorization. In a first century context, however, it was unlikely to be a social category based on skin color—a connotation that almost always attends the English word *race*.

17   Article 12 of the "Statement on Social Justice" seems to move in this direction. Though the statement correctly asserts that race is not a biblical category, it also seems to regard race as a social construct in a way that is not true of ethnicity and nationality. https://statementonsocialjustice.com/#affirmations-and-denials.

18   See Joe R. Feagin and Eileen O'Brien, "Studying 'Race' and Ethnicity: Dominant and Marginalized Discourses in the Critical North American Case," in *The Sage Handbook of Race and Ethnic Studies*, ed. Patricia Hill Collins and John Solomos (Los Angeles: Sage, 2010), 53.

19   The national discourse in Germany has stigmatized the language of "race" (*Rasse*) as a response to the racially motivated horrors of the Holocaust during the Second World War. This does not mean that there is no racism in German society, only that there has been a conscious effort to conceptualize collective identity away from race and toward ethnicity.

been emptied of its hierarchical significance and supremacist premises. Scripture itself attests the possibility of a society in which differences in skin color are acknowledged but have little or no relevance for collective identity.[20]

However, as we have seen, cultural identity is formed, in part, through social interactions between groups, and this, tragically, includes interactions that fall short of the glory of God. This means that many cultural identities are partly constructed through the experience of oppression. Thus, while no individual and no group should adopt or construct a racial identity to oppress others, it is far from clear that those whose cultural identity has been forged in part through the experience of racial oppression at the hands of others should necessarily reorient their identity around ethnicity rather than race.[21] Societies that conceptualize peoplehood in terms of ethnicity rather than race are not immune to claims of supremacy.

Moreover, we can state unequivocally that cultural identities shaped in part by the shared experience of injustice and exploitation will be abundantly present in the eschatological worship of the crucified and risen Messiah. Thus, we rightly lament that race as a form of identity

20 In an important study of skin color in ancient Israel, David Goldenberg writes, "To biblical Israel, Kush was the land at the furthest southern reach of the earth, whose inhabitants were militarily powerful, tall, and good-looking. These are the dominant images of the black African in the Bible, and they correspond to similar images in Greco-Roman culture. I found no indications of a negative sentiment toward Blacks in the Bible. Aside from its use in a proverb (found also among the Egyptians and Greeks), skin color is never mentioned in descriptions of biblical Kushites. That is the most significant perception, or lack of perception, in the biblical image of the black African. Color did not matter." Goldenberg, The Curse of Ham: Race and Slavery in Early Judaism, Christianity, and Islam (Princeton: Princeton University Press, 2009), 195. Some argue that a form of racism did exist in antiquity, though in ways that distinguish it from the modern form. See David G. Horrell, Ethnicity and Inclusion: Religion, Race, and Whiteness in Constructions of Jewish and Christian Identities (Grand Rapids, MI: Eerdmans, 2020), 80–82.

21 Distilling the view of Cornell and Hartmann, Horrell argues that "race is assigned, ethnicity is asserted," making the former an "outsider" categorization and the latter an "insider" categorization. Horrell, Ethnicity, 78–79. That may reflect how racial identities originate, but many groups do continue to construct a racial identity for themselves regardless of the origin of the identity. In addition, examples of imposed or assigned ethnicity also exist.

was ever conceived and imposed as a claim of supremacy, even as we acknowledge with gratitude and wonder the divine grace that draws the cultures of those shaped by that experience into God's purpose to fill the earth with a diversity of peoples.

Given its history, we must take particular care that no group experiences race as a form of identity through imposition by an oppressive majority, but only as the group's own cherished and valued expression of its unique experience of the world. For this reason, for those outside the group to advocate for a "colorblind" society can be seen as yet another way of imposing identity from the outside. Or, to take another example, those who think of themselves as "Black" in the United States often do so as a way of describing their sense of belonging to a group whose cultural and social experience is widely shared by those who have black skin. This, however, does not apply to everyone with black skin, many of whom do not think of themselves as Black in this specific racial sense. Very few first-generation African immigrants think of themselves as Black in the American sense. We could hardly respond to those who do not identify as Black by insisting that they do. It is one thing for a group to come to embrace a racial form of identity despite it having been imposed in the past. It is quite another for such an identity to be imposed by others in the present despite it being foreign to the group members' experience.

4. *Implications.* We have focused on three especially prominent forms of cultural identity—nationality, ethnicity, and race. But these are merely representative. Many other forms could be included in a more comprehensive list; for example, the clans of Somalia or the countries of the United Kingdom (Wales, Northern Ireland, Scotland, and England). Having considered the various ways in which groups of people conceive and construct cultural identity both in Scripture and contemporary experience, it is important to draw out several crucial implications.

First, although the various forms of cultural identity are neutral in and of themselves, they must be carefully distinguished from their ideological perversions. Identity becomes ideology when those who hold it assert the intrinsic superiority of one identity over another. Nationality easily becomes nationalism, ethnicity slides into ethnocentrism, and race is readily corrupted by racism. This happens when members of a given group forget that all people are made in the divine image with equal dignity and responsibility for culture-creating stewardship of God's rule.

Second, these differing forms of cultural identity often exist alongside one another. In a given context, one can find not only multiple cultural identities but also multiple *forms* of cultural identity. We see rudimentary indications of this in the varied terms for cultural identity that we meet in Scripture. There are certain situations today when clarity around this fact proves vital. Not all people whose skin is black are culturally Black. I teach at a seminary with a significant number of students from Africa. Few, if any, of these students think of their identity in primarily racial terms. But there are also students who do. In the interactions between students from Africa and African American students, it is important for those who *are* culturally Black to be aware that many with black skin think of their cultural identity in ethnic rather than racial terms. Such issues are more easily navigated when they are clearly understood.

Failure to recognize the possibility of multiple forms of cultural identity often leads to trouble. A few years ago, I walked past a "Black commencement" ceremony while attending a graduation at Harvard. Some on social media bristled when they heard of the event, wondering resentfully what would have happened had someone organized a "white commencement." As in most things, context is everything. Holding a "white commencement" would deepen the dark stain of white identity in the United States because a "white" event of any kind could only be understood as a "white only" event, perpetuating a long history of exclusion and oppression. In the United States, to construct a racial identity based on whiteness is typically hostile. By contrast, as the organizers of the Black commencement event explained, "black graduations are not anti-anyone. They just celebrate black students, their accomplishments, and their supporters."[22] However, it would be difficult to regard a "white graduation" as anything but antiblack. For the same reason, "Black lives matter" is clearly racial; "white lives matter" is racist.[23] The point is that *the racial identity of one group does not mean that neighboring groups must construct a racial identity in opposition.*

In some contexts, the opposition of identities would evoke the specter or memory of oppression. The affirmation of Blackness as a cultural identity need not require the counter-assertion of whiteness in opposition, especially when alternative forms of cultural identity are available. In such moments, it may not be important for me to think about my cultural identity at all. I might think of my Irish forebears and of the obstacles they overcame, but the more important response would be simply to delight in another group's celebration of cultural achievement, especially in the face of oppression. The one thing I should absolutely resist is the temptation to give "whiteness" salience as an identity.[24]

Third, for complex reasons, the way one group constructs its cultural identity often impacts the construction of identity by neighboring groups. This can be caustic when the construction of identity becomes a form of opposition. But it can also be helpful, even beautiful, when differences positively shape the construction of identity. This bears importantly on the sometimes-fraught discussion of "cultural appropriation." The use of this expression has proven unhelpfully imprecise and has blurred the distinctions between behavior that belittles and the appreciative exploration of the cultural practices of another group.

22 Eryn Mathewson, "Don't Hate on Black Graduation Ceremony at Harvard University," *The Undefeated*, May 23, 2018, https://theundefeated.com/.

23 My intent here is not to assess the Black Lives Matter movement but to note that the slogan "Black lives matter" is an expression of racial identity, evoking a widely shared experience of what it is like to be Black in America.

24 One particular strand of critical race studies called "whiteness studies" insists that a feature of whiteness is its denial as a strategy for maintaining cultural dominance. It is worth noting, however, that white supremacists, far from denying their whiteness, have historically insisted on it.

While the former must be eschewed, the latter is not only laudable but inevitable in the context of meaningful relationships between people of different backgrounds.

Fourth, for many people, cultural identity is hybrid and contextual. Virtually everyone in Africa, for instance, has both an ethnic and a national identity. Ancient Israelites had both tribal and national identities. Not only is identity likely to be multiple, the way in which a given person interacts with the various cultural identities from which he or she derives a sense of self is highly related to context. Whenever I meet a Kenyan in America, it is almost always national identity that comes to the fore. But in Kenya, that same person's ethnic identity might emerge more strongly in some situations.

Cultural Identity, Gender, and Sexuality

Although this is not a book about gender or sexuality, it is important to see the way in which the early biblical narratives distinguish gender and sexuality from cultural identity. We shall see that whereas cultural identity is constructed as part of the divine mandate, gender and the sexual bond that the difference in genders makes possible are givens— part of the created order of things. As such, they are important building blocks for cultural identity, but are not themselves constructed.

This has not always been clear in the interpretation of Genesis 1–2 or in the contemporary discussion of gender and sexuality. As interpreted by many, the command to fill the earth relates to gender and sexuality only inasmuch as the command to fill the earth requires reproduction. That certainly is part of the picture, but, as we have seen, the narrative arc of both Genesis 1–11 and Scripture as a whole envisions the filling of the earth not simply with people but with peoples. Gender and sexual union are essential to the fulfillment of this purpose, as is evident in the use of the genealogical material to differentiate peoples.

In much contemporary discussion, gender and sex have been distinguished from one another, and the link between sex and sexuality severed. Whereas sex is understood as a biological trait, gender "is socially, culturally, and personally defined."[25] In a similar way, contemporary discussion of sexuality in many countries has generated an expanding list of "sexual identities." Though many of the sexual behaviors associated with these identities were known in the ancient world, a new development in contemporary discussion is the treatment of various forms of sexuality and gender as identities equivalent in kind to ethnicity and race. Thus, many now refer to sexual and gender "minorities."[26]

My purpose here is not to lay out a biblical theology of gender and sexuality, but it is important to consider the relationship between gender and sexuality on the one hand and cultural identity on the other. In Scripture, gender and sexuality are not constructs, but they do play an important role in the construction of cultural identity. Scripture thus admits considerable variation across cultures in the way that the two genders relate to one another; how they present themselves to one another; patterns of courtship; marriage customs; cultural norms for gender in relation to work, play, and raising children; and much more. However, gender itself is not socially constructed. Rather, it is a divine gift: God created humanity "in his own image, / in the image of God he created them; / male and female he created them" (Gen. 1:27 NIV).

This is not to say that culturally constructed beliefs, values, and behaviors related to gender and sexuality might not be corrupted by

25 Krista Conger, "Of Mice, Men, and Women: Making Research More Inclusive," *Sex, Gender and Medicine*, Spring 2017, https://stanmed.stanford.edu/. The terms *sex* and *gender* were synonyms for five centuries, until *sex* took on the additional connotation of "sexual intercourse" early in the twentieth century and *gender* took on the additional connotation of "gender identity" in the late twentieth century to refer to a person's internal sense of being a man or a woman. So, https://www.merriam-webster.com/dictionary/gender#usage -1. More recently, the idea that a person's internal sense of gender identity is unrelated to biological sex has opened up the possibility of other forms of gender identity. For some, the objective nature of *gender* as formerly used has carried forward into the newer use to designate "gender identity." This is evident in the claim that a biological male who identifies as a woman *is* a woman not simply as a matter of identity but as a matter of objective fact.

26 See Nate Collins, "What Transgender People Need from Conservative Christians," *Christianity Today*, June 22, 2018, https://www.christianitytoday.com/.

human rebellion. In fact, gender and sexuality are so close to the core of human personhood that we should expect to see sin's effects especially here in practices normalized across whole groups. For instance, in many cultures in Africa, what is euphemistically dubbed "female circumcision" but more accurately described as "female genital mutilation" can only be understood from a biblical perspective as horribly wrong. It is a cultural practice, generated by distorted beliefs about female sexuality, that seeks to curtail in the female body what Scripture contains within marriage. At the same time, Scripture takes a neutral stance toward a host of culturally specific practices related to gender and sexuality. The payment of dowries, the romantic imagery of the Song of Songs, and the role of parents in the marriages of their children are all examples of practices related to gender and sexuality generated by a particular cultural group's ever-changing construction of cultural meaning and identity.

The biblical narratives recognize inherent, as opposed to constructed, differences between male and female as part of the world made good by God. These differences give rise to widely varying social patterns that delineate the nature of relationships and roles across these differences and thus help generate distinct cultural identities.

This discussion highlights the importance of critical engagement with the ways in which particular cultures conceptualize masculinity and femininity. We should expect that cultures will differ from one another. No culture will get it right because even if there are wrong ways to be a man, there is also no one right way to be a man. The same is true for women.

The Garden as Temple

There is one final feature of the creation story that we need to consider in order to make sense of the divine intention in ordaining differences among the peoples of the earth. The first humans are placed in a garden and told to fill the earth, not by leaving the garden but by extending it. But in doing so, they would not just be extending a garden. They also would be expanding the dwelling place of God.

Recent studies have shown that the garden was also a temple—a place specially prepared for divine habitation. The identification of gardens with temples was simply assumed within the worldview of many ancient peoples. As John Walton comments, "Without hesitation the ancient reader [of the creation account] would conclude that this is a temple text."[27] In Scripture, subsequent descriptions of the temple are stamped with the memory of Eden.

Our earlier discussion of creation focused on the first six days, but what did God do on the seventh day? He rested. In the ancient Near East, resting was what gods did in temples after they had established order and stability. "We might even say that this is what a temple is—a place for divine rest."[28] Thus, Psalm 132 describes the temple as God's "resting place" (132:8, 14), but also as the place of the divine throne (132:11–12). God's rest on the seventh day marks the transition from his creative activity to his ruling activity, from creation to the governance of creation.[29]

Many of the motifs that tie gardens to temples and represent the garden-temple as a place of divine rest and rule are mirrored in other texts of the ancient Near East. But one feature of the biblical account that sets it apart from others is the depiction of the garden-temple as a place of shared rule and shared habitation. Though this understanding of the garden as a temple has gained broad acceptance within biblical scholarship, it has not yet been fully integrated into our understanding of God's purposes for humanity. Greg Beale rightly highlights the fact that the outward expansion of the garden was meant to serve "the goal of spreading the glorious presence of God."[30] However, if the command to fill the earth is not simply a command to populate it with people but with *peoples*, we get a sense of the divine vision of a unified humanity filled with distinct peoples within God's presence and under his rule.

27 John Walton, *The Lost World of Genesis One* (Downers Grove, IL: InterVarsity Press, 2009), 71.

28 Walton, *Lost World*, 71.

29 Walton, *Lost World*, 72–73.

30 G. K. Beale, *A New Testament Biblical Theology: The Unfolding of the Old Testament in the New* (Grand Rapids, MI: Baker Academic, 2011), 622.

Conclusion

Graeme Goldsworthy distills the framework of the biblical story as "God's people in God's place under God's rule."[31] Thus, the opening movement of the story has Adam and Eve in the role of God's people, living in Eden, and charged with obedience to God's word. Though not without its uses, the rubric doesn't quite capture something that seems to have been important to the Creator from the very beginning. The narrator tells the story as one of God-intended diversity. The command to fill the earth is not simply a directive to populate the earth, but to fill it with diverse families, clans, and nations who will share in God's rule through their creative interaction with the rest of creation. As they do so and thereby expand the garden, the whole earth becomes fit for the presence of God. Strongly implied within the commission to fill the earth with diverse cultures and languages is a conception of the peoples of the earth as unified in the shared task of building a temple.

Instead, they come together to build a tower.

---

31 Graeme Goldsworthy, *Gospel and Kingdom: A Christian Interpretation of the Old Testament* (Exeter, UK: Paternoster, 1982), 54.

3

Children of Cain, Heirs of Babel

Cultural Identity in Rebellion

The violence in the Bible is appalling.
ATTRIBUTED TO CHRISTOPHER HITCHENS

AS WE DROVE OFF the escarpment that follows the Great Rift Valley
and down into the western lowlands of Ethiopia, the asphalt gave way
to gravel and stone. As the elevation dropped, the temperature rose.
Great plumes of choking dust billowed behind us. Less than an hour
from the lush highlands, we now passed through red-earth fields dotted
with acacia, stubble, and the occasional thatched-roof hut. During the
nine-month dry season, daytime temperatures soared with little relief
at night. This, I thought, would be a tough place to live.

A few colleagues and I were headed toward a small village called
Gesses. Some years before, our mission had established a small station there in the hopes of planting and nurturing churches among a
lowland people called the Gumuz. The work was going reasonably
well. The education and veterinary projects seemed to be appreciated
in the community. The church was slowly growing. But life was hard
and hot. Water was hard to come by. When the Gumuz burned the
stubble from their fields in preparation for planting, black mambas,

puff adders, and cobras—a fun trifecta by any measure—took refuge on the station.

Life there was challenging for other reasons as well. In Addis Ababa, Ethiopia's capital city, it seemed we were always hearing reports of shootings and conflict in the area. It wasn't that the Gumuz were especially violent. Not infrequently, they were subject to poor treatment and discrimination from the highland peoples who looked down on their lowland neighbors. But violence and revenge had long since become a part of the culture. A fair bit of it took place across lines of clan or ethnic difference.

While we were there, we heard talk of a recent revenge killing. Someone had come up behind one of the believers at a gathering and put a bullet in the back of his head. It wasn't for anything he himself had done but for who his people were. Many years before, a member of his clan had killed someone from another group. This was payback.

Someone explained to us the way in which revenge had been woven into the culture. "If someone from another group kills someone from your group, the identity of the killer is often known. Your group may not be able to do anything about it right away, but the next child born into your family or clan is given the name of the murderer."

At this point, I stopped him. "Wait, why would anyone want to give their baby the name of a murderer?"

"It's simple," he said. "To ensure they will never forget. Even if it takes years, they will have their revenge."

In the wake of the rebellion of Adam and Eve, the early chapters of Genesis narrate the effects of sin not simply on people but on peoples. In the previous chapter, we saw that God's intent is for a world filled with diverse peoples unified in the worship of God and endowed with the dignity and shared responsibility of governing his world. Humanity, however, resists the divine purpose in two quite different ways. Prior to the flood, the narrator presents us with a world filled with diversity but also filled with violence. At least temporarily, the flood ends the violence, but as the world begins once again to fill with diverse peoples, human rebellion takes a different form as humanity gathers at Babel to bring diversity to an end. The unity of all peoples in worship of one God is perverted in the dissolution of difference and the glorification of human power over others.

Children of Cain

1. *"The First Genocide."* The first branch in the family tree goes badly. God gives life to Adam and Eve and endows them with the power to beget life. The life they beget is the life they receive, so God-given life passes to two sons. Then the unimaginable happens. One recipient of begotten life takes what belongs to God alone; he takes life from his brother.

Though the story initially focuses on the two brothers, they are not the only characters in the story or even the most important. Woven through the story are the actions and attitudes, the will and words of God. The Lord looks with favor on Abel and his offering, but not on Cain and his. He sees Cain's angry response and warns him of sin crouching at the door. And he holds Cain to account for the murder of his brother.

If this much is clear, one particular feature of the story has puzzled interpreters both ancient and contemporary. Why does the Lord regard Abel's offering with favor but not Cain's? It cannot be that God loves herders but hates farmers, though this has been suggested.[1] Neither can it be that God prefers the produce of the flock over the produce of the field, though again many have supposed otherwise.[2] Perhaps the most commonly held view is that God shows favor to Abel because "only those who offer the best in their sacrifices are acceptable to God."[3] But even this goes beyond what the text actually says. Abel brings from the firstlings of his flock, but Cain brings his offering first.[4]

---

1   Hermann Gunkel, *Genesis*, trans. M. E. Biddle (Macon, GA: Mercer University Press, 1997), 43.

2   Commentators make frequent reference to the prescriptions of the Mosaic law to explain God's rejection of Cain's offering, but not only does this require knowledge that Cain does not possess, but the law prescribes both agricultural and animal offerings.

3   Gordon J. Wenham, *Genesis 1–15*, Word Biblical Commentary (Dallas: Word, 1987), 117.

4   The superiority of Abel's offering cannot have arisen from the fact that it is a blood offering because the text is explicit that Abel offers the fat of the firstlings. At the same time,

It is possible that the narrator did not intend us to know why the Lord has no regard for Cain and his offering.[5] Perhaps not even Cain knows. However, the question that virtually every reader asks about the story seems not to occur to Cain. Before he is murderous, he is incurious. Instead of asking why the Lord has not favored him or his offering, he grows angry and casts a malign eye toward his brother.

Though he does not ask, the Lord comes to him and tells him anyway. "If you do the good, will you also not find favor?" (Gen. 4:7 AT). This simple statement has received surprisingly little attention from commentators. Most assume that the Lord's words anticipate the choice between right and wrong that Cain will soon make. On this understanding, the Lord is cautioning him to "do what is right" (e.g., NIV). But coming on the heels of the Lord's assessment of Cain's offering and Cain's angry response, it is perhaps better understood as the Lord's explanation of why he and his offering have not found favor. The warning comes in what follows: "If you do not do the good, sin is crouching at the door" (AT). As this warning is typically read, not doing good is identified with the sin Cain has committed. But this is banal, equivalent to saying, "If you sin, you will sin."[6] But if the sin in view is Cain's violent attack on his brother, Cain's vulnerability to this sin comes from the same failure that led to the Lord's rejection of his sacrifice—his failure to embrace the good. But what is the good that Cain has failed to do?

---

the inferiority of Cain's offering cannot be demonstrated from the fact that Abel alone brings firstfruits. The grammar of Gen. 4:3–4 suggests that Cain brings an "offering" and Abel "also" brings the firstfruits. John H. Sailhamer, "Genesis," in *Genesis–Leviticus*, rev. ed., Expositor's Bible Commentary (Grand Rapids, MI: Zondervan Academic, 2017), 97.

5   So John Walton, *Genesis*, NIV Application Commentary (Grand Rapids, MI: Zondervan), 263.

6   Kristen M. Swenson equates doing good with anger management, i.e., "if you do not control the sin of anger, the sin of murder will overtake you." Swenson, "Care and Keeping East of Eden: Gen 4:1–16 in Light of Gen 2–3," *Interpretation* 60 (2006): 379, cited in and followed by Mari Jørstad, "The Ground That Opened Its Mouth: The Ground's Response to Human Violence in Genesis 4," *Journal of Biblical Literature* 135 (2016): 706. While this avoids the tautology, it implies that Cain's failure to control his anger led to the Lord's rejection of his offering rather than the other way around.

As I noted in chapter 2, the sevenfold "good" that God pronounces over his creation is moral only in an indirect sense. The most immediate sense is that the various elements of creation are not only well-suited for their intended purpose but also teeming with the diversity that God intends for each sphere. As each sphere of creation abounds with richly varied life, God pronounces it "good."

As we turn from the initial account of creation (Gen. 1:1–2:3), the command God gives to the humans to fill the earth and exercise dominion over it becomes the focus (2:4–25). This chapter has often been regarded as a second creation narrative, but Genesis 2 is not so much a second account of creation as a slow-motion replay of the climax of God's creative act. If Genesis 1 says simply that God created humanity male and female, Genesis 2 breaks this part of the divine creative act into discrete scenes. Here we learn that before God said that the creation of the sixth day was "good" or pronounced the whole of his creation "very good," he said that one thing was "not good." After the creation of Adam, God said, "It is not good that the man should be alone" (2:18). The problem was not loneliness—at least not only. As the resolution to the problem implies, the problem was that, alone, Adam could not accomplish either element of the divine command to fill the earth and govern it in keeping with God's purpose. Only with the creation of the woman could the divine intent for a world teeming with diverse peoples be fulfilled. With the creation of the woman, humanity became suited to this purpose—that is, "good."

My suggestion is that God's disapproval of Cain and his offering stem from Cain's failure to pursue the good in this sense. The story begins with the characters apparently keeping step with the divine commission to fill the earth with diverse peoples, unified in their worship of God. Adam and Eve bear two sons, and they pursue different paths: Abel keeps sheep and Cain tills the ground. The rapid emergence of two very different ways of life—pastoral and agricultural—appears promising, as does the desire first of Cain and then of Abel to return a portion of the fruits of their work to the Lord as worship. As one commentator notes, "There are the makings of a rich pattern in these complementary skills and the attempted interweaving of work and worship."[7]

However, there are indications that God does not approve of Cain's choice of vocation, but not because the text reflects an antipathy toward farmers. This, after all, is the vocation assigned to Adam before the fall (Gen. 2:5) and affirmed after the fall (3:23). The problem is not with farming as a way of life, but with farming as a way of life *for Cain*. If the "good" that Cain must do in order to find favor in God's sight is the good defined in the creation narrative, Cain's fault lies not in farming *per se* but in choosing to do exactly what his father does.

We can confirm this by attending to the role of the "ground" in the story.[8] Note the following points:

1. Following Cain's murder of Abel, the punishment is that the ground will no longer produce crops. Clearly this dimension of Cain's punishment is unique to him. The ground continues to bear crops for Adam, but, following the murder, it no longer yields its produce for Cain. As a result, he is forced to forage; he becomes "a restless wanderer on the earth" (Gen. 4:12 NIV).

2. By contrast, the punishment for Adam's disobedience is that he *must* work the ground, but it will yield its produce only through hardship and toil (Gen. 3:17, 23).[9] The juxtaposition of God's choice of work for Adam at the end of Genesis 3 and the note about Cain's choice of work at the beginning of Genesis 4 is striking. The work that Adam *must* do, Cain does by choice. By placing this choice alongside Abel's choice to tend flocks, the author highlights the fact that Cain chose to work the ground, but he need not have.

3. Following God's rejection of Cain's offering of "the fruit of the ground," the author shows us what Cain thought of God's warning.

7   Derek Kidner, *Genesis,* Tyndale Old Testament Commentary (Downers Grove, IL: Inter-Varsity Press, 2016), 80.

8   As Jørstad notes, "It has almost become a truism that the ground in Gen. 1–11 is a character in its own right." Jørstad, "Ground," 705.

9   Cf. Gary A. Herion, "Why God Rejected Cain's Offering: The Obvious Answer," in *Fortunate the Eyes That See*, ed. Astrid B. Beck et al. (Grand Rapids, MI: Eerdmans, 1995), 52–65.

Cain takes his brother out to a field and kills him there. The term for "field" usually refers to cultivated ground. If so, the author is suggesting that Cain's choice of the place to kill Abel is meant to send a message to God. This murder is not simply an act of envy toward Abel, but one of rage toward God for rejecting his offering. If God will not take his offering from the ground, he will take what belongs to God—the life in his brother's blood (Gen. 9:4)—and spill it on the ground.

4. Following the murder, God comes to Cain and says, "Your brother's blood cries out to me *from the ground*" (Gen. 4:10 NIV).[10] The ground that he has chosen to till in defiance of the good now bears witness to the evil he has done. This last point is not immaterial. If this first branch of the family tree should have been shaped by the divine commission to fill the earth, now the earth itself cries out against the one who has rejected the divine vision of the good.

5. In Genesis 2:5, the ground lacks anyone to work it, so the Lord forms Adam and settles him in the garden to "work" and "keep" it (2:15). The same two words recur in the story of Cain and Abel. Cain works the ground (4:2). But when the Lord comes to him following the murder of Abel, Cain famously rejects the divine insinuation that he should be the "keeper" of his brother. Perhaps he means that, like his father, he works and keeps the ground. If the Lord wanted his brother kept, he should have seen to it himself! The Lord will not have it. The Lord's commission to humanity was not to farm the ground but to fill the earth. Since Cain did not work to keep his brother, he cannot work and keep the ground.

There is no small irony in the fact that Cain's rejection of the divine purpose to fill the earth with diverse peoples culminates in an assault on his brother, who had embraced that purpose. As one commentator puts it, in killing Abel, Cain asserts a defiant choice to "remain in

---

10 The portrayal of blood as a living thing that cries from the ground may correspond to the premise that the life of a thing is in the blood (Gen. 9:4) and serves as a reminder of God's exclusive prerogative over life.

an undifferentiated world."[11] But there is one further irony. God had warned Cain that if he did not embrace the good, "sin is crouching at the door and desires to rule over you" (Gen. 4:7 AT). In rejecting the divine intention to rule over the earth in the way God intends, he succumbs to sin's desire to rule over him. If Abel represents what it means to reflect the image of God, Cain rejects that meaning in the most palpable way possible.

Though the account of Cain and Abel is often told as a story of fratricide or interfamily conflict, we should see it, rather, as a story of willful resistance to the divine purpose that the human family comprise many families united in worship of the one God. As such, Cain's murder of Abel is not just the first fratricide but "the first genocide."[12] Cain's initial resistance to this purpose may seem benign—what harm can come from following in the footsteps of one's father? But his resistance turns violent. The story of Adam places all alike within one human family; the story of Cain and Abel apportions all alike into particular families. The story of Adam introduces sin as a deadly force within the human family; the story of Cain and Abel introduces violence as one form sin takes when the creatures made in God's image rebel against the divine desire for a world teeming with diverse peoples.

2. *A World Full of Violence.* If Adam's sin sets off a chain reaction, the links in the chain perpetuate the violence across families. Banished from the presence of the Lord for his act of violence, Cain is terrified that he will fall prey to violence. We might well ask, "From whom?" but the text answers neither that question nor the question of where Cain found a wife. Instead, the author keeps our eyes focused on the rapid descent of a world made good by God into a world made violent by people.

However, woven into this story is another thread. As the descendants of Cain increase, so, too, does the cultural differentiation

11 David W. Cotter, *Genesis*, Berit Olam (Collegeville, MN: Liturgical Press, 2016), 43.
12 The expression was coined by Elie Wiesel, "Cain and Abel: The First Genocide," in *Messengers of God: Biblical Portraits and Legends* (New York: Random House, 1976), 37–68.

between the branches of his family tree. One branch innovates a nomadic way of life (Gen. 4:20). Another creates musical instruments (4:21). Still another is known for the invention of tools and work with metal (4:22). In locating this explosion of cultural diversity within the genealogy of Cain, the author shows that despite Cain's assault on the divine purpose to fill the world with diverse peoples, it happened anyway.

If the divine purpose cannot be destroyed, it can be distorted. We see this most vividly in the author's depiction of Lamech. God forms a wife for Adam and provides a wife for Cain. Lamech takes two. We would not be without basis in the text to think that Lamech possesses the charms of a poet, but the poem he writes for his two wives is more chilling than charming:

> Adah and Zillah, hear my voice;
>   you wives of Lamech, listen to what I say:
> I have killed a man for wounding me,
>   a young man for striking me.
> If Cain's revenge is sevenfold,
>   then Lamech's is seventy-sevenfold. (Gen. 4:23–24)

Lamech might be a lover of sorts and a poet to match, but this is no love poem. We might have expected one of the earliest poems in Scripture to serve as still further evidence of the cultural innovation that marks humanity from the earliest stages. In one sense, it does. But Lamech somehow manages to subvert an art form that does not yet exist. The poem he writes for his wives is a violent boast.

But it is more than that. Six generations after Cain, the memory of the Lord's words of mercy to Cain still lived. In response to Cain's fear that he would become a target of violence away from the Lord's presence, the Lord had issued a warning: "If anyone kills Cain, vengeance shall be taken on him sevenfold" (Gen. 4:15). Life belongs to the Lord alone, so vengeance for life taken belongs to the Lord alone. However, on Lamech's lips, the Lord's warning is twisted into a boast of personal revenge meted out as disproportionate violence.[13] Worse, he distorts the memory of God's mercy toward Cain into a model of merciless revenge. The Lord had warned that, should anyone kill Cain, divine vengeance would be "sevenfold." The numerical idiom points to a full measure of life-for-a-life justice. Lamech, however, not only claims the Lord's prerogative as his own but exchanges proportional justice for escalated violence: "If you hit me, I will crush you; if you disrespect me, I will destroy you; if you harm me; I will kill you."

Placed within a genealogy that highlights the growing cultural differentiation between the families that are beginning to fill the earth, the jarring note about Lamech highlights violence and conflict as a growing part of the social order. There is, in other words, a straight line from Cain's slaughter of Abel to Lamech's normalization of revenge to the Lord's verdict about the world just before the judgment of the flood:

> Now the earth was corrupt in God's sight, and the earth was filled with violence. And God saw the earth, and behold, it was corrupt, for all flesh had corrupted their way on the earth. And God said to Noah, "I have determined to make an end of all flesh, for the earth is filled with violence through them." (Gen. 6:11–13)

Called to fill the earth with culturally diverse peoples, humanity fills the earth with violence as well. The whole narrative sequence focuses simultaneously on the *formation* of cultures and on the *corruption* of cultures with violence. Lamech, the vengeful poet, serves as a representative of both.

The biblical author's intention, it seems, is to show us that the rebellion of Adam does not simply sow the seed of sin in every human heart, but also that sin characteristically manifests itself in a deep-seated antipathy toward difference. It does no good to object that the violence

---

13 The translation of Gen. 4:24 is disputed. The ESV suggests that Cain vows sevenfold revenge, whereas the NIV and NET indicate that Cain is avenged by the Lord. The ESV is difficult to sustain if Lamech accurately recalls the whole of the Lord's promise, which was to avenge Cain if anyone took his life.

perpetrated by Cain against Abel is simply a case of family rivalry. Both are children of Adam. But then again, we all are. And this is the author's point. We are all part of one human family. In this sense, every act of violence has a sibling as its victim. At the same time, Abel does not just go missing in the field; he goes missing from the genealogy that follows. In God's design, that one family is meant to comprise many families. And yet, antipathy toward diversity worms its way into the fabric of human social interaction as a manifestation of the rebellion that mars every human heart.

One flashpoint of contemporary debate is whether or not we should describe the antipathy toward difference as "systemic." Do expressions such as "systemic ethnocentrism" or "systemic racism" reflect what Scripture teaches about the nature of sin? On the one hand, such expressions rightly highlight the impact of sin on social structures. Sin can and does shape cultural sensibilities that normalize the mistreatment of the members of one group by those of another. Sin can and does blind members of dominant cultural groups to the ways in which the practices and norms—legal and otherwise—of one cultural group work to the disadvantage of other groups.

At the same time, it is important to see that racism and ethnocentrism become embedded in systems because the repudiation of the divine purpose is rooted in the rebellious hearts of every individual. This means that these sins are often more damaging in systems controlled by dominant groups. But antipathy toward difference is common to all groups because the sin that gives rise to it is common to all individuals. This is perhaps to make the rather obvious point that sin affects and infects all cultures because cultures are formed by sinful individuals. Still, it remains a point worth making, given the tendency of some to locate "systemic racism" or "ethnocentrism" only in some groups and the tendency of others to locate this antipathy toward others in some individuals but not others.

Both Scripture and experience attest our universal resistance to the idea that cultural difference is a divinely intended good. Long before anyone subscribes to an "ism," he or she succumbs to the sin that crouches at *everyone's* door. That capitulation need not be willful. Our sin is evident not only in what we do but what we leave undone, not only in conscious acts but in unconscious dispositions. The underlying predilection, sin, is always there and readily erupts into any one of a myriad of harmful attitudes toward those who live across lines of difference. Under the right conditions, those attitudes fester until the blister bursts, sometimes violently. Our paternity may work itself out in a thousand different forms, but we are all children of Cain.

Heirs of Babel: The Post-Flood Move toward Totalizing Uniformity

1. *On Rainbows: Does the End of Violence Require the End of Difference?*
Within Genesis, the flood functions not only as a judgment but also as a kind of re-creation. In the beginning, the earth is covered in the chaotic primordial waters. In the original creation, the dry land emerges as the waters are subdued and contained, separated and constricted. In the flood, the waters return. The violence is gone, but so, too, is the blessing of a world teeming with diverse peoples. Still, the divine purpose for humanity remains after the flood. Three times over we hear the original charge: let the creatures that filled the earth, both animals and people, once more "be fruitful and multiply and fill the earth" (Gen. 9:1; cf. 8:17; 9:7).

Even so, God is under no illusion that the judgment poured out in the flood has brought the problem to an end. Noah may have survived the flood along with his wife, their three sons, and their sons' wives, but so has the pulse of sin that activates the impulse to violence. Thus, as they exit the ark, God gives humanity's surviving remnant a ritual, a reminder, and a symbol.

First, he provides them with a ritual through which they will regularly rehearse a foundational theological truth: life belongs exclusively to God. They are permitted to eat the flesh of animals, but they must not "eat flesh with its life, that is, its blood" (Gen. 9:4). The blood must be poured out because the life it sustains belongs to God. The enactment of that truth whenever they eat meat serves to drive the exclusivity of God's claim over all life deep into their worldview.

Second, God tells the survivors that they have been created in his image. This truth was central to the creation story, but as God sets about the task of re-creating the world, he reaffirms it. This time, however, he makes explicit the implication of this truth: there must be no violence. Thus, the ritual of pouring out blood is tied to a sober reminder:

For your lifeblood I will surely demand an accounting . . .

> *Whoever* sheds human blood,
>   by humans shall their blood be shed;
> for in the image of God
>   has God made mankind. (Gen. 9:5–6 NIV)

Third, he gives them a symbol. In our own day, the rainbow has come to symbolize diverse sexual and gender identities. In Scripture, however, the symbol has a completely different meaning. It represents in some way the divine promise to never again "strike down every living creature" (Gen. 8:21; cf. 9:11, 15). As I demonstrated in the preceding chapter, the command to "fill the earth" is not simply an order to populate the planet, but a directive to fill the earth with peoples, who are to govern the earth for God's glory and the good of its inhabitants—both human and nonhuman.

Some commentators argue that the bow in the clouds is the warrior bow of God, now "pointed away from earth and made a thing of beauty."[14] Though we cannot be certain of this, clearly the flood is an act of judgment that brings an end to violence. The promise symbolized by the bow, however, cannot be understood as a divine vow to never again destroy *any* life. The power both to give and to take life remains God's exclusive prerogative—one that he exercises repeatedly through the Scriptures. The promise, rather, is that he will never again destroy *all* life. Though the inclination of the human heart is evil (Gen. 8:21), God will never again address the sinful proclivities of human hearts toward corruption and violence by destroying every

14 Cotter, *Genesis*, 60.

living thing. If, in fulfilling God's purpose to fill the earth with diverse peoples and cultures, they again fill the earth with violence, he will never again address the latter by eradicating the former. He will never again wipe life in all its diverse forms from the earth. Understood in this way, the rainbow symbolizes the divine commitment to a world of cultural diversity.

2. *The Assault on Difference: Sameness and Subjugation.* God's commitment to a diverse world must be understood in order to grasp the significance of what happens next—the construction of a massive "tower" at Babel. However, between the exit from the ark and the building of the tower, the narrator pauses to remind us once more of the divine intent to restore blessing to humanity, conceived as a family of culturally distinct families united in the worship of God. Along the way, he reminds us of the persistence of sin and its role as a barrier to the fulfillment of the divine purpose. However, that sin takes a new form. If violence can be understood as human resistance to fill the earth, the sin that characterizes the postflood period is the corruption of the unity of the peoples that fill the earth.

We might have guessed that the peoples and nations who come to fill the earth descend from Noah's three sons. The author, however, does not leave this to inference. He tells us as much—twice. At both the beginning and close of the postflood segment that stretches from Genesis 9:18 to 10:32, we are told that the peoples that eventually fill the earth all derive from Noah's three sons—Shem, Ham, and Japheth (Gen. 9:19; 10:32). The repetition of this note just before the story of what happens at Babel suggests that the author intends us to have it well in mind as we read that story. As noted earlier, the genealogy of the three brothers forms the Table of Nations that serves as a kind of symbolic representation of the earth filled with tribes and tongues, all in their appointed territories in keeping with the divine purpose.

Following the disastrous preflood history, the outcome pictured in the genealogy would be heartwarming were it achieved as obedience to the divine will. Sadly, it is not. Two stories make this clear—the story of Ham's sin against his parents and humanity's sin against God at Babel.

The first story is equal parts sordid and curious. It is puzzling because the ugly truth has been cloaked in the language of discretion. Noah plants a vineyard, harvests grapes, makes wine, and gets drunk. But then the story takes a darker turn. Ham enters the tent and sees "the nakedness of his father" (Gen. 9:22). He then tells his brothers. For the older brothers, this poses a problem that they resolve with a garment and backward walking. Entering the tent with faces turned, they cover their "father's nakedness" but do not see. When Noah recovers from his stupor and learns of it, he curses not Ham but Ham's youngest son, Canaan. The curse is enslavement to his brothers (identified in the genealogy as Cush, Egypt, and Put) and to his two uncles (Shem and Japheth).

Two questions arise from the surface meaning of the text, both related to the propriety of the curse placed on Canaan. First, is not servitude far too harsh for simply seeing his father naked? Second, whatever the fault of Ham in the incident, why does the consequence fall on his son Canaan?

The compressed and oblique storytelling here cautions against dogmatism about the meaning of the text, but several conclusions seem warranted. First, though the nature of Ham's offense is disputed, most agree that there is a sexual dimension to it. Ancient rabbinic interpretation infers that Ham either castrates or rapes his father.[15] However, a growing number of interpreters have found the use of the same idiom in Leviticus 18:7 instructive. There, we are told that to "uncover the nakedness of your father" is to uncover "the nakedness of your mother" in the context of a law that categorically forbids sexual intercourse between a man and his mother. This would suggest that the concern of the

15 On the rabbinic interpretation of this passage, see David M. Goldenberg, "What Did Ham Do to Noah?" in "The Words of a Wise Man's Mouth are Gracious" (Qoh 10,12), festschrift for Gunter Stemberger, ed. Mauro Perani (Berlin: de Gruyter, 2005), 257–65, accessed in slightly expanded form at https://www.sas.upenn.edu/~dmg2/what%20did %20ham%20do.pdf.

Genesis narrator is not that Ham sees his father disrobed. Rather, Ham sees the nakedness that properly belongs to his father by uncovering the nakedness of his mother.[16] In short, the narrator regards the event as so unspeakable that he refuses to speak it, choosing instead to use a known euphemism for maternal incest.[17]

If this is the case, we can make sense of why the narrator repeatedly notes that Ham was the father of Canaan (Gen. 9:18, 22). This story explains *how* Ham becomes the father of Canaan. The curse falls on Canaan as the offspring of this illicit union.[18]

It is important to note that the curse Noah pronounces need not be read as a punishment imposed by God. Rather, the curse names the social reality that results from Ham's impregnation of his mother. While "first degree" incest is taboo across all cultures, we must ask why this is the case. Contemporary discussions of the taboo converge with the biblical text in two ways: incest resists differentiation in favor of sameness and destroys social cohesion. A few chapters later, in Genesis 19, in an episode widely seen as parallel to this one, Lot's two daughters ply their father with wine and then sleep with him. They have escaped Sodom and Gomorrah but have evidently brought some of Sodom and Gomorrah with them. Both daughters become pregnant. The first names her child Moab, meaning "from my father." The second is no less brazen. She names her son Ben-ammi—"son of my own people" (19:37–38). The text assumes that we are hardwired to look for mates beyond the bounds of immediate kinship. This ensures

---

16 That Ham's "seeing" implies uncovering is indicated by the response of his brothers, who avoid seeing as they cover the nakedness of their father.

17 Jacob Milgrom argues that "the nakedness" of a woman refers euphemistically to her sexual organs, but the same Hebrew expression used in constructions with a man denotes his marital rights over the sexual function of his wife. Milgrom thus renders Leviticus 18:7a as follows: "The sexual jurisdiction of your father, namely, the sexual organs of your mother you shall not uncover." Milgrom, *Leviticus 17–22*, Anchor Bible (New York: Doubleday, 2001), 1537. For a detailed defense of this meaning in Genesis 9, see especially J. S. Bergsma and S. W. Hahn, "Noah's Nakedness and the Curse on Canaan (Genesis 9:20–27)," *Journal of Biblical Literature* 124 (2005): 25–40.

18 The notations in Gen. 9:18, 22 are superfluous unless the story means to tell us how Ham came to be the father of Canaan. Bergsma and Hahn, "Noah's Nakedness," 35.

not only that new families are formed, but also that ties are formed between families.[19]

Incest is also taboo because it disrupts social cohesion and destabilizes the social order. Within the created order described in Genesis, the offspring produced by such acts have no clear place. As the offspring of Ham's mother, is Canaan Ham's son or his brother? Not only is Canaan's place in Noah's line rendered irremediably ambiguous, some commentators suggest that Ham's motivation is to displace his father. His heinous act lays claim to his father's authority. This would explain why he immediately goes and tells his brothers. The author has introduced the episode by identifying Noah's three sons as the ones from whom come the peoples who fill the earth (Gen. 9:19). Those peoples are then identified in the genealogical Table of Nations that follows the episode. If Shem, Ham, and Japheth are presented as the source of the diverse families that fill the earth, Ham's heinous action seriously undermines the unity between them.

This is confirmed not only in the curse that Noah pronounces over Ham's son Canaan, but also in the blessing he pronounces over Shem and Japheth. Noah's pronouncement, like other patriarchal pronouncements in Genesis, is not a prophecy from God, but depicts the social

---

19 The contemporary discussion of incest is wide-ranging and conflicted, driven by two quite different theoretical frameworks—one arising from the field of evolutionary biology and the other arising from socioanthropology. For a brief survey of the history of this discussion, see Johanna Stiebert, *First-Degree Incest and the Hebrew Bible: Sex in the Family* (London: Bloomsbury, 2016), 26–32. For a brief sketch of the two theoretical frameworks and their application to the topic of incest, see Gregory C. Leavitt, "Tylor Vs. Westermarck: Explaining the Incest Taboo," *Sociology Mind* 3 (2013): 45–51. Leavitt advocates and updates Edward Tylor's "social alliance" theory, which holds that a preference for marriage outside one's own immediate group serves the interests of the group by creating survival-enhancing alliances with other groups. In contemporary discussion, the view that evolution has hardwired humans for aversion to incest because it renders the offspring less fit is especially associated with Arthur P. Wolf. He usefully summarizes the discussion and defends his view in *Incest Avoidance and the Incest Taboo: Two Aspects of Human Nature* (Stanford: Stanford University Press, 2014). Some recent discussion seeks to combine the two perspectives, e.g., E. Shor and D. Simachai, "Incest Avoidance, the Incest Taboo, and Social Cohesion: Revisiting Westermarck and the Case of the Israeli Kibbutzim," *American Journal of Sociology* 114 (2009): 1803–42.

reality created by Ham's action and projects it into the future. Without a clear place in Noah's line, Canaan will find himself marginalized and relegated to subservience, while a future of prosperity, cooperation, and commensality opens up to Shem and Japheth: "May God enlarge Japheth, / and let him dwell in the tents of Shem" (9:27).

We must note here that the interpretation of this text has a history even more repulsive than the event it describes. Over the course of many centuries, it was used as a warrant for the enslavement of Africans, as though the bitter fruit of Ham's sin was somehow an expression of the divine will. Among the many problems with this, within Genesis, Canaan and his descendants are not associated with Africa but with the land occupied by Israel after the exodus (Gen. 10:15–19).[20] But if the author's intent is not to justify slavery, the story does clearly show that the preflood problem of conflict between the families of the earth has taken root in postflood soil. The alienation that marred relationships between diverse peoples before the flood has taken a new form—the subjugation of one people to another. If the nature of Ham's sin represents resistance to the divine will for a world filled with diverse peoples, the fruit of his sin is true to its root. The perversion of the unity of all peoples into unitarian sameness results in a social order in which one people is subordinate to another. Resistance to difference in one generation begets subordination of difference in the next. The narrative makes the claim that relationships of hierarchical power between peoples are not a divinely intended social order but an intrinsic (and divinely pronounced) consequence of human repudiation of cultural difference as a divinely intended good.

3. *Twisting Unity into Uniformity: The Dissolution of Difference.*
The second postflood story portrays the rejection of difference in

---

20 David Goldenberg begins his book by commenting, "This biblical story has been the single greatest justification for Black slavery for more than a thousand years." Goldenberg, *The Curse of Ham: Race and Slavery in Early Judaism, Christianity, and Islam* (Princeton: Princeton University Press, 2009), 1. The exegetical justification is not uniquely Christian, as Goldenberg shows, but can be traced in Jewish and Islamic exegesis of this story as well.

another form. In the story of Babel, the human assault on the divine vision of diverse peoples filling the earth and unified in their worship takes a surprising and surprisingly literal form. At least temporarily, the flood destroys violence from the earth, but the underlying sin continues to lurk in human hearts (Gen. 8:21). As the story of Ham shows, the serpent has many heads. No sooner does God deal with the problem of violence than another manifestation of its corrupting influence takes shape on the plains of Shinar. This time, it is not violence but its absence that grabs our attention. The scene at Shinar opens with the world at peace and its inhabitants engaged in a common task, speaking a common language, and unified by a common purpose.

In the history of interpretation, the peaceful unity portrayed at the opening of this passage has been regarded as a God-honoring good. As a result, many continue to understand "the story to mean that ethnic pluralism was largely the unfortunate result of human sinfulness."[21] On this reading, the ethnic differentiation prior to the flood was the root of the violence that provoked the flood. Following the flood, however, humanity was one, and this was good. Surely it was better when everyone spoke the same language, and it would be better still if everyone spoke *my* language!

Many years ago, as new arrivals in Ethiopia, we were struggling to learn Amharic. This had for many years been the "national" language, even though it was the language of just one of Ethiopia's eighty-plus ethnic groups. However, because the Amhara were the ethnic group of a centuries-long imperial dynasty, it had become the language of education and commerce. Ethiopian friends would encourage us by telling us in jest that "Amharic is the language of heaven," as if mastering it would give us a head start on the language we would all one day speak! Ironically, Ethiopia was just commencing a controversial initiative to encourage the nation's many peoples to speak their own

---

21 Bernhard W. Anderson, "Babel Story: Paradigm of Human Unity and Diversity," in *Ethnicity* (New York, 1977): 63–64.

languages with a new policy that allowed children to learn in their mother tongues until seventh grade, at which point all students would learn in English. In many cases, resistance to that idea came from those who believed that Ethiopia would be better off with a single national identity. If everyone spoke the same language, they reasoned, then ethnic tensions would surely recede.

The idea that humanity would be much better off if we all shared a single language and culture has a long and checkered history. As we have seen, however, this is not the ideal set out by God. And this, it seems, takes us to the heart of the rebellion at Babel.

The relationship between the episode at Babel and the Table of Nations in the preceding chapter is theological rather than chronological. As many commentators note, the portrait of humanity drawn in the Table of Nations (Gen. 10) reflects the situation after the incident at Babel (Gen. 11), not before. As noted in chapter 2, the table of seventy peoples represents the *fullness* of the nations, distributed across the earth, each in its own land and speaking its own language (10:5, 20, 31). This is God's intent. It is not *all* that God intends, but it is not *at all* what humanity intends. As the incident at Babel demonstrates, God's purpose is achieved *in spite of* human intention, not because of it. The achievement of that purpose is a blessing that the people who come together at Babel do not want and attempt to avoid.

Within the Table of Nations, there are already signs that all is not well. The table mostly focuses on lines of descent and the peoples who develop from them. But there is an extended sidebar concerning Nimrod, a descendant of Cush who is a "mighty warrior" (Gen. 10:8 NIV). Nimrod, it seems, does not fill the earth by spreading out but by subsuming others under his authority. Several things alert us to this. First, although Cush is regularly associated with the area below Egypt across to the southern tip of the Arabian Peninsula, the kingdom he establishes sprawls across Mesopotamia. If Nimrod is a Cushite, he is far from home. Second, like Cain, he builds cities, but he also establishes a kingdom. Third, the text describes him as "a mighty hunter before the LORD" (10:9). As Gordon Wenham notes, "before the LORD" "is probably no more than a superlative."[22] Such a view leans into the stereotype of ancient Mesopotamian warrior-kings, who were often portrayed as hunters.[23] In short, within the Table of Nations, Nimrod stands out as the only individual whose name does not become the name of a people. He is not the founder of one people but the conqueror of many.

The author's note that the Tower of Babel is on the plains of Shinar (Gen. 11:2) connects the tower to Nimrod. Both Babel and Shinar are centers of his kingdom (10:10). We may not be far from the truth in supposing that Nimrod, like many imperial overlords after him, styles himself as a uniter of nations. This is the stated ambition of those who gather around a kiln at the heart of Nimrod's kingdom. In doing so, they seek to prevent what God intends—the dispersion of peoples who will fill the earth and govern it on his behalf. The initiative begins with a stroke of cultural innovation: "Come, let us make bricks, and burn them thoroughly" (11:3), followed by, "Come, let us build ourselves a city and a tower . . . and let us make a name for ourselves" (11:4). This sequence of self-directing proposals serves a very definite purpose: "lest we be dispersed over the face of the whole earth" (11:4).

It is not certain how the construction of a tower serves this end, but the proximate goal is clear enough—they will be one people, with one language, gathered in one place, under one name. This is not so much a bid for fame as a bid for solidarity. It is not that they desire to make a name for themselves in the eyes of others, but that they wish to form a single *identity*. The text highlights the impressive innovation in material culture—the firing of bricks and the construction of an imposing tower. But the text gives no indication of a religious function for the project. Rather, it focuses only on the tower's role in expressing the people's common identity and in giving that identity a geographic and symbolic center. As one writer puts it, "The narrator's primary interest

---

22 Wenham, *Genesis 1–15*, 223. A number of early Jewish and Christian interpreters, including Augustine, understand the idiom in a negative sense, connoting his arrogance and opposition to the Lord. See especially Mary Katherine Y. H. Hom, "'. . . A Mighty Hunter before Yhwh': Genesis 10:9 and the Moral-Theological Evaluation of Nimrod," *Vetus Testamentum* 60 (2010): 63–68.

23 Hom, "'A Mighty Hunter,'" 68.

is not in the tower but *in the cultural homogeneity* that was the purpose of humanity's building project as a whole."[24] The preflood narrative takes note of a generation that "began to call upon the name of the LORD" (Gen. 4:26). The people who gather at Babel evince no such concern. They give no thought to the will of the one God; their sole focus is to be one people. They reject the divine will for a unity of diverse peoples based on the worship of God for the glory of God. Instead, they seek uniformity across peoples based on a single language and culture for the glory of a name they will make for themselves.

When humanity at Babel moves to unite under one name, God moves to block them. After surveying their work, the Lord comments on their extraordinary unity, "Behold, they are one people, and they have all one language, and this is only the beginning of what they will do. And nothing that they propose to do will now be impossible for them" (Gen. 11:6). We should not understand the construction of the tower as a genuine threat to God's authority. Rather, the divine concern is that if humanity can unite to bring off this massive cultural and technological achievement, there is no human obstacle to their intention to not "be dispersed over the face of the whole earth" (11:4). In response to the proposals that serve that end, God comes with his own: "Let us . . . confuse their language" (11:7). In doing so, he counters their intention with his: "So the LORD dispersed them from there over the face of all the earth" (11:8). In short, what they refuse to do in obedience to the divine will, he does for them. If they will not pursue the diversity God intends, he will impose it.

We see, then, a straight line from Ham's sin and Canaan's curse to Nimrod's aggression to Babel's tower. At the risk of oversimplification, we might say that the preflood narrative is one of a diverse humanity in rebellion against the unity God intends, while the postflood story is one of a unified humanity in rebellion against the diversity God intends. After the flood, the storyline begins with Ham's subversion of

---

24 Theodore Hiebert, "The Tower of Babel and the Origin of the World's Cultures," *Journal of Biblical Literature* 126 (2007): 39.

the human family's unity by his unspeakable sin of sameness and by the resulting destruction of social cohesion. It then turns to Nimrod's impulse to empire before arriving finally at Babel, where a rebellious form of unity is mortared in place brick by brick.

Much of biblical history unfolds in Babel's wake. After the incident at Babel, Scripture places God's dealings with one nation in the foreground, but Babel's distorted version of human unity remains in the background. If not Babel, then Babylon. It is certainly not hard to pick out the similarities between the cultural homogenization symbolized by the tower on the plains of Shinar and the totalizing forces epitomized in the towering image set up by Nebuchadnezzar on the plains of Dura (Dan. 3). But the same will to homogenizing power, not least cultural power, asserts itself again and again in a succession of kingdoms—Assyrian, Babylonian, Persian, Greek, and finally Roman. The polytheism of these kingdoms was not a happy-faced pluralism. These empires regarded the peoples they conquered as children of lesser gods. These empires may have been happy to incorporate the lesser gods of conquered peoples into their pantheons, but they left little doubt that the peoples of lesser gods were lesser peoples. When it served their purposes, they happily laid waste to the cultural and national identities of those they conquered. Little wonder, then, that Israel's prophets described exile as national death. Later on, when cultural dispossession took the apparently more benign form of assimilation—as under the Greeks—many rightly feared that the result would be the total loss of the cultural identities of subjugated peoples. For many, it was.

This, of course, is not simply the arc of biblical history but of human history as well. We may think first of totalitarian regimes where not just political but cultural hegemony is elevated to a virtue. The vision of an Arabized, monolingual world—the hoped-for Ummah of Islamic eschatology—is another useful example. But we also see it wherever the lofty language of unity belies a unitarian cultural vision. The rhetoric of "one America," "one China," or one anything can easily become a seductive cipher for an ideological commitment to cultural uniformity. Such a vision deals in the currency of fear. Whether benignly or baldly, it presses an agenda of assimilation, often by stoking fear that a dominant culture is about to be assimilated. But as we shall see, the biblical vision of unity *requires* diversity. Without difference, there is nothing to unify.

Conclusion

The chapters of Genesis that immediately follow the creation story are often read as a tale of personal sin. But just as the creation story casts a vision not just for a world full of people but a world full of peoples, the sin that worms its way into the world through the rebellion of individuals corrupts not only individual hearts but relationships—relationships between people, but also relationships between peoples. The stories that lead up to the flood portray a world full of peoples in keeping with God's intent. However, as the earth fills with peoples, the peoples fill the earth with violence. The flood brings violence to an end, at least temporarily. But the sin lurking in human hearts soon surfaces again. The stories that lead from the flood to Babel focus not so much on violence between the peoples that once more fill the earth but on a distorted vision of unity that deprives the world of its God-intended diversity. Yet, God's purpose for his creation remains.

By the end of Genesis 11, the stage is set for God to bring that purpose to fulfillment. But he does so in a most surprising way. He does not fashion a system to manage conflict between peoples, as useful as that might be. Instead, he acts to form a new kind of people.

4

One for All

The Restoration of Blessing
in a People of Peoples

A tree can only be as strong as the forest that surrounds it.

PETER WOHLLEBEN, IN *THE HIDDEN LIFE OF TREES*

ON OCTOBER 3, 1935, Italian Prime Minister Benito Mussolini sent a vast army from Eritrea, an Italian colony at the time, into Ethiopia. Italy's first attempt to bring Ethiopia into its colonial fold had failed at the Battle of Adwa in 1896. However, forty years later, Italy's army was far more formidable, and Mussolini had decided it was time to rewrite the national humiliation at Adwa with the ink of colonial glory. The forbidding mountains of Ethiopia's highlands had served its defenses well in 1896. But the mountains were no match for bombers, especially when their bowels were heavy with poison gas.

Shortly after the onslaught began, Ethiopia's emperor, Haile Selassie I, was forced to flee the country for London, where he proved to be a relentless advocate for the reversal of the unprovoked invasion of his country. In June 1936, he laid out the atrocities being perpetrated against Ethiopia before the League of Nations in Geneva:

Special sprayers were installed on board aircraft so that they could vaporize, over vast areas of territory, a fine, death-dealing rain. Groups of nine, fifteen, eighteen aircraft followed one another so that the fog issuing from them formed a continuous sheet. It was thus that, as from the end of January 1936, soldiers, women, children, cattle, rivers, lakes and pastures were drenched continually with this deadly rain . . . to kill off systematically all living creatures.[1]

The League had been formed in the wake of World War I to ensure that relations between nations remained just and that conflicts were justly mediated. It had been instrumental in the resolution of several disputes between smaller nations. The League believed that the diminutive emperor's appeal was justified and put the matter to Mussolini. He scoffed, "The League is very well when sparrows shout but is no good at all when eagles fall out."[2] His point was clear: the League of Nations might have a role in sorting out the disputes of small countries, but if the conflict involved a powerful nation, the League was powerless. It had no army with which to stop Mussolini, and given that many of its members had asserted colonial control over other nations, it had little moral ground to object to Italy's actions. So the League did nothing. Only when the Italians attacked British colonial interests in the region several years later did Britain intervene.

In June 2020, a brief epilogue to the episode unfolded in London. A British family who had hosted Haile Selassie for a time during his exile in England had erected a statue of the emperor in a small London park. However, in the unrest that followed the killing of an ethnic Oromo singer and activist, Hachalu Hundessa, London-based members of the Oromo, the largest of Ethiopia's ethnic groups, angrily toppled the likeness of the emperor. Haile Selassie was an Amhara, and, for centuries, the Amhara had claimed the right to rule. As an

---

1   Haile Selassie, "Appeal to the League of Nations," June 1936, https://www.mtholyoke.edu/.
2   Cited in Allan Phillips, "Historical Background on the Declaration," in *The United Nations Declaration on Minorities: An Academic Account on the Occasion of Its 20th Anniversary (1992-2012)*, ed. Rainer Hofmann and Ugo Caruso (Leiden: Brill, 2015), 5.

Amhara proverb put it, "An Amhara rules; he is not ruled."[3] Haile
Selassie was an "emperor" not because he asserted colonial control
over other countries, but because he exercised imperial control over
the ethnic groups of Ethiopia. Eighty-five years after his moving
speech in Geneva and forty-five years after his death, ethnic resent-
ment smoldered still.

The emperor viewed the Italian occupation of Ethiopia as a grave
injustice, but he did not see Amhara control of Ethiopia as a problem.
Perhaps he distinguished his own rule as an Ethiopian from that of
outsiders. Indeed, many have seen in his rule a concerted effort to
build a multiethnic society.[4] Nevertheless, many others look back at
his rule as one predicated on ethnic hierarchy. A passionate defender
of equality between countries, in the eyes of many, he failed to see the
peoples of his own country in the same light.

The account raises a question that arises every day. It is the question
with which we began this study: How should nations and peoples relate
to one another? To ask this question is to ask about God's purposes. If
God's intention is that humanity fill the earth with culturally distinct
peoples, does this mean they should live apart from one another? Or is
there also a divinely intended configuration of peoples, a form of unity
between peoples of differing cultural identities? To those accustomed
to thinking of Scripture as a guide to a personal relationship with God,
the question of God's intention for the relationship between peoples
may seem out of bounds. But is it? The consequence of assuming that
it is an unimportant question is that many Christians hold views of
the relationship between nations and peoples that are formed less by
Scripture than by one of the political conceptions of the state surveyed
in the opening chapter. However, in a way that differs markedly from
these contemporary approaches to cultural multiplicity within states,
Scripture sets out a distinctive vision for the way in which the peoples
of the earth ought to relate to one another. We catch the first glimpse

3   In Amharic, *Amhara yazzal, inji aytazzazim.*
4   Donald N. Levine, *Greater Ethiopia: The Evolution of a Multiethnic Society,* 2nd ed. (Chi-
    cago: University of Chicago Press, 2000).

of this vision in the story of God's dealings with a Chaldean herder named Abram.

Particularity and Its Point

We have lingered over the early chapters of Genesis because they set the stage for a drama that unfolds over the pages of Scripture. The first eleven chapters keep our attention on the whole stage. Still, the individuals that cross the stage matter, and their choices as individuals are heavy with moral meaning. We learn this in part from the nonhuman characters in the story. The serpent coaxes rebellion from untested innocence, sin crouches at the door, and blood unjustly spilled cries its grievance from the ground. We also learn that individuals matter and have meaning in relation to the character who takes the stage before all others and makes the stage before he takes it: "In the beginning, God . . ."

If the first eleven chapters set a universal stage designed by the lead character in the drama, the story that unfolds on this stage is not simply one of individuals and their interactions with each other and with God. The author also populates the stage with families and clans, nations and peoples. As such, the story is necessarily about the relationships between these peoples and the place of each in God's design.

As we have seen, the story goes badly twice and in two ways: first, the perversion of diversity with violence strikes against the unity of humanity, then the perversion of unity with uniformity strikes against the diversity of humanity. God addresses the former with the flood and a kind of re-creation with a renewed separation of the waters. However, in some ways, the situation at Babel is worse. Prior to the flood, Noah, at least, was described as righteous. But there is no Noah at Babel—no one through whom the Lord might seed the re-creation of creation. The story of Babel concludes with only one piece of the divine purpose in place. Diverse nations and peoples have filled the earth, but they are far from united in the worship of God. The God-achieved diversity of humanity has not yet been unified in a God-honoring end.

This is the dramatic moment that brings us to Genesis 12. Judging from the space allocated, we might say that the achievement of diversity within the human family was the easy part. To be sure, it took two decisive actions—the destruction of all people in the flood and the dispersion of all peoples at Babel—to bring us to this point. But what happens next sets a course that will occupy the attention of the biblical writers right through to the end of the canon. To achieve his purposes for peoples, God acts in a surprising way. He comes to a man named Abram and says, "Go from your country and your kindred and your father's house" (12:1). This is to be a new beginning, one that opens with the formation of a new family—a new people—in a new land.

This new beginning has much in common with the re-creation of the world at the time of Noah. Once more, God takes the initiative in the form of a unilateral covenant with an individual. Yet, there are also significant differences. The covenant with Noah was simply a promise of something God would never do again. But the oath God makes to Abram is a promise to make something of the diversity he fashioned through his action at Babel. Through the one family that he will make from Abram, he will restore blessing to all the families of the earth. In blessing one people, he promises to bind all peoples together in a community of blessing with himself as the source of blessing.

A Community of Blessing:
The Covenant with Abraham in Two Parts

It would be difficult to overstate the centrality of this text or the centrality of blessing to this text. In some discussions, a dispute over a point of Hebrew grammar has obscured a straightforward but profoundly beautiful idea. This idea is summarized in Genesis 12 as an initiative with two parts. The first part is then revisited in Genesis 15, followed by an exploration of the second part in Genesis 17.

In the first part of God's initiative, he promises to restore blessing to one people, enabling them to fulfill their intended purpose. God's oath thus begins with a promise to bless Abram—to make from him a great nation. The second part is contingent on the first. Once blessing is restored to one people, that people will mediate blessing to other peoples—a divine intention marked by a change in Abram's name to Abraham. Further, these peoples will return blessing to the people of Abraham. Then, as the peoples bless the people of Abraham, God in turn will bless them. In this way, all the peoples of the earth will find blessing "in you" (Gen. 12:3)—that is, God's covenant will establish a community of blessing that will embrace all peoples. God himself will initiate a dynamic movement of blessing that forms a people whom he blesses. In doing so, he constitutes that people as a community of reciprocal blessing within which all peoples both receive and return blessing to one another and to God. As the initiator of this blessing, God is a member of this community of reciprocal blessing and, as such, he, too, receives blessing in the form of worship.[5]

This way of conceptualizing the relationship between nations and peoples was unique within the ancient world and especially among the peoples of Canaan. Among the Canaanite peoples, each people or nation had its own god, and the well-being of each people turned on two things: the god's power to secure the well-being of the people and the willingness of that god to do so. Scholars have sometimes described this "henotheistic" worldview as a kind of halfway house between polytheism and monotheism, but this is mistaken. A henotheist was simply a polytheist who recognized the special obligations of a particular people to a particular god. This idea typically arose when a god had a particular connection to a people's land—a worldview that Daniel Block describes as "territorial henotheism."[6] Within this worldview, the primary link

5   When God is the object rather than the source of blessing in Scripture, the content of the blessing is the worship of his covenant people who bless the Lord in response to blessing received as a covenantal benefit. See, for example, Ps. 67.
6   Daniel Block coins the expression "territorial henotheism" in relation to Canaanite religion to reflect evidence that the gods of Canaanite peoples were primarily territorial deities. A people came to give primary loyalty to a deity by virtue of living in the territory of that deity. Israel's God differed in the claim that he was primarily the God of a people and only of a territory in the secondary sense. He became their God prior to his gift of land.

was between god and land. The blessings afforded the land by its deity might be withheld if the people failed to induce the favor of that god. But because the primary connection was between the god and the land, the people of that land did not consider the deity's blessing on the land shareable with or relevant to the peoples of other lands.[7]

The covenantal language of Genesis 12 points in quite a different direction. In philosophical terms, the covenant constructs what Charles Taylor calls a "social imaginary."[8] As we will see, the social imaginary of Genesis locates individuals within peoples, all peoples within one people, and one God in the midst who initiates a reciprocal exchange of blessing, imparting blessing to one for the sake of all. The people are given land, *but the fundamental relationship of the covenant is not between God and the land but between God and the people.*[9] The bedrock affirmation of the covenant underscores this: "I will be your God, and you shall be my people" (Jer. 7:23). Within this relationship, the core commitment of God is to bless his people and then to bless all peoples in them or through them.

1. *What Is Blessing?* Before elucidating this two-part idea in Genesis 15 and 17, we must clarify the nature of the blessing that God is promising to restore. In the preceding chapters, the blessing God imparts to the various spheres of his creation is a dynamic force that enables each recipient to function in robust fulfillment of the divine design. In Genesis 1, God creates the creatures with which the sea and sky teem. He then "blessed them . . . [and] said to them, 'Be fruitful and multiply'" (1:28). As Gordon Wenham rightly notes, God's "blessing"

Block, *The Gods of the Nations: Studies in Ancient Near Eastern National Theology*, 2nd ed. (Eugene, OR: Wipf & Stock, 2013), 63.

7   According to Block, "The function of a nation's territory was to respond to the deity's blessing by yielding abundant harvests for the inhabitants." Conquest might be understood as proof of the superiority of the conquering nation's god or gods, but it also secured material benefits derived from conquered lands. Block, *Gods*, 152

8   The term "social imaginary" comes from Charles Taylor, *Modern Social Imaginaries* (Durham, NC: Duke University Press, 2004), 23. He uses the expression to describe the way in which ordinary people imagine the social world.

9   Block, *Gods*, 149–53.

continues the work of creation in that it enables the creatures to do what they were made to do, to flourish in the fulfillment of their purpose as creatures of sea and sky.[10] Thus, God creates diverse forms of life and, then, by blessing them, endows them with the power to produce fullness from that diversity.

On the seventh day of creation, God rests from the work of creation (Gen. 2:2). He then blesses that day (2:3). When God blesses the seventh day, it is a way of saying that the work of creation has ended and the work of governance begins—a governance shared with humanity, whom he blesses for that purpose.[11] Thus, when he blesses humanity and blesses the seventh day, God infuses the governance he shares with humanity with the vitality essential for the fulfillment of its purpose. If the proper end of human governance is worship, the governance itself is the creative task of filling the earth with peoples through the development of diverse patterns of work and ways of life. God's blessing enables this governance and enables all that results from it to be returned to him as worship. This blessing is what God sets out to restore through the covenant with Abraham.

In imparting blessing to one people, God purposes to restore blessing to all peoples *in the same sense.* In other words, he restores to Israel properly functioning peoplehood with a view to restoring that same blessing to all peoples. Israel will be the people by whom and in whom the peoples of the earth experience this blessing. Renewed in this way, the peoples of the earth will innovate ways of being in the world for the good of the world and the glory of God. *Because this blessing flows from God to one people, initiating a cycle of reciprocity, blessing can be experienced only through the interactions of one people with another.* This goes

10 Gordon J. Wenham notes "how here and in 1:28; 2:3; 5:2 a statement about God's blessing, ברך [brk] immediately follows a mention of his creating, ברא [br']. Divine blessing continues God's benevolent work in creation, and the writer exploits the verbal similarity between the terms to draw attention to their theological relationship." Wenham, *Genesis 1–15*, Word Biblical Commentary (Dallas: Word, 1987), 24.

11 For a brief summary of the evidence and additional bibliography, see John Walton, *The Lost World of Genesis One: Ancient Cosmology and the Origins Debate* (Downers Grove, IL: InterVarsity Press, 2010), 71–77.

to the heart of why God's purpose to restore blessing does not unfold as a general initiative toward all individuals or even to all peoples, but as a particular initiative to one people. The fulfillment of this purpose requires that the relations between peoples be marked not by oppression and acrimony, but by a disposition to cultivate the good that God has woven into the fabric of all he has made.

Genesis 3–11 narrates the way in which sin drains the life-giving vitality of divine blessing from humanity, leaving their culture-creating, people-forming, earth-filling efforts in ruins. On five occasions, the author designates the rebellious abandonment of blessing as a curse. In Genesis 12, however, the covenant that God initiates with Abraham can only be understood as the divine initiative to restore blessing to humanity. In this covenant, the fivefold curse is countered with God's promise of fivefold blessing.[12]

The initial promise of blessing in Genesis 12 is subsequently developed in Genesis 15 and 17, where the two dimensions of blessing are explored in turn.

2. *The Restoration of Blessing to One People—Genesis 15.* The restoration of blessing initiated through God's covenant with Abraham takes the form of national identity. The national focus of the covenant can be obscured in treatments that see it as an expression of God's intent to restore blessing to all people. Though this adequately captures the universal intent of the covenant, it flattens the covenant's clear focus on peoples and undermines the preparation for that focus in the preceding narrative.

Several key elements of collective identity come to the fore in Genesis 12, but the promise of blessing restored takes an even clearer national form in the rearticulation of the covenant promise in Genesis 15. We may see this by setting these elements alongside the characteristics of ethnicity set out by John Hutchinson and Anthony Smith:[13]

---

12 Wenham, *Genesis 1–15*, 270. The five references to "blessing" in Gen. 12:2–3 correspond to the five declarations of "curse" in Gen. 3–11 (3:14, 17; 4:11; 5:29; 9:25)

13 John Hutchinson and Anthony D. Smith, "Introduction," in *Ethnicity*, eds. John Hutchinson and Anthony D. Smith (Oxford: Oxford University Press, 1996), 6–7.

Hutchinson and Smith	Genesis 12, 15
"a common proper name"	"I will make your name great" (i.e., not "Abram" per se but the name of the people descended through Isaac then Jacob—that is, Israel)
"a myth of common ancestry . . . kinship"	"Count the stars . . . so shall your offspring be" (i.e., the people descended from Abraham)
"shared memories of a common past"	Abraham's descendants will be enslaved for four hundred years before possessing the land
"elements of a common culture," normally including "religion, customs, or language"	a covenant with Yahweh; ratification through sacrifice; plus, sign of circumcision (17:10)
"a link with a homeland"	"I brought you out of Ur . . . to give you this land"
"a sense of solidarity"	the people bound together by the covenant with Yahweh

Table 4.1. Elements of Collective Identity.

If there is a gap between these depictions of collective identity, it is in the nature of the link to a homeland. For many groups, that link lies in a vague and distant past. But for Abraham, the promised land is definite and demarcated—"from the river of Egypt to the great river, the river Euphrates, the land of the Kenites, the Kenizzites, the Kadmonites, the Hittites, the Perizzites, the Rephaim, the Amorites, the Canaanites, the Girgashites and the Jebusites" (15:18–21). Two different words are used in the Old Testament to describe the descendants of Abraham—words that are regularly translated as "people" ('am) and "nation" (goy). One author has suggested that a "nation" is a "people" with its own land.[14] Whether or not this linguistic distinction holds up

14 Steven Grosby, "Religion and Nationality in Antiquity: The Worship of Yahweh and Ancient Israel," *European Journal of Sociology* 32 (1991): 231.

for the Hebrew terms, we readily recognize the difference between the two concepts. At this point, we need not concern ourselves with how and when a "national" identity enters into the collective psyche of this people. The key point is that nationhood is held out to Abraham in an entirely *ordinary* sense. The Israelites will be a people who trace their origins back to Abraham, to whom God promised a specific territorial inheritance. The blessing is not, therefore, a generalized promise of prosperity or well-being. Rather, it takes the form of nationhood.

I stress this point because it is easy to lose sight of the fact that the blessing given to Abraham is not an abstraction, though, as we shall see, there is a clear spiritual dimension to it. At the same time, to say that the blessing is concrete is not to identify the blessing promised to Abraham with personal prosperity. Rather, blessing is the concrete experience of nationality, of cultural identity, of being a particular people in a particular place. To the extent that material well-being is enjoyed by individual members or families within the nation or by the nation as a whole, it is a result of being a particular people in a particular place, doing what God commissioned them to do. I describe this blessing of nationality or peoplehood as "ordinary" because it bears the same traits of cultural identity attributed to the peoples listed in the Table of Nations in Genesis 10, all with their own lands and languages.[15]

And yet, there is something different. The blessing restored is not ethnicity or nationality as experienced by every other nation, but nationality as it was *meant* to be experienced. This, as we have seen, is what it means for God to bless something. When God blesses something, it functions in keeping with the divine purpose and design.

Much of the discussion of Genesis 15 has focused on the meaning of "covenant." Many have spoken of the covenant as a promise

---

15 It is useful to note that Karl Barth placed the discussion of nationhood and national identity within the section on ethics in his *Christian Dogmatics*. He did not regard nationhood or national identity as part of the creation order but saw nations and the experience of belonging to a particular people as the sphere within which Christians are called to obey God. As Carys Moseley distills Barth's view: "Nations are the context for Christian discipleship." Moseley, *Nations and Nationalism in the Theology of Karl Barth* (Oxford: Oxford University Press, 2013), 178, with reference to *Church Dogmatics*, III/4, 289.

of relationship and redemption. John Walton, by contrast, places the emphasis on revelation.[16] However we think about what God does within the covenant, we must not forget the nature of the blessing that God's covenantal actions secure. Revelation, relationship, and redemption all prove necessary for the blessing of the covenant to be realized. God's initiative to reveal himself, to establish a relationship with himself, and to secure redemption from sin must do its work in individual lives. At the same time, this must not obscure the fact that Genesis 12 and 15 cast the outcome of God's covenant initiative as the blessing experienced in the form of national identity.

Though the blessing promised to Abraham is the blessing of people-hood, the covenant is not formed, in the first instance, with a people but with a person. The scope of covenantal blessing is national and collective, but it begins with an individual who responds to God's covenantal initiative in faith. When God promises to form from him a great nation, we are told that Abraham "believed the LORD, and he counted it to him as righteousness" (Gen. 15:6).

The narrator's comment is crucial, and we must not rush by it. The term *righteousness* is not so much a characterization of a status conferred on Abraham as a characterization of his faith. In other words, Abraham is not considered righteous because of his faith; rather, his faith is righteousness in the eyes of God. This is not simply saying that in believing God's promise, Abraham does the right thing. Rather, as Bruce Waltke notes, *righteousness* connotes "behavior that serves the community according to God's norms . . . and establishes the well-being of the community."[17] In commenting on the earlier assessment of Noah as "righteous" (Gen. 6:9), Waltke states that the righteous are those who "are willing to disadvantage themselves to advantage others."[18] Abraham's faith is counted as righteousness in this specific sense. He

---

16 John Walton, *Genesis*, NIV Application Commentary (Grand Rapids, MI: Zondervan, 2001), 400–404.

17 Bruce K. Waltke, *Genesis: A Commentary* (Grand Rapids, MI: Zondervan Academic, 2016), 242.

18 Waltke, *Genesis*, 133.

leaves his own people and land in the expectation that blessing will flow to a people that God will form from him, and from that people to all peoples.

3. *The Restoration of Blessing to One People for the Sake of All Peoples—Genesis 17.* In Genesis 17, Abram becomes Abraham. His new name unveils God's intent to make him the "father of many nations" (Gen. 17:5 NIV). This is the second part of the dual idea introduced in Genesis 12. If the focus of Genesis 15 is the restoration of blessing to one people, the focus of Genesis 17 is the restoration of blessing to all peoples.

However, the difference between these two initiatives does not lie only in the fact that the first is particular and national, whereas the second is universal and international. Beyond that, the Genesis 15 initiative to restore blessing to the people God will form from Abraham is unilateral and unconditional, while the initiative of Genesis 17 is bilateral and conditional. The point seems to be that if blessing is to flow from this new people to all peoples and if all peoples are to experience the restoration of blessing through that new people, that new people will have to be a certain sort of people. Abraham could not "become 'father of a multitude of nations' unless he first became the father of a 'great nation.'"[19] In what does this people's greatness consist and how does it serve as a channel of blessing to all peoples?

Genesis 17 and the biblical tradition that builds on it highlight three things in particular. First, this nation will be characterized by a righteousness that comes from faith. At least initially, the greatness promised to it seems to take the form of numerous descendants and land. Doubtless these two features of the promise are essential if this is to be a great nation. At the same time, these two features of the promise have little basis in Abraham's experience at the time God gives him the promise: his wife, we have been told, is unable to conceive (Gen.

---

19 Paul R. Williamson, *Abraham, Israel, and the Nations: The Patriarchal Promise and Its Covenantal Development in Genesis*, Journal for the Study of the Old Testament Supplement Series (Sheffield: Sheffield Academic Press, 2000), 262.

11:30), and Abraham, he has been told, must leave his own land (12:1). Nevertheless, Abraham believes God's promise to form from him a nation of blessing, and God counts it to him as righteousness.

The faith that God counts as righteousness is manifest in actions in which Abraham's trust in God leads him to disadvantage himself for the sake of others. Commanded to leave his country and relatives, he leaves. In the ensuing narrative, the primary threats to the promise of nationhood take the form of threats to Abraham's faith. Not once but twice, the promise of descendants is put at risk by Abraham's faithless misrepresentation of Sarah as his sister to a foreign king who sought to wed her (Gen. 12:13; 20:2). If not for divine action, the promise of "seed" would have been lost. Moreover, because of Abraham's failure of faith, the kings who had sought to wed Abraham's "sister" are beset with disaster. His sin puts at risk the formation of the people in whom God had purposed to restore blessing and, in doing so, compromises the flow of blessing to all peoples. Nevertheless, after God provided the promised heir, Abraham did not withhold him when God required that the heir be given back. Since God had promised that the great nation would be formed through Isaac, Abraham believed that "God was able even to raise him from the dead" (Heb. 11:19). This would be a people formed through faith.

The narrative portrays a kind of preliminary fulfillment of the promised community of blessing among peoples through Abraham's faith-fueled righteousness, a preview of what it means to be a "great nation." In Genesis 14, Abraham acts to restore justice and peace among warring kings. In response, a king named Melchizedek comes to Abraham, offering a shared meal of bread and wine. As "priest of God Most High," he pronounces blessing over Abraham and blesses the Creator who has granted success to Abraham's efforts. Abraham responds to this blessing with blessing in kind, conferring on Melchizedek "a tenth of everything" (14:18–20).[20]

---

20 The point is made in a negative way in relation to the king of Sodom. Abraham acts to repulse the dispossession of Sodom. But the king acknowledges neither God nor the dynamic of blessing at work through Abraham. Instead, he attempts to strike a deal: "Give

Second, the greatness of the people to whom God restores blessing will be manifest in their love for God and for people, made possible by the presence of God in their midst. In Deuteronomy 4:5–8, we again find Abraham's descendants depicted as a "great nation." The expression occurs infrequently, so its recurrence in another pivotal text commands our attention. If its use in Genesis 12 conveys the promise of national identity, in Deuteronomy 4 it contemplates the fulfillment of that promise through the constitution of Israel as a nation at Mount Sinai. Moses declares,

> See, I have taught you statutes and rules, as the LORD my God commanded me, that you should do them in the land that you are entering to take possession of it. Keep them and do them, for that will be your wisdom and your understanding in the sight of the peoples, who, when they hear all these statutes, will say, "Surely this *great nation* is a wise and understanding people." For what great nation is there that has a god so near to it as the LORD our God is to us, whenever we call upon him? And what great nation is there, that has statutes and rules so righteous as all this law that I set before you today? (Deut. 4:5–8)

Here, as Israel is about to enter the land, the greatness of the nation is set forth in terms of the wisdom of a people who live in keeping with God's righteous law and its provision for the corresponding presence of God in their midst. In Deuteronomy 5, this law is articulated as a covenantal commitment to God and to the well-being of one's neighbor. This, in Deuteronomy, is what it means for Israel to be a "great" nation—a greatness that God intends to be a source of wonder and blessing to the nations.

The import of Israel's righteousness for the nations is already anticipated in Genesis 17. Unlike the covenantal initiative of Genesis 15, the language of Genesis 17 is bilateral. If Abraham is to be the father of many

---

me the persons, but take the goods for yourself." But Abraham will not have it. The king of Sodom does not want a righteous community of blessing but a commodified exchange of obligation—a proposition that Abraham rejects (Gen. 14:21–24).

nations, he must "walk before me, and be blameless [*tamim*]." The term signifies not perfection, as some have suggested, but wholeness—a fit description of a person whose heart and action are united, whose loyalty to God is undivided, and whose treatment of people is of a piece with his or her devotion to God. If the nation formed from Abraham is to be not only the recipient of blessing but an agent of blessing to all nations, the people must be wholly devoted to God and wholly committed to the well-being of others. The blessing consists in being what God intended them to be—a community in which life received from God is lived with God and for God, and with others and for the good of others. To be constituted as this kind of people is already to be a people concerned not just about the well-being of itself but of all peoples.[21]

Third, Israel's greatness is to be realized in the establishment of a royal line within the nation that would spring from Abraham and Sarah. This expectation is embedded in the covenantal promise to make Abraham a father of many nations (Gen. 17:5–6, 11). As a result, the paired expectation of many kings might be understood as an entailment of Abraham's designation as a "father of a multitude of nations." But the text forestalls such an understanding with the note that kings would come from Sarah through Isaac, not from Hagar through Ishmael (cf. Gen. 35:11).

As Paul Williamson notes, though this expectation of royal progeny links Abraham's role as the father of a nation to his significance

---

21 The practice of circumcision, appointed as a sign of the covenant in Genesis 17:9–10, may relate to the question of collective identity. In this text, the practice is tied to the covenantal requirement that Abraham be *tamim*—a word that designates wholeness. In ritual contexts, wholeness is tied to fitness for the intended sacrificial purpose. In metaphorical contexts, "uncircumcised" hearts, eyes, or ears are incapable of doing what hearts, eyes, and ears are intended to do in God's purpose. "This metaphorical concept of suitability presumably lay at the heart of physical circumcision also; circumcision connoted the idea of suitability for participation in God's plan and purpose for his covenant people." P. R. Williamson, "Circumcision," in *Dictionary of the Old Testament: Pentateuch*, ed. T. Desmond Alexander and David W. Baker (Downers Grove, IL: InterVarsity Press, 2003), 124–25. Circumcision thus identified Abraham's descendants as a people in whom the blessing of a properly functioning humanity had been restored. They were *tamim* (Gen. 17:1) in being a "before God and for others" kind of people, enabling them to play their part in a community of blessing made up of all peoples.

as the father of many nations, the nature of the link is developed not in Genesis but in Psalms. In one of the few Old Testament texts that evokes the covenant with Abraham, Psalm 72 makes this link clear in the expectation of a Davidic king in whom the nations would be blessed. The ideal king of the psalm "is clearly depicted as the mediator of the Abrahamic blessing; the role formerly associated with Abraham is assumed by the author to have been inherited by this Davidic king."[22] Here we find a clear precursor to the "in Messiah" theology of the New Testament. This is not to abandon the promise of nationhood made to Abraham, but to recognize the ideal king as the one who embodies both the righteous rule of God and the righteous people who live under that rule:

> Endow the king with your justice, O God,
>   the royal son with your righteousness.
> May he judge your people in righteousness,
>   your afflicted ones with justice. (Ps. 72:1–2 NIV)

But a people ordered in righteousness will not simply flourish under the blessing mediated through the king; their king will be a source of blessing for the nations, who in turn will bless the king of this people (Ps. 72:3–17). Here again, we see the divine intention of a community of blessing, with God himself as the source of blessing poured out on one people for the sake of all peoples. The greatness of this people will be realized in and through the greatness of their king.

Identities of Power or Blessing?

In much contemporary rhetoric, the nature of cultural identity is understood in inherently oppositional terms. Indeed, some theorists do not simply describe the experience of cultural identity as frequently oppositional, but *define* cultural identity as the experience of opposition. To experience cultural identity, they say, is either to oppress or

22   Williamson, *Abraham*, 169.

be oppressed. Thus, to speak about identity is to speak about power. This lens on the way we experience our sense of belonging to particular groups is often described as "identity politics"—an expression that arises from the perception that the most salient thing about the relationships between groups is disparity in power.

Karl Marx famously analyzed human history as a struggle between oppressors and the oppressed. For Marx, the struggle for power was between groups defined by economic class. Today, some theorists use a similar analysis in their assessment of the relationship between ethnic or racial groups within a society, blending it with postmodern philosophical perspectives on power. For postmodernists, knowledge is perspectival, so claims to truth function as assertions of power over others. Not just politics, but history, law, religion, and language itself are forms of power. The role of Critical Theory has been to construe these various acts of power as the acts of groups, including cultural groups. Racism (or ethnocentrism) is not simply attributable to individuals who regard some groups as innately inferior to others. Rather, these "isms" are characteristic of racial or ethnic groups and the cultural systems that perpetuate the power and privilege from which their members benefit.[23]

The use of power as the dominant lens for considering the relationships between peoples is also evident on the other end of the political spectrum. National populists fuel a sense of group grievance with a belief that their racial, ethnic, or national identities were once *rightfully* dominant but are now threatened. In one sense, the nationalist form of identity politics poses the greater threat to a Christian way of thinking about the world because it not only embraces the notion that cultural groups are power identities but celebrates and pursues the dominance of one group over another.

Though we must not embrace this way of looking at the world, it certainly reflects the reality that oppression often mars relationships

23 Though the meaning of the expression "critical race theory" has become politicized and, therefore, blurred, Critical Theory as a concept that existed prior to its application to racial or ethnic groups is helpfully explored by Tim Keller, "A Biblical Critique of Secular Justice and Critical Theory," *Life in the Gospel*, August 2020, https://quarterly.gospelinlife.com/.

between groups. Scripture can and often does portray nations and peoples in relationships defined fundamentally by disparities in power. Such relationships are invariably characterized as unrighteousness.[24] The premier example of this in Scripture comes when Abraham's descendants find themselves enslaved in Egypt. Although such disparities often reflect the way things are, it is not the way things are meant to be. The circumstances that precede the enslavement of Abraham's descendants in Egypt illustrate that God's covenant with Abraham is meant to restore humanity as a community of blessing between peoples. The actions of the individuals who make up this nascent nation demonstrate the necessity of a grace-wrought transformation. If this nation is to be the people in whom and through whom blessing is restored to all peoples, they will have to change. The pride, malice, and envy that mark the twelve sons of Israel must give way to forgiveness, mercy, and love.

The story of transformation unfolds as a story of God's providential involvement in individual lives, not least the life of Joseph. But as the closing chapters of Genesis make clear, Israel's twelve sons become twelve tribes. Here we learn that the one nation itself will be a people of peoples. Before they can be a nation that mediates righteousness and blessing to all peoples, they must learn to live as one people whose unity depends on the righteousness of their collective life and the presence of God as the source of life and blessing in their midst. That, in turn, will require a king they do not yet have—a king who will administer God's justice for the nation and lead all nations to obedience (Gen. 49:8–12).

Conclusion

Despite a widespread perception that Scripture has little to say about the relationship of one people to another, the early chapters of Genesis suggest the opposite. The relationship between peoples turns out to be

24 This is true even when the oppression is an outcome of divine judgment. Though the Old Testament frequently portrays divine judgment as God's act of giving a people over to its enemies, these enemies carry out the divine will unintentionally. As a result, they are themselves held accountable for their unrighteous acts toward the others.

a central concern. The narrative that opens Scripture does not view humanity as simply a collection of individuals, but situates individuals within families and families with peoples. This in no way suggests that the arc of Scripture bends away from Enlightenment individualism (e.g., classical liberalism and its contemporary variants) toward one or another of the communitarian constructions of reality (e.g., Marxism or various versions of identity politics) in which the significance of individuals fades to nothing. Over against these two extremes, the Scriptures strongly assert both the extraordinary significance and value of individuals made in the image of God *and* of the peoples within which individual lives have moral meaning. To view reality in this way means that Scripture necessarily focuses on both individuals (and their relationships) and on peoples (and the relationships between them).

The encounter between God and Abraham unveils the divine purpose to restore blessing to humanity by restoring the blessing of a properly functioning nationhood. When God promises to make Abraham a great nation, he means that he will form from Abraham an ordinary people, one whose greatness will consist in the righteousness of a collective life lived before God and for God. But the greatness will also consist in the way this nation mediates divine blessing to all peoples. The peoples of the earth are neither to collapse their differences into unitarian sameness (as at Babel) nor to distort their diversity into a hierarchy of oppression and violence (as with Cain and Nimrod). Rather, in the divine vision revealed to Abraham, the peoples are to come together in a community of blessing with God in their midst as the ultimate source of blessing. This "blessing" is not a cipher for material prosperity. Instead, it is a depiction of every people doing what they are meant to do—living with one another in righteousness and peace, but doing so in a myriad of expressions of the creative stewardship of God's creation. For that to happen, every nation and people must regard every other nation and people not only as important to God but as essential to their own well-being. The blessing that originates with God is not simply allocated to all peoples, as though each nation and people were independent of all others or able to experience this blessing in isolation from all others. Rather, it originates with a God who blesses one people, who in turn mediate that blessing to other peoples. Those peoples, in turn, return blessing to the one people and to God, who then imparts his blessing to them, as part of an ongoing relationship of reciprocity.

Articles of Separation

Desecration, Dissolution, and
the Death of Nations

*The disappearance of nations would impoverish us no less than
if all peoples were made alike, with one character, one face.
Nations are the wealth of mankind; they are its generalized
personalities: the smallest of them has its own particular
colors and embodies a particular facet of God's design.*

ALEXANDER SOLZHENITSYN, NOBEL LECTURE (1970)

A FEW YEARS AGO, I was involved in an effort to assess the progress
of the gospel among the various peoples of Ethiopia. Although we had
several different data sets, we worried that there were too many gaps
and mistakes in the data to guide the efforts of churches and mission
agencies. As we compared the sources of information, it was clear
that one of the least reached areas of the country lay in the southwest
corner of Ethiopia, where a large number of small people groups dot
the Omo River valley. On a political map of Ethiopia, these peoples
are lumped together in a region called "Southern Nations, Nationalities and Peoples," though the difference between the three terms was

never very clear. We noticed that one group—the Dime (*di-may*)—was especially small: only 891 people remained. Other groups were smaller still. One report found only 115 Biraile people, of whom only twelve older adults could still speak their native Ongota language.[1] According to the report, the group's cultural identity has been absorbed into that of a neighboring people.

Linguistic and cultural extinction is not as rare as we might suppose. Of the 225 living languages of the United States, 164 are classified as "dying" and fifty-nine more are "in trouble." Dozens more have already disappeared. Between 1998 and 2019, sixty languages of peoples indigenous to the United States became extinct.[2] Sometimes the extinction of languages coincides with the disappearance of the cultural identities of those who spoke them. When that happens, it is not just languages that disappear but cultures. We rightly lament their loss.

This is not a new phenomenon. The names of nations and peoples that no longer exist are scattered across the pages of Scripture. We read of Arameans and Moabites, Ammonites and Amorites—and many more. None of these peoples survives today. People die. So do peoples. That was a reality of the ancient world as much as it is our own.

Given the fact that cultural identities are socially constructed, we readily grasp that all cultures change over time. Though the persistence of certain names and the durability of certain cultural forms across many centuries can create an impression of cultural stasis, a moment's reflection suggests otherwise. What it means to be "English" today differs from what it meant a hundred years ago, let alone five hundred years ago. The dynamic nature of cultural identity may explain why some identities gradually disappear. But there are other factors as well. Assimilation, atrocities perpetrated by other groups, diseases, and political upheaval have also erased certain identities from living memory.

Whenever a people passes from the earth, we tend to regard it as an accident of history or recoil at the injustice that caused it. However, if

1   See Ethnologue: Languages of the World (website), https://www.ethnologue.com/.
2   Nick Martin, "What's Lost When a Language Disappears," *The New Republic*, December 12, 2019, https://newrepublic.com/.

we are to do justice to all that Scripture says, we must squarely face the fact that some nations have perished *as a direct result of divine action.* How can we make sense of this, especially given the fact that many critics and not a few Christians have come to see the biblical accounts of the Israelite conquest of Canaan, recorded in the book of Joshua, as divinely mandated genocide?[3] If God truly prizes cultural diversity within his grand design for humanity, why does he command the Israelites to leave alive "nothing that breathes" (Deut. 20:16; cf. Josh. 6:21).

Answering that question will help us answer another. Earlier, we asked the foundational question "What are nations?" Now we ask a no-less-important question: "What are nations for?" In the preceding chapter, we saw that God initiates a covenant in pursuit of his purpose to restore humanity as one people within which all peoples are constituted as a community of blessing by means of a covenant. However, in order for that to happen, Israel, the people formed by that covenant, must be holy. Israel's holiness is central to the blessing conveyed to all peoples.

Idolatrous Identities

When God promised to form "a great nation" from Abraham (Gen. 12:2), the promise necessarily included land. This was part of what it meant to be a nation. However, the land chosen by God for this nation was not a vast, empty tract, ready for occupation as soon as Abraham could get there. Instead, the land was inhabited by seven nations. Sometimes Scripture refers to these nations collectively as the Canaanites (12:6)[4] and the land as a whole as Canaan (11:31), a name apparently derived from the child born of Ham's incestuous trespass of his mother. In other texts, the Canaanites are simply one of several nations who live in the land that God promised to give to Abraham as the territorial inheritance of the nation that he will form from him.

---

3   This perspective is simply presupposed in some studies of the topic. Note, for instance, the subtitle in C. S. Cowles, *Show Them No Mercy: 4 Views on God and Canaanite Genocide* (Grand Rapids, MI: Zondervan, 2010).

4   Occasionally, the name of one of the other nations similarly stands for all the others. See, for example, the reference to the Amorites in Gen. 15:16.

The Table of Nations in Genesis 10 lists several nations that not only are descended from Canaan but also appear alongside the Canaanites in the various lists of the nations that live in the land. By the time we get to Deuteronomy 7, the number of nations living in the land is specified as seven—perhaps a stylized way of representing the fullness of the land, just as the seventy nations in Genesis 10 represented the fullness of the earth.

When Abraham arrived in Canaan, however, the land had not yet reached another kind of fullness—a fullness that had to be completed before Abraham's descendants could inherit the land. The Lord comes to Abraham in a dream and tells him that the inheritance of the land would not happen for another four hundred years, "for the sin of the Amorites has not yet reached its full measure" (Gen. 15:16 NIV).[5] In the meantime, God removes Abraham's descendants from the land and takes them to Egypt. As the stories of the Joseph cycle (Gen. 37–50) demonstrate, not only is the land not yet ready for this new people, this new people is not yet ready for the land. First, they fall under the influence of their Canaanite neighbors. Then, as soon as there is differentiation within this people with Joseph and his eleven brothers, their unity dissolves into rivalry, jealousy, and acrimony.

Even so, the divine determination to restore blessing through the descendants of Abraham in the form of a flourishing and properly functioning humanity finds preliminary fulfillment in the life of Joseph. His faithfulness to the Lord becomes the unexpected means by which blessing flows to the whole world (Gen. 41:57). Crucially, the restoration of divine blessing to all peoples turns directly on a divine gift of revelatory wisdom—a capacity to interpret dreams that effects a restoration of sorts for Joseph and, through that blessing, the restoration of a worldwide community of blessing received and blessing returned. God imparts understanding of his ways to Joseph, and Joseph's faithful response to the Lord results in "the saving of many lives" (50:20 NIV).

---

5   By metonymy, the "Amorites" stand for all the peoples of the land.

To be sure, this preliminary fulfillment of the divine purpose revealed in God's covenant with Abraham does not represent the fullness of all that God intends for and through his people. Before that can happen, the fullness of judgment must fall on the fullness of human rebellion in the land where God had promised to form a holy people for the benefit of all peoples. This will require the destruction of idolatrous nations in the land in order for it to serve as the cohabitation of a holy God and a holy nation.

1. *Conquest More or Less?* To modern readers, the book of Joshua is a troubling narrative of divinely mandated violence. The stories that follow Israel's miraculous crossing of the Jordan River are often collectively designated "the Canaanite genocide" and compared with horrific episodes of "ethnic cleansing." The narratives do indeed raise challenging questions about the ways of the Lord. But they also raise questions for biblical theology. How do we explain the juxtaposition within the canon of Scripture of the divine command to destroy the nations that live within the land with the divine intent to restore blessing to all peoples?

According to some, Israel crosses the Jordan and wages a campaign of utter annihilation against the people that dwell within the land. A literal reading of both narrative and legal texts supports this view. Thus, in Joshua 10–11, we find statements that summarize Israel's conquest of first the southern part of the land, followed by the northern part:

> So Joshua struck the whole land, the hill country and the Negeb and the lowland and the slopes, and all their kings. He left none remaining, but devoted to destruction all that breathed, just as the Lord God of Israel commanded. (Josh. 10:40)

> And all the cities of those kings, and all their kings, Joshua captured, and struck them with the edge of the sword, devoting them to destruction, just as Moses the servant of the Lord had commanded. . . . Every person they struck with the edge of the sword until they

had destroyed them, and they did not leave any who breathed. Just
as the LORD had commanded Moses his servant, so Moses commanded Joshua, and so Joshua did. . . . For it was the LORD's doing to
harden their hearts that they should come against Israel in battle, in
order that they should be devoted to destruction and should receive
no mercy but be destroyed, just as the LORD commanded Moses."
(Josh. 11:12–20)

The reference to the commandment of Moses points back to Deuteronomy and its definitive prescription of extermination of the peoples
of Canaan:

When the LORD your God brings you into the land that you are entering to take possession of it, and clears away many nations before
you, the Hittites, the Girgashites, the Amorites, the Canaanites, the
Perizzites, the Hivites, and the Jebusites, seven nations more numerous and mightier than you, and when the LORD your God gives
them over to you, and you defeat them, then you must devote them
to complete destruction. (Deut. 7:1–2)[6]

It is easy to see why many readers have understood such texts as
divinely mandated genocide. However, there are indications that there
is more to these statements of complete annihilation than meets the
eye. We shall see that these texts call for the permanent dissolution of
national identities centered in idolatry within the land. Though the
cultural identities of these peoples could continue with divine sanction
as part of Israel, they could do so only as forms of peoplehood freed of
idolatry. If ancient nationhood was constituted by the nexus of land,
god, and king, these texts prescribe the end of idolatrous forms of nationhood through the destruction of pagan worship and kingship that
mediated the rule of pagan gods. Only through the end of idolatrous

6 Deuteronomy 20 sets out greatly curtailed laws of war for other enemies. Women and
children, for instance, are not to be harmed (20:14). Nevertheless, the decree for the
peoples within the land is reaffirmed in starkly comprehensive terms.

nationhood could properly functioning nationhood be restored to one holy people for the sake of all peoples.

2. *Rhetoric and Reality*. To understand the language of complete destruction, we must grapple with not only what the words mean but also what they do. First and foremost, we must observe the rather obvious difference between the rhetoric of total annihilation and the reality of what actually happens. Peoples described as totally destroyed continue to inhabit the land. This is presupposed in Judges. The book describes a postconquest land still teeming with non-Israelite peoples whose gods repeatedly seduce the Israelites who settle there. Even within the book of Joshua, the statements of comprehensive destruction are followed by much more modest assessments of the circumstances that prevail at the end of Joshua's life. In a kind of farewell speech just before he dies, Joshua describes the allocation of land to each of Israel's tribes but freely recognizes the *ongoing* need to possess the land. Just so, he warns an assembly of "all Israel" not to mix with "the survivors" of nations that remain in their midst (Josh. 23:2, 12 NIV). God has accomplished great victories, to be sure, but Israel must take care not to normalize social discourse with the survivors who remain in the land.

The reference to survivors might suggest the continued presence of a beleaguered few—a handful of shell-shocked refugees who had somehow escaped the Israelite onslaught and who, with a bit more effort, could be easily expunged from the land. But that seems not to be the case. Indeed, the Lord intentionally leaves a number of nations as a punitive response to Israel's infidelity:

> And [God] said, "Because this people have transgressed my covenant that I commanded their fathers and have not obeyed my voice, I will no longer drive out before them any of the nations that Joshua left when he died, in order to test Israel by them, whether they will take care to walk in the way of the LORD as their fathers did, or not." So the LORD left those nations, not driving them out quickly, and he did not give them into the hand of Joshua. (Judg. 2:20–23)

If the command to leave none alive and the narration of Israel's claim to have kept the command are to be understood as an ancient form of rhetoric, what precisely did the rhetoric mean?

Some suggest that the language should be understood as a meta-phorical proscription of political and social intercourse. A number of the biblical texts insist that Israel is not to establish typical patterns of social interaction with the peoples of the land. Above all, they are not to intermarry with them or enter into treaties with them. In short, they are not to relate to them as one people might relate to another.[7]

Others contend that the command to exterminate the seven nations from the land is hyperbole—a literary exaggeration that serves a theological point. God's intent is simply that these nations be driven out of Canaan; the language of total annihilation does not mean that they are to be eradicated from the earth but that they are to be destroyed *from the land*. K. Lawson Younger rightly notes that the rhetoric of complete destruction designates complete defeat.[8] This helps us understand what the biblical authors meant when they claimed that there were "no survivors" (Josh. 10:40; 11:8 NIV). But what, concretely, was Israel to achieve? How would they know they had obeyed a command couched in the hyperbolic rhetoric of total annihilation?

We gain the footing we need to answer this question by noting that within Scripture, the preservation of survivors suggests the possibility that a nation that had undergone the catastrophe of national dissolution might one day recover. Gerhard Hasel speaks of this in characterizing the Old Testament theology of the remnant. To speak of survivors is not simply to speak of those who manage to escape an enemy intent on killing everyone. Rather, it is to speak about a national remnant

7   Christa Schäfer-Lichtenberger, "JHWH, Israel und die Völker aus der Perspektive von Dtn 7," *Biblische Zeitschrift* 40 (1996): 194–218. For a summary of her view, see Arie Versluis, *The Command to Exterminate the Canaanites: Deuteronomy 7*, Old Testament Studies (Leiden: Brill, 2017), 8.

8   On the use of hyperbole in ancient conquest narratives both biblical and extrabiblical, see especially K. Lawson Younger Jr., *Ancient Conquest Accounts: A Study in Ancient Near Eastern and Biblical History Writing*, Journal for the Study of the Old Testament Supplement Series 98 (Sheffield: Sheffield Academic, 1990).

out of which a new nation could one day rise.[9] Their survival does not suggest that the nation itself has survived. Rather, the survival of a remnant denotes the hope of future *national* restoration. To put it another way, the fact that individuals are spared does not make them a "remnant." A remnant is a group that not only survives but forms a thread of continuity between the nation's past and a future restoration of its national life. Even if for a time the nation ceases to exist, the possibility of restoration remains.

If the command to destroy the Canaanites so as to leave no survivors is not to be taken literally, how then should we understand it? I suggest that this is not the language of genocide but the language of national dissolution in which all hope of national restoration has been destroyed. Hundreds of years after Israel's "conquest" of the land under Joshua, we still read of survivors in the land from "the Hittites, the Amorites, the Perizzites, the Hivites, and the Jebusites" during the reign of Solomon (2 Chron. 8:7). Ezra 9:1 sets out a similar list of groups and depicts them as still in the land *after the exile*. Thus, as individuals or even groups, Hittites remain in the land, but they have no *national* existence there. To leave no survivors is to ensure that the destruction of national identity is so complete that those Canaanites who remain in the land do not dream of a restored national identity apart from Israel. This does not dismiss the reality of violent conflict, but it does suggest that the aim of such conflict is very specific—not the destruction of every individual within a nation, but the destruction of national identity.

We do not know the extent to which people from the seven nations in the land remained culturally distinct, though it seems unlikely that the designations would have persisted as names with no relevance.[10]

9   G. F. Hasel, "Remnant," in *International Standard Biblical Encyclopedia*, ed. G. W. Bromiley (Grand Rapids, MI: Eerdmans, 1988), 4:130–34.

10 "Although Uriah, a Hittite, was sufficiently integrated into Hebrew society to serve in the king's army, marry a Hebrew woman, and be listed among David's mighty men, the distinction between Hebrews and other ethnic groups was still maintained, and his ethnicity was an essential part of his identity." Gregory McMahon, "Hittites in the OT," in *The Anchor Bible Dictionary*, ed. David Noel Freedman (New York: Doubleday, 1992), 3:232. The designation "Hittite" has been ascribed to as many as four different ancient

In such cases, though certain features of cultural identity survived, constituent elements of ancient conceptions of national identity did not. We point to three in particular—land, deity, and king.

The Lord's promise to make Abraham a great *nation* entailed another—the promise of land. As we noted earlier, some scholars have even suggested that this is what distinguished "a people" from "a nation" in the ancient world. At the conceptual level, if not the lexical, one can conceive of a people without land, but not of a nation without land.

As previously noted, a sense of national identity in the ancient world was bound up with territory, in part because of the connection between a nation's god and the land. Nationality was not tied to a constitution but to a god and land. In the ancient world, "the corresponding element in the constitution of nationality was the saliency of the belief in the 'god of the land' relative to the other deities by the people (and other 'peoples') who dwelt in the land."[11] As a result, each people bore the name of its god. The prophet Micah expressed this idea when he declared, "All the nations may walk / in the name of their gods, / but we will walk in the name of the LORD / our God for ever and ever" (Mic. 4:5 NIV). In other words, the nations were given their "character and identity . . . by the gods they worship."[12]

Closely related to this reality was the fact that the will of a nation's god was mediated through its king, the image of its god.[13] It was not so much that the god ruled over his people, including the king, through

---

ethnic groups, whose relationships to one another and to the Canaanite nation that bears that name is disputed. Phillip E. Satterthwaite and David W. Baker, "Nations of Canaan," *Dictionary of the Old Testament: Pentateuch*, ed. T. Desmond Alexander and David W. Baker (Downers Grove, IL: InterVarsity Press, 2003), 602.

11 Steven Grosby, *Biblical Ideas of Nationality: Ancient and Modern* (Winona Lake, IN: Eisenbrauns, 2002), 29. Grosby distinguishes between nationality and other forms of collective identity—e.g., empires or city-states—in part, by noting the degree to which a territorial god was either exclusively worshiped or given priority in relation to other gods that might also have been worshiped.

12 James L. Mays, *Micah*, Old Testament Library (Philadelphia: Westminster, 1976), 99.

13 For a discussion of ancient Near Eastern kingship and its relation to the divine image, see especially John Richard Middleton, *The Liberating Image: The "Imago Dei" in Genesis 1* (Grand Rapids, MI: Brazos, 2005), 93–145.

the law. Rather, the king's words *were* law. The strong link between national identity and kingship is reflected in Israel's desire to have a king "like all the nations" (1 Sam. 8:5). This request angers Samuel. It also angers the Lord. But the issue is not kingship *per se*. Indeed, the Deuteronomic "law of the king" lays down the terms on which kings will rule in Israel. It even permits the Israelites to ask for a king *like all the nations*:

> When you enter the land the LORD your God is giving you and have taken possession of it and settled in it, and you say, "Let us set a king over us like all the nations around us," be sure to appoint over you a king the LORD your God chooses. (Deut. 17:14–15 NIV)

Here we see the expected nexus of land, god, and king in keeping with ancient notions of national identity. The problem in 1 Samuel is not the entirely lawful desire to have a king "like all the nations," but the pursuit of kingship as an *alternative* to divine kingship. The people couch their request to Samuel in the language of Deuteronomy, but what they really want is to cut God out of the picture.

When Samuel mirrors back to them the description of the sort of king they want, it is a rather astonishing repudiation of Deuteronomy's law for the king. According to Deuteronomy, the king is to eschew the conventional prerogatives of kingship—the accumulation of wives, wealth, and capacities for war (Deut. 17:15–17). Instead, he would lead the people in obedience to the divine King and his law (17:18–20). The people are not wrong to make kingship central to their notion of the nation or to pursue a form of nationhood "like all the nations." But they are rebellious in seeing human kingship as a way to free themselves from divine kingship. The author of Judges had lamented the absence of a king and saw it as the reason for the people's recurring rebellion against divine rule. Perversely, the Israelites of Samuel's day see the presence of a king as a new way to rebel against God's rule. One might even say that in severing the king's rule from God's rule, they seek what no other nation imagined. If other nations saw their kings as those who mediated the rule of their gods, Israel regards the king as an alternative to God.

Once we have seen how the nexus of land, god, and king lies at the heart of ancient conceptions of national identity, we can see the way in which both the laws and the narratives regarding the conquest in Deuteronomy and Joshua portray the conquest as a divinely mandated termination of national identity. That is, the conquest is fundamentally a divine action that brings an end to pagan worship and pagan kingship, and the connection of both to the land. God has declared the land holy as preparation for its habitation by a holy people and by his own holy presence. Understood in this way, the conquest does not aim at the extermination of every Canaanite person or the end of every vestige of Canaanite cultural identity. Instead, the laws and narratives of the conquest reflect the divine determination to bring a specific group of *national* identities to an end. The identities of these nations were rooted in an idolatrous commitment to pagan gods, in loyalty to the kings who cultivated devotion to those gods, and in the land putatively owned and ruled by those gods. *Read through the lens of Western individualism, the command to leave no survivors sounds like genocide; read through the lens of ancient conceptions of national identity, it is rightly understood as a metaphor for national death without the hope of national restoration.*

In support of this idea, we may note the way in which the laws and narratives regarding the conquest focus on the eradication of idolatry and kingship within the land as a way of speaking about the termination of the Canaanite national identities *within the land*. First, as others have noted, the mandate of no survivors applies only to the nations living within the land.[14] This land was to be the dwelling place of a holy God and a holy nation (Ex. 19:6), unmarred by pagan deities and the perverse worship they required, including child sacrifice.

Second, the reason for the distinction between distant nations and those living within the land is that the latter pose an immediate and

---

14 Deuteronomy 20 proscribes the practice of *this kind of* warfare against nations outside of the land.

ongoing threat to Israel's fidelity to the Lord. Such nations must not persist within the land lest they "teach you to do according to all their abominable practices that they have done for their gods, and so you sin against the LORD your God" (Deut. 20:18). Though commentators tend to focus on the divine command to destroy the peoples living in the land, in several key texts the central concern is essentially icono-clastic. The integral relationship between a nation's cultic apparatus and its identity might seem strange to a modern secularist, but it lies at the heart of the ancient worldview. As a result, God commands the Israelites to "break down their altars and dash in pieces their pillars and chop down their Asherim and burn their carved images with fire" (7:5).

Walter Moberly takes this iconoclasm to be the meaning of the language of total destruction. In other words, the language functions as "a metaphor for religious fidelity."[15] Moberly rightly sees that the command is made practical in two key prohibitions: Israel is not to make cove-nants with the nations living in the land or to intermarry with them (Deut. 7:2b–3). However, Moberly fails to appreciate the significance of these two proscriptions. Both speak to the formation of alliances between *nations*.[16] For Israel to enter into alliance with another nation, whether through treaties or marriages, would be to accept its validity and affirm its existence as a nation within the land.

Third, we must pay particular attention to the narrative's focus on the termination of non-Israelite kingship within the land. Thus, the

---

15 Walter Moberly, "Toward an Interpretation of the Shema," in *Theological Exegesis: Essays in Honor of Brevard S. Childs*, ed. Christopher Seitz and Kathryn Greene-McCreight (Grand Rapids, MI: Eerdmans, 1999), 135.

16 The Bible, of course, does not forbid *interethnic* marriage per se. The primary issue is with *interreligious* marriage, but this is not the only point to the prohibition in Deuter-onomy 7. In this text, the prohibition against intermarriage with the sons and daughters of the Canaanite nations is paired with a prohibition of covenants with those nations. This suggests that the problem is with the religious threat posed by political and social relations *between nations*. Peter C. Craigie argues that the mixed marriages serve the specific purpose of sealing treaties or covenants between nations. Such covenants pose an immediate danger to Israel's prior covenant with Yahweh. Craigie, *The Book of Deu-teronomy*, New International Commentary on the Old Testament (Grand Rapids, MI: Eerdmans, 1976), 178–79.

primary narrative of Israel's conquest—Joshua 6–12—concludes with a lengthy list of kings whose reigns end with Israel's entrance into the land. The message is clear: there must be no rival to the reign of Yahweh.

None of this is to suggest that there was no conquest or that the conquest did not involve war. Rather, the claim is that the form divine judgment took was not genocide; the biblical texts do not enjoin or depict the annihilation of every individual who belonged to a particular ethnicity, nationality, or race. They do, however, mandate the destruction of nations whose national identities were rooted in the worship of false gods and the reign of kings who rejected the exclusive worship of Yahweh and his exclusive right to rule within a land set apart as holy to him.

The Unholy Land: Desecration and Sacral Destruction

For some time, it has been customary to refer to the campaign against the Canaanite peoples as "holy war"—an early Israelite form of *jihad*.[17] However, this may not capture the point the biblical authors seek to make in their use of the Hebrew term *herem*, which has led some to describe the conquest as "holy war." The term is rendered in various ways in the translations—none of them entirely satisfactory. At its core, the word describes two possible outcomes when that which is holy comes into contact with that which is not: contamination and consecration. In some contexts, the outcome of contact between the holy and the unholy is the desecration or contamination of the holy. But what happens when the holiness is such that it cannot be contaminated? In that case, the unholy thing is "made holy"—consecrated by holiness that cannot be altered or adulterated. The consequence of this consecration is the permanent devotion of the thing to God and its withdrawal from ordinary use. Applied to the Canaanite nations, God's claim over their land makes their presence an encroachment

---

17 This view was made popular by Gerhard von Rad, *Holy War in Ancient Israel*, trans. and ed. Marva J. Dawn (Grand Rapids, MI: Eerdmans, 1958). It remains influential, despite weighty criticisms. See especially Versluis, *Command to Exterminate*, 60.

on the holy. Under the *herem* decree, the Canaanite nations "become absolutely holy; they cannot be returned to everyday usage."[18] This necessarily results in their destruction *as nations*.

Although the term frequently occurs in the context of Israel's wars with Canaanite nations, the issue is not that Israel engages in a war made holy by careful observance of particular religious procedures, as some have supposed. It is not war that is holy, but God. This God asserts his claim over the land in order to make his dwelling there. This not only makes the land holy as a matter of fact, but renders problematic all that sets itself in opposition to God's righteous rule within the land. In particular, land over which God has asserted his ownership and rule can no longer accommodate the presence of other gods or the nations who derive their identities from them.

Fundamental to the Old Testament's theology of the land is the notion that the land belongs to God (Lev. 25:23)—the God before whom there must be no other gods. Many have noted that Exodus is in reality an account of a conflict between Yahweh and the gods of Egypt. It is not so frequently noticed that the account of the conquest is a conflict between Yahweh and the gods of the Canaanite nations. The text we have been considering in Deuteronomy 7 is rightly understood as an elaboration of the first two of the Ten Commandments. The giving of these commands is recalled in Deuteronomy 5 and their positive form is articulated in the Great Commandment of Deuteronomy 6. These commandments insist that Israel must have no other gods beside Yahweh. He alone must be worshiped and loved because he alone is God. Thus, even if the real presence of other gods may be contained within images, Israel must never permit such images a place within the land. And the Israelites must certainly never think that the presence of the uncreated God can be constrained in any created thing.

Later, Deuteronomy 12 elaborates the incompatibility of God's presence in the land with that of other gods in relation to the third commandment:

---

18   John Goldingay, *Old Testament Theology: Israel's Life*, vol. 3 (Downers Grove, IL: Inter-Varsity Press, 2010), 149.

You shall surely destroy all the places where the nations whom you shall dispossess served their gods, on the high mountains and on the hills and under every green tree. You shall tear down their altars and dash in pieces their pillars and burn their Asherim with fire. You shall chop down the carved images of their gods and destroy their name out of that place. You shall not worship the LORD your God in that way. But you shall seek the place that the LORD your God will choose out of all your tribes to put his name and make his habitation there. (Deut. 12:2–5)

The language here is striking. In dispossessing the Canaanite nations, Israel must not only destroy the cultic apparatus that supports the worship of other gods—altars, pillars, Ashera poles, and images—but must also "destroy their name out of" the places where such worship takes place. These "sacred" places are not simply to be repurposed for the worship of Yahweh. No, Yahweh will choose a place "to put his name" and make his dwelling there.

We see the way in which the holiness of God's presence, represented in his name, conveys holiness to a place in the initial revelation of the divine name to Moses at Mount Sinai in Exodus 3. As Moses approaches a bush filled with unearthly fire, a voice addresses him: "Do not come near; take your sandals off your feet, for the place on which you are standing is holy ground" (Ex. 3:5). This is the first time in Scripture that we meet the word *holy*, though it is ubiquitous from this point forward.[19] The command that Moses remove his sandals effectively distinguishes holy ground from common ground. In this context of consecrating holiness, Moses asks to be told God's name. The name of the God who is present only in his word turns out to be remarkably like the all-consuming, unconsuming fire from which he speaks. His name identifies him as the one who simply is and will be. The holiness of that name, like unapproachable fire, threatens all who draw near.

19 See Richard Bauckham, *Who Is God? Key Moments of Biblical Revelation* (Grand Rapids, MI: Baker, 2020), 37–38.

In the wider sweep of Scripture, the sacralization of the land in preparation for the divine presence anticipates the sacralization of the world. The land of Israel becomes a kind of microcosm of the whole earth. Already within the Old Testament, the prophets anticipate a day when the holy presence of God—his glory—will fill the earth "as the waters cover the sea" (Hab. 2:14). However, the destruction of the Canaanite nations when God's presence fills the land augurs ill for the nations that fill the earth. To be sure, as Daniel anticipates, the advent of God's kingdom will be like a stone that fills the earth, crushing the kings and kingdoms of the world (Dan. 2:44–45). But that is neither the whole story nor the end of nations.

The Death and Resurrection of Israel

1. *A Treasured Possession.* One might suppose that God's determination to cause his name to dwell in the land of Israel might make it impossible for *any* nation to dwell there with him. And indeed, the Scriptures suggest that this was very nearly the case. Following the exodus, God brings Israel to Mount Sinai, where he declares that the people will be—they *must* be—a holy nation:

> You yourselves have seen what I did to Egypt, and how I carried you on eagles' wings and brought you to myself. Now if you obey me fully and keep my covenant, then out of all nations you will be my treasured possession. Although the whole earth is mine, you will be for me a kingdom of priests and a holy nation. (Ex. 19:4–6 NIV)

But what if they did not obey? What if they were not a holy nation? The holiness of the nation was predicated on faithfulness to the covenant, which was to function as a kind of constitution, stipulating what it meant for Israel to be a nation that bears the name of the Lord, with an identity wholly dependent on the Lord's determination to dwell among them. The terms of that covenant are then set out in the chapters that follow and lead directly to the revelation of a detailed plan for the Lord's dwelling—the tabernacle—in the midst of the people. However, within the covenant is a warning to anyone within Israel who repudiates the covenant by worshiping other gods: "Whoever sacrifices to any god, other than the LORD alone, shall be devoted to destruction" (Ex 22:20). Here the ESV's "devoted to destruction" renders the same Hebrew term (*herem*) that dictates the destruction of Canaanite nations from land claimed by the Lord for his dwelling. The point is not simply that idolatry is to be treated as a capital crime within Israel. Rather, the tragic irony is that idolaters are "made holy" by the act of idolatry, separated from the realm of ordinary human existence. And so, they must die.

If *herem* can befall an individual idolater, the incident with the golden calf provides a window to what happens when the whole nation succumbs to idolatry. Before Israel even enters the land, the people breach the covenant. As a result, the Lord declares to Moses, "Now leave me alone so that my anger may burn against them and that I may destroy them. Then I will make you into a great nation" (Ex. 32:10 NIV). Although the language of *herem* is not used, the implication is clear: Israel's idolatry is incompatible with God's holy presence. So the Lord will destroy the Israelites and fulfill his promise to Abraham by forming a great nation from Moses. That Moses himself would survive may explain why the destruction of the people is not depicted as an act of national *herem*. The Lord would preserve Israel's national identity, even if only through a single thread.

In response, Moses puts forth two initial reasons why the Lord should reject his own proposed solution to the problem of the broken covenant. While the solution would preserve the Lord's faithfulness to his promise to make a great nation from Abraham, the Egyptians would not see it that way. They would think that the Lord was like a capricious pagan god, who brought disaster and death on Egypt to free his people, only to "wipe them off the face of the earth" (Ex. 32:12 NIV). Moreover, in his covenant with the patriarchs, the Lord had promised to make their descendants as numerous as the stars in the sky and to give the land to them (Gen. 26:4). The point seems to be that God had promised to give the land to *innumerable* descendants of the patriarchs, not just to one.

Even when the Lord relents following Moses's intercession, Israel's identity as a nation remains in jeopardy. The plans for the sanctuary are cancelled. The Lord will honor the oath he made to Abraham to give the people the land, but he will not go with them into the land and cannot dwell in their midst within the land. To do so would constitute a permanent threat of annihilation to them and an enduring affront to him. Moreover, the covenant remains broken. Even were they to inherit the land God promised the patriarchs, God's insistence that he will not dwell there with them calls their status and identity as a nation into question.

So, Moses again returns to the Lord. His previous effort to make atonement for Israel's covenantal breach had failed. It is not immediately clear that atonement is even possible. Moses asks God simply to forgive. But if that is not possible, Moses asks God to take his life in exchange for that of the nation. The Lord, however, rejects this out of hand: sinners must die for their own sin (Ex. 32:30–33).[20] The nation as a whole has been implicated in the idolatry. The nation as a whole has been cursed with plague. But if the nation as a whole is not to die, what remedy is there? Moses, it seems, is running out of arguments.

The case Moses brings is subtle, even oblique, and the divine response more so. Moses says, in effect, "You have told me to lead this people and promised to send someone with me, but you haven't told me whom you will send. You have told me that I have found favor in your sight, but I have to know how you live your life, so that I can continue to find favor with you. Remember as well that this nation is your people." The Lord initially ignores much of this, but he responds by telling Moses that his presence will go with *him* (Ex. 33:14). Still, Moses pushes. "If you have told me to lead this people and that your presence will go with me, does that not mean that your presence must go with *us*? If not, then do not send us up from here. How will anyone know that I have found favor in your sight—that is, *I together with your people?* Is

---

20 "Sinners, not the guiltless, will be blotted out—for now at least." So Peter Enns, *Exodus,* NIV Application Commentary (Grand Rapids, MI: Zondervan, 2014), 577.

it not in your going with us that we will be distinguished—*I together with your people*—from every other people?" (33:15–16, paraphrased).

Moses seems to be alluding back to the Lord's initial commission at Mount Sinai in Exodus 19:6. In constituting the Israelites as his covenant people, God said they would be his treasured possession, a priestly people able to mediate his rule to the nations, and a holy nation. But this could only happen as a matter of divine grace. God's purposes for this people could be accomplished only if he were to renew the covenant and, with it, the promise to dwell in the midst of his people. Only so could this people become the nation through which God would accomplish his purposes for the world—a nation holy to the Lord. Only so could this nation become a source of divine blessing to all nations.

2. *The Land That Vomits.* The incident with the golden calf anticipates what will become the greatest obstacle to the fulfillment of God's purpose for all peoples through this one people—the problem of idolatry among his own people. If the realization of God's purpose for all peoples requires that this one people be holy to the Lord—a people who know the Lord and walk in his ways—the greatest obstacle to that realization is their ongoing dalliance with other gods.

We should not think that God simply excuses Israel's idolatry. However, it is important to acknowledge the difference between the way the Lord deals with nations and the way he deals with individuals. We noted earlier that one of the reasons Scripture gives for the centuries that passed between the time of God's promise of land to Abraham and the entrance of Israel into the land was that the sins of the nations living in the land were not yet complete (Gen. 15:16). A similar rationale in Leviticus serves as a warning to Israel not to walk in the ways of the Canaanites: "If you defile the land, it will vomit you out as it vomited out the nations that were before you" (Lev. 18:28 NIV). Later, the Lord exhorts the nation to keep faith with the covenant, "that the land where I am bringing you to live may not vomit you out" (20:22 NIV). The catalog of land-defiling sins that precede these warnings does not contain a special kind of national sin. Rather, these sins, like all sins, are acts of individual human rebellion.

However, over time, individuals defile not simply themselves by their idolatrous acts; they also defile the land. Their sins accumulate over time like rancid food in the belly until the land itself "vomits" the nation out. Ezekiel 36 draws on these texts from Leviticus to explain the exile that brought Israel's national existence to an end several centuries later:

> The word of the LORD came to me: "Son of man, when the house of Israel lived in their own land, they defiled it by their ways and their deeds. . . . So I poured out my wrath upon them for the blood that they had shed in the land, for the idols with which they had defiled it. I scattered them among the nations, and they were dispersed through the countries. In accordance with their ways and their deeds I judged them." (Ezek. 36:16–19)

The texts from Leviticus and Ezekiel take special care to highlight the fact that the fate that befell the people of Israel was no different from the fate of the nations before them. The depiction of the land disgorging itself of idolatry and of the nations that practice it provides a graphic picture of the political reality of dispossession and exile. The cutting off of kingship and the Lord's abandonment of the temple to destruction both mirror the end of national identity experienced by the Canaanite peoples at the time of the conquest. Like the nations that preceded it, Israel, too, becomes *herem* to the Lord.

3. *"Can These Bones Live?"* In his justly praised book *The Resurrection of the Son of God*, N. T. Wright distills his survey of the ancient beliefs about death with characteristic pith: everyone knew that "dead people stayed dead."[21] The same can be said of nations in the ancient world—once dead, they stayed dead.

The prophet Ezekiel knew this as well as anyone. In the famous vision of Ezekiel 37, the Spirit of the Lord sets him down in a vast valley, full of desiccated bones. This is not the darkened valley of the shadow of

---

21 N. T. Wright, *The Resurrection of the Son of God* (Minneapolis: Fortress, 2003), 9.

death. This valley is sunbaked and exposed. Death has long since come and gone. The sea of bones he sees is dry. As if to imprint the image in the prophet's mind, the Spirit takes him on a tour through the bones, "and behold, they were very dry" (37:2). The vision goes on to the identify the bones as the nation of Israel in its experience of national death—its kingship cut off, its connection to the land destroyed, and its covenant with God broken.

Following the tour, the Lord poses a curious question to the prophet: "Can these bones live?" (Ezek. 37:3). The answer to the question would seem to be an obvious no, but the prophet resists it. Instead, he says, "O Lord GOD, you know." What follows can be described only as an act of new creation. The word of the Lord goes forth over the bones and the prophet hears a great rattling as the bones come together. Muscle and flesh appear on the bones, followed by skin. Then, as at creation, the breath of God enters these newly formed (or re-formed) bodies, and they live (37:7–10).

It is easy to see why later interpreters understood the image as a literal depiction of individual, bodily resurrection.[22] But its primary force is that of a metaphor—a depiction of something just as unexpected as the resurrection of a long-dead person. What the prophet sees is a collective event—the resurrection of a nation accomplished as an act of new creation.

I have described Ezekiel's vision as a metaphor, but I am not suggesting that the event it depicts is unreal. In fact, there is reason to think that the renewed humanity that results from this event is more real than anything that precedes it. This is uncorrupted and incorruptible humanity. It is

---

22 Both Jewish and Christian interpreters came to understand Ezekiel 37 as a prophecy of the literal resurrection of individuals. This was especially important in the early Christian polemics against the antimaterialist views of Gnostic opponents. John Taylor comments, "When Tertullian, for instance, tried to refute the Gnostics, who held that Ezekiel 37 referred only to the restoration of Israel, and not to personal resurrection, it is probable that for once the heretics were in the right." Taylor, *Ezekiel: An Introduction and Commentary*, Tyndale Old Testament Commentary (Downers Grove, IL: InterVarsity Press, 1969), 230. This is essentially correct, but as the New Testament makes clear, the resurrection of Israel takes place through the bodily resurrection of the Messiah and all who are "in him."

the humanity of the new creation, the humanity in which God achieves his purpose to create for himself one holy people made up of all peoples.

This re-created Israel will be quite unlike the unresurrected Israel that died by the Lord's hand. All the marks of nationhood will be there— a Davidic king will shepherd them, a new covenant will be formed, and their God will again dwell among them in the land he has appointed for them (Ezek. 37:24–27). At the same time, this reconstituted nation will be markedly different from the preexilic version. This Israel will be holy, as the Lord is holy, because the Lord will make the people holy (37:28).

4. *Raised to Life for the Life of the World.* As with the notion of resurrection itself, many of the implications of Israel's restoration to a qualitatively different kind of life are not fully worked out within the writings of the prophets. Nevertheless, a handful of prophetic texts suggest that God's restoration of Israel to life will ultimately bring life to all nations. When God raises Israel from the dead, the result will be a people whose exclusive loyalty to Yahweh will be manifest "in truth, in justice, and in righteousness." Only in this way will the promise of blessing to all nations and peoples be fulfilled:

> If you return, O Israel, declares the LORD,
>   to me you should return.
> If you remove your detestable things from my presence,
>   and do not waver,
> and if you swear, "As the LORD lives,"
>   in truth, in justice, and in righteousness,
> then nations shall bless themselves[23] in him,
>   and in him shall they glory. (Jer. 4:1–2)

The prophet's evocation of the covenant with Abraham highlights the ultimate purpose of God in raising the nation to new life. New life for Israel will mean life for the world.

---

23 The NRSV and HCSB read "be blessed."

What Are Nations For?

The conquest narratives and their recapitulation in Israel's experience
of exile provide a powerful answer to the question "What are nations
for?"—or, to put the question in another form, "What are cultures for?"
The answer, in brief, is that they are for God. In both their diversity
and their unity, they reflect and refract the glory of God. They do so as
the people that comprise them refrain from idolatry and injustice, but
also as they fulfill their obligations to the good as beings who worship
God within a specific time, place, and people.

A long-standing problem of liberal democracies has been their
failure to allow for the existence of distinct cultural groups within a
political order predicated on the freedom of individuals. The Canadian
philosopher Will Kymlicka has sought to address this problem by
thinking about what cultures are for. He argues that cultures provide
a necessary structure of meaning within which individuals exercise
their freedom to choose.[24] In other words, cultures are a vehicle for
expressing individual freedom. It is easy to see why societies shaped
by liberalism have come to be marked by what Charles Taylor calls
"expressive individualism." This is the belief that "each one of us has
his/her own way of realizing our humanity, and that it is important
to find and live out one's own, as against surrendering to conformity
with a model imposed on us from outside, by society, or the previous
generation, or religious or political authority."[25]

There is a sense in which Kymlicka's way of thinking about what
culture is within a liberal order ultimately undermines culture: culture
frames the choices that we make, but to be "authentic" we must reject
the choices offered by culture. With respect to the culture it claims to

24 "For it is only in the context of a given culture ... that people can exercise their (intrinsi-
cally valuable) freedom to choose among different life-plans." Daniel Sabbagh, "Nationalism and Multiculturalism," in *Revisiting Nationalism*, ed. Alain Dieckhoff and Christophe
Jaffrelot, The Ceri Series in Comparative Politics and International Studies (New York:
Palgrave Macmillan, 2005), 101, referencing Will Kymlicka, *Liberalism, Community, and
Culture* (Oxford: Clarendon, 1989), chap. 8–11.
25 Charles Taylor, *A Secular Age* (Cambridge, MA: Harvard University Press, 2007), 5,
475.

sustain, liberalism fails by succeeding.[26] But is the facilitation of individual expressive choice what culture is *for*?

The material surveyed in this chapter suggests that it is not. Instead,
humans flourish within a divine economy in which a holy God, not the
perfectly liberated individual, is the center of culture. The result is not
a culture of theocratic sameness but a multiplicity of cultures within
one holy people whose holiness orients the ever-emerging phenomena
of culture toward the love of God and the love of neighbor.

Conclusion

The judgment that fell on the Canaanite nations at the time of the
conquest should not be understood as genocide, though it often has
been. Rather, we have seen that the biblical texts utilize ancient literary conventions to depict the deaths of the Canaanite nations as the
unavoidable consequence of encroachment by the unholy on holiness
itself. Made in the image of God, the people of these nations made
images of gods. Placing themselves under the rule of those gods, they
subverted the meaning of nationality and defiled land deemed holy
to the Lord.

That same judgment fell on Israel for the same reason. The agent of
God's judgment on the Canaanite nations became the object of that
judgment. If God drove the Canaanite nations from the land they
defiled with their idolatry, he also drove the Israelites from the land
that they polluted with idolatry and injustice. This dissolution through
dispersion is represented in Israel's Scriptures as the death of the nation.
Their status as "not a people" consigns them to historical oblivion. In
the prophetic imagination, only with an act of resurrection can the
nation be restored. However, once restored, the prophets envision this
reconstituted people as the agent of God's purposes for all peoples.

---

26 Though framed in different terms, the overarching critique resembles that of Patrick De-
    neen, *Why Liberalism Failed* (New Haven, CT: Yale University Press, 2018), 64. Deneen
    refers to classical liberalism as "anticulture" in that it weakens and destroys particular
    cultures without creating a coherent culture of its own.

6

Bread for Dogs, Bread for the World

Privilege and Hospitality in
the Gospel of Matthew

There may be many unexpected feasts ahead of you.
J. R. R. TOLKIEN, IN *THE FELLOWSHIP OF THE RING*

SEVERAL YEARS AGO, I received an email from an older colleague.
We had never met, but he had spent many years in Ethiopia before
being forced out by the communist revolution of 1974–1975. Still, even
twenty years later, his network inside Ethiopia was far better than mine.

I don't remember why he was writing, but after he introduced himself, he said that he had heard about me from one of my Ethiopian
students. He wrote, "I hear that you are the sort of professor who has
students in his home and shares meals with them." I was taken aback
because my initial thought was that it wasn't true. The fact was that
we didn't have students in our home as much as he seemed to think.
I was with my Ethiopian students all the time and frequently shared
meals with them, but we usually shared those meals somewhere near
the school. The student had evidently misinformed him, and now it
would be my embarrassing obligation to set him straight.

However, after mulling it over, it occurred to me that the student who had described me that way had probably never been in our home. What he had described was not an experience he had had with me, but an impression he had of me. And he was describing that impression in the most Ethiopian way possible. His impression was that I was a person who genuinely enjoyed spending time with students, was welcoming toward them, and ate with them. I hope they all thought that!

If our years in Ethiopia taught us anything, it was the high value that Ethiopians place on eating with others, especially those they consider guests. Coming from a culture where people "go out" to eat, I grew to value a culture in which people come together to eat. We've now been gone from Ethiopia for several years, but just this week I received a note from an Ethiopian student, telling me about his work in southern Ethiopia: "When you come to Ethiopia, I want to invite you." His English wasn't perfect, but the meaning was clear: "I will be your host, and you will be my guest."

Within our own cultural contexts, we all understand what hospitality is. We don't simply come together to eat; we eat together in order to come together. In order for that to happen, it is nearly always necessary for someone to play the host, especially when the individuals are from different backgrounds. Hosts must prepare the table and invite others in. In doing so, hosts take what is properly theirs—the comforts of their homes, their gardens, their food, their culinary skills, their stories—and welcome guests to enjoy what is theirs as an expression of honor, friendship, and love. Even when hospitality is offered outside the home, its basic dynamic is the same—blessing received becomes blessing shared, strengthening the bond between host and guest.

That same dynamic applies not just to people but to peoples. But what does that look like? How does an entire people receive another people into itself? That question is central to the Gospel of Matthew and to Matthew's understanding of God's purposes for humanity. The prophets declared that Israel's idolatrous nationhood had to be destroyed, but they also held out the hope that Israel would be restored and the promise to Abraham fulfilled. Matthew's account of the fulfillment of God's purposes begins with the memory of that promise.

The Beginning of Matthew and the Ends of the Gospel

To ancient readers, genealogies were more than lists of names—much more. Apparently, some could become unhelpfully obsessed with them (1 Tim. 1:4; Titus 3:9). Still, they were important, not least because they told you who you were by telling you who your people were and your place among them. They established, in other words, the identity and social solidarity of a people.

In many American settings, the shared sense of the past that defines a people might not be too specific and certainly could not be conveyed in a genealogy. But that is not true everywhere. I recently read an account in which a Somali immigrant named Gilad described an exchange with an African American:

> An African American was talking to me, and he said his biggest problem is that he knows he is from Africa, but he doesn't know which part of Africa. I told him that I can count all my ancestors' names, in Somali, up to thirty. I asked, "Do you know the name of your grand-grand-grand-grandfather?" . . . He didn't know, because his name is a Christian name, a Western name. [As a Somali, his father's name is his second name, his grandfather's name is his third name, and so on.] So I tell my sons every day they have to know their relatives . . . and where they come from.[1]

Gilad's African American friend most certainly shared a sense of the past with those who make up the cultural group to which he belonged, but that shared sense of history was not the sort that could be communicated with a lengthy genealogy.[2] But for Jesus, it was. Though not

---

1 Cited in Kimberly A. Huisman, *Somalis in Maine: Crossing Cultural Currents* (Berkeley, CA: North Atlantic Books, 2011), 269.
2 The brevity of a genealogy might well tell a very different and traumatic story, as would surely have been the case with Gilad's African American friend.

embedded in a thirty-generation name, his people's identity is certainly embedded in the forty-two generation genealogy that opens Matthew's Gospel. This is not just history; it is *shared* history. Thus, like other genealogies we meet in Scripture, it has an ideological point. It is not just the family tree of Jesus, but a claim about the kind of people to which he belonged—or, rather, the kind of people who belonged to him.[3]

1. *Canaanites in Israel?* Matthew constructs the genealogy, in part, from the Judahite strand of the nine-chapter genealogy that begins 1 Chronicles (2:1–4:23). Some of the features of this genealogy anticipate the ideological emphases of the more abbreviated genealogy in Matthew. The thirty names from Abraham to Zerubbabel in Matthew's genealogy correspond to names listed by the Chronicler. As in Matthew, the Chronicler includes unexpected annotations—brief side comments that advance the genealogy's claims. Also as in Matthew, these annotations evoke rather than rehearse stories from the past. At the outset of Judah's line, for instance, the Chronicler refers to the sons born to Judah by a Canaanite woman, the daughter of Shua [Bath-Shua] and to the fact that the Lord put the first of these to death. He notes as well Judah's impregnation of his daughter-in-law Tamar, another Canaanite (1 Chron. 2:3–4). One need not recall all the shocking details of the original story to see the family's dirty laundry piling up on the porch. The genealogical aberration—Judah's daughter-in-law bore Perez and Zerah *to Judah*—tells us all we need to know.

But it is not just the ugly family secrets that would have caught the ancient reader's eye. In contrast to the many ancient genealogies that sought to demonstrate the ethnic purity of a people, the Chronicler goes out of his way to highlight the profusion of non-Israelites who find their way into Israel through interethnic relationships, especially in the line of Judah. Sometimes the evocation is very subtle. The first Bath-Shua anticipates a second—the wife of David. The woman well-known in

---

3   For a discussion of genealogies as genre, see Steven M. Bryan, "The Missing Generation: The Completion of Matthew's Genealogy," *Bulletin for Biblical Research* 29 (2019): 162–84. Much of the discussion below is presented in more detail in this article.

biblical history as Bathsheba is, through a slight adjustment, given the same Canaanite name as Judah's first wife—Bath-Shua (1 Chron. 3:5). The resemblance of their names highlights another similarity. Like Judah's first wife, the wife of Israel's first Judahite king is also identified as a Canaanite by virtue of her previous marriage to Uriah, a Hittite.[4]

Matthew paints the Chronicler's interest in outsiders into his own genealogical portrait of the Messiah's people and finds several ways to enhance it. For example, of the five references to women (including Mary), only Bathsheba is not mentioned by name. Instead, she is identified as "the wife of Uriah" (Matt. 1:6).[5] To Tamar (1:3) and the wife of Uriah, he adds references to Rahab and Ruth (1:5). The Rahab he has in mind, it seems, was the Canaanite woman who abetted the early efforts of Joshua to defeat Jericho. Though Ruth was not a Canaanite, she belonged to the neighboring Moabite people, whose refusal to let Israel pass through their land earned them permanent exclusion from the temple (Deut. 23:3-4). All told, within the Messiah's people, Matthew includes three individuals from nations excluded from the land and one from a nation excluded from the temple.

The inclusion of individuals from excluded nations not only subverts the genre's conventional use to support claims of ethnic purity but also challenges conventional notions about Israel's identity as a holy nation. The genealogical annotations evoke the memory of Israel's most well-known figures at their widely known worst and prepare us to see this people as very much in need of deliverance from the rebellion that marked them as a nation. Immediately following the genealogy, Joseph is told to name the child "Jesus" because "he will save his people from their sins" (Matt. 1:21). Further, the outsiders find their place within Israel as those whose righteousness and faith in Israel's God exceed that

---

4 For the historical case that Uriah was a Hittite of Canaanite identity, see Bryant G. Wood, "Hittites and Hethites: A Proposed Solution to an Etymological Conundrum," *Journal of the Evangelical Theological Society* 54 (2011): 239–50.

5 For the argument that the use of "wife of Uriah" instead of "Bathsheba" indicates that Matthew's primary interest is in the status of the women as non-Israelites, see especially Jason B. Hood, *The Messiah, His Brothers, and the Nations (Matthew 1.1–17)*, The Library of New Testament Studies (London; New York: T&T Clark, 2011).

of their Israelite contemporaries. Uriah is more faithful than David. Ruth is more devoted to Israel's God than her embittered mother-in-law. Rahab is more confident in the power of Israel's God than the faithless spies who cautioned against entry. Even Tamar, whose actions are less than laudable, is unexpectedly acclaimed as righteous: when Judah realizes that he is responsible for her pregnancy, he exclaims, "She is more righteous than I" (Gen. 38:26).

The point is not that Israel needs forgiveness while the outsiders who become a part of Israel do not. Rather, Matthew holds up Tamar, Rahab, Ruth, and Uriah as outsiders who became model members of Israel. Even as strangers to the covenant, they exemplified the faith-filled righteousness that was to be the hallmark of Israel's covenant commitment to God. In this respect, they anticipated the outsider about whom Jesus says, "With no one in Israel have I found such faith" (Matt. 8:10), and a "Canaanite" woman whose faith connects her to the Canaanite women of the genealogy (15:28).

2. *The Brothers of the Messiah and the Fulfillment of God's Promise to Abraham.* While Matthew's genealogy takes many cues from Chronicles, there are differences as well. Among the most important of these is where it begins. The Chronicler starts with Adam; Matthew starts with Abraham. The Chronicler embeds the particular story of Israel in the universal story of humankind. Matthew embeds the universal story of humankind in the particular story of Israel. His telling of this story moves from national constitution through national dissolution to national restoration. By beginning with Abraham, Matthew intends for us to recall the moment when the universal story of God's purposes for humanity became a very particular story about Israel. The divine blessing lost through human rebellion would be restored to humanity within the people formed from Abraham.

Matthew highlights Israel's constitution as a nation of twelve tribes with his reference to "Judah and his brothers" (Matt. 1:2) early in the first of the genealogy's three segments. But the constitution of Israel as a nation of twelve tribes does not bring to pass God's promise to form a people of peoples. Instead, the nation spirals toward dissolution—a moment marked by another genealogical annotation. "Jeconiah and his brothers" (1:11) are sent away into captivity, resulting in the death of the nation—the event that brings the second segment of Matthew's genealogy to a close.

The third segment of the genealogy thus poses a question—the same question that God posed to Ezekiel as he surveyed the valley of bones that represented Israel's national death: "Can these bones live?" (Ezek. 37:3). Matthew frames the question in kinship terms. If "Judah and his brothers" represent the nation in its initial constitution, and "Jeconiah and his brothers" represent the nation in its dissolution, does God's promise to Abraham remain viable? The expected reference to "brothers" in the third segment is missing, like a piece from a puzzle. To find the missing piece, we must read the Gospel through to the end to see the way in which Matthew deploys kinship language to speak about Israel's reconstitution as a people of peoples.

Midway through the Gospel, Jesus's immediate mother and brothers come looking for him. Pointing to a group of disciples, he declares, "Here are my mother and brothers"—those who do "the will of my Father in heaven" (Matt. 12:46–50). Here Matthew anticipates the climax of the Gospel in the resurrection narrative, where an angel directs Mary Magdalene and "the other Mary" to "go . . . and tell his disciples" (28:1–7). As they go, Jesus meets them on the road. He repeats almost verbatim the angel's words to the women at the tomb. But there is an important shift: "Go and tell *my brothers* . . ." (28:9–10).

By this time, Judas has betrayed Jesus. When the eleven meet Jesus, his words are heavy with messianic meaning: "All authority in heaven and on earth has been given to me" (Matt. 28:18). These words show us why the disciples' response upon meeting Jesus is exactly that of the women who meet him on the road: they worship him. The scene is almost certainly meant to evoke the memory of Genesis 49:8–10, when the original Judah, depicted as a lion, is told that the scepter will not depart from him and that his brothers will bow to him. This, we now understand, is Matthew's way of completing the third table of the genealogy.

If "Judah and his [eleven] brothers" at the beginning of the genealogy recalls Israel's constitution as a nation of twelve tribes, the Messiah and his eleven worshiping brothers bring to fulfillment Israel's reconstitution as a nation of nations.[6]

For this reason, worship is not their only work. Jesus immediately commissions the eleven to make disciples of all nations, baptizing and teaching them to obey everything he commanded them (Matt. 28:18–20). But the eleven will not go alone. The Messiah they worship will go with them. In that sense, they will always be the twelve; they will always be Israel, reconstituted to fulfill God's purpose to make from Abraham a people of peoples. These disciples do not leave their kinship ties behind, but they do find new kinship ties with the brothers, sisters, and mothers of the Messiah, bound to him by obedience within one people who bear the name of the one God, now revealed as Father, Son, and Holy Spirit (28:19).

Taking Meals with the Messiah

Jesus's encounters with non-Jews in Matthew's Gospel are infrequent. When they happen, it is because someone seeks him out, not the other way around. These encounters end well, but they do not always start well. Within scholarship on Matthew, this has been one of the most puzzling features of the Gospel. How can a Gospel that ends with Jesus commissioning his disciples to make disciples of all nations constrain the mission of Jesus himself to Israel alone (Matt. 10:6; 15:24)? Can the Great Commission redeem the ethnic exclusivism that marks Jesus's mission prior to the resurrection? Significant clues to how Matthew resolves this tension may be found in two exchanges, as first a Gentile soldier and then a woman whom Matthew provocatively labels a "Canaanite" come to him with their needs.

---

6   On the significance of the reference to Jesus's brothers in Matthew 28 for the completion of the genealogy in Matthew 1, see Bryan, "Missing Generation," 162–84. The article builds on Hood's insight (in *The Messiah*) that the reference to the disciples as "the brothers" of the Messiah in the resurrection narrative creates a literary envelope with the two references to "brothers" in the genealogy.

The first encounter is set within a sequence of miracle stories that Matthew brings together in chapters 8–9 of his Gospel. Most treatments of these chapters rightly highlight Matthew's focus on the authority of Jesus. The two chapters follow the Sermon on the Mount (Matt. 5–7), which concludes with a comment about Jesus's authority. The healings, cleansings, exorcisms, and miracles in Matthew 8–9 form a collage that draws our eye to a rich variety of images that vividly portray that authority. But there is more here than meets the eye.

Spliced between the three sets of miraculous displays of Jesus's authority (Matt. 8:1–17; 8:23–9:8; 9:18–34) are two pairs of vignettes on discipleship (8:18–22; 9:10–17). Their presence within this carefully constructed sequence of miracles alerts us to the fact that Matthew's characterization of the community of disciples in the Sermon on the Mount does not end when the sermon ends. Still, Matthew does not develop the theme in the way we expect—that is, by highlighting instances in which those whom Jesus heals, cleanses, or delivers from demonization go on to become faithful followers. Not even the disciples whom Jesus saves from a storm at sea (Matt. 8:23–27) are held up as models of faith-filled discipleship. "Why are you afraid?" Jesus asks. "You have so little faith!" (8:26 NLT).

So, what does Matthew want us to see? The answer, it seems, is that he wants us to look past the individuals and to see the characters as a group formed and bound together by what they have in common. The beneficiaries of Jesus's authority bring him their need, their affliction, their distress. In many of the episodes, those who come to Jesus approach him with a social, moral, or ritual status that has left them marginalized, excluded, cut off from Israel. Most of them are not disciples and do not become disciples. Rather, they *represent* disciples. Their physical, ritual, and social conditions mirror the spiritual conditions and status of those who will follow Jesus. Collectively, they serve as a picture of the restored people whom God is calling into existence through the authoritative work of Jesus to save his people from their sins (Matt. 1:21).

We can now see why Matthew weaves discipleship material into the sequence of healings and miracles. Matthew transitions to the first pair of vignettes (8:18–22) with an unexpected citation of Isaiah 53:4: "He took our illnesses and bore our diseases" (Matt. 8:17). Matthew does not think that Isaiah was speaking about the healing ministry of the suffering servant. However, he sees more clearly than many commentators that there is a powerful analogy between the Messiah's healing ministry and his mission to save his people from their sins—an analogy already present in Isaiah 53.

Similarly, the second pair of discipleship vignettes (Matt. 9:10–17) depicts the Messiah's people as composed of the tax collectors and "sinners"—individuals whose willful rebellion has placed them outside of the covenant. They are people whose moral defilement has resulted in their exclusion from Israel—the spiritual analog to the ritual condition of the leper (Matt. 8:2–4), the dead girl (9:18–19, 23–26), or the woman with continuous menstrual bleeding (9:20–22).[7] Strikingly, Jesus describes his role in relation to such a people as that of a physician who heals the sick (9:12). This is not allegory. Rather, it is Matthew's way of indicating that we must see an analogy between Jesus's ministry of healing and his mission to form his people. The evangelist is drawing a meaning-filled comparison between the desperate physical and ritual conditions Jesus resolves and the desperate spiritual conditions they represent. The onlookers—most especially the Pharisees—do not see this. But Jesus insists. He heals, he says, so that they may "know that the Son of Man has authority on earth to forgive sins" (9:6 NIV). His mighty acts in these two chapters do not form his new people. That will happen only as he exercises his authority to forgive sins.[8]

---

7   These are each severe forms of impurity. Corpse impurity was the most severe form of defilement, and many suppose that impurity generally is associated with death. The symbolic value of this ritual status is to signal the threat of moral defilement to the life of Israel.

8   We may have incidental confirmation of this way of reading these chapters from an important literary device that Matthew employs. Though there are nine stories in Matthew 8–9, organized as three stories in three panels, three of the stories involve two acts of deliverance. All three of these are drawn from Mark, but only one of them involves two people in Mark. The other two are "doublets" introduced in Matthew. The effect is to produce not nine but twelve saving acts. That number proves significant in the narrative that follows. The first saving act in the middle panel rescues the disciples from death at

We are now able to see the significance of Jesus's encounter with the centurion (Matt. 8:5–13). Whatever privilege he may enjoy as a part of the Roman occupation of Israel, he does not come to Jesus with a sense that any of those privileges count for anything. Instead, he comes with an acute awareness that he is among the unprivileged when it comes to receiving the bounty of Israel's God. In that sense, he is not out of place in this collage of marginal, desperate, and desperately needy people. As he freely admits, he is not worthy (8:8).

His encounter with Jesus stands out within the collection of healing miracles in three ways. First, with the probable exception of the Gadarene demoniacs (Matt. 8:28–34), he is the only non-Jew in the group. He is an outsider, not simply with respect to his ritual status, as the leper in the story that precedes (8:2–4), but with respect to his ethnic status. In short, he is outside of Israel. Second, as a result of his outsider status, he alone confesses his unworthiness before Jesus. With respect to the privilege he seeks—access to the power of Israel's God to deliver—he acknowledges that he has no claim on the benefit he desires. Third, like the four men who bring their paralyzed friend to Jesus in the following chapter (9:1–8), he does not seek the benefit for himself but for a neighbor—in this case, his (probably Jewish) servant.

Despite his status as an outsider—and, in part, because of it—Jesus holds the centurion up as a model Israelite: "With no one in Israel have I found such faith" (Matt. 8:10). Jesus commends the man for his faith-filled intuition about the nature of Jesus's authority. When Jesus agrees to heal his servant, the man insists not only that his unworthiness means that Jesus should not come to his house but also that the nature of Jesus's authority means that he *need* not come. He replies, "Like you, I am under authority, so when I give orders, things happen because my commands carry the authority of Caesar himself. So, since

---

sea. Immediately following these two chapters, Matthew places his account of the calling of the twelve, whom Jesus sends to "the lost sheep of the house of Israel" (Matt. 10:6) There is wide agreement that the number evokes the memory of Israel's original constitution as a nation and symbolizes Jesus's belief that God is now acting through him to restore Israel. The twelve who represent Israel are thus saved and then sent as witnesses to Israel.

God's authority resides in you, if you give the word, my servant will be healed" (8:9, paraphrased). One might expect Jesus to bristle at the analogy the centurion uses to explain his belief that Jesus could heal his servant from afar—the projection of Caesar's authority from Rome into Jewish lands. Instead, Jesus commends him.

The centurion's faith makes him a model member of this Abrahamic people of peoples, not only because he perceives that the authority of Jesus is the authority of God, but also because he demonstrates his faith in practical concern for his servant. The differences in ethnicity and social status between the centurion and his servant are vast. And yet, the centurion cares for his servant's well-being. No less than his trust in Jesus's ability to speak the authoritative word of God to save his servant, the centurion's unlikely love for a neighbor demonstrates the faith that should characterize Israel. And yet, it does not.

This contrast casts a worrying light on the response of many of Jesus's contemporaries. Jesus's ensuing declaration about the coming messianic banquet underscores the condemnation implicit in his words to the centurion: "I tell you, many will come from east and west and recline at table with Abraham, Isaac, and Jacob in the kingdom of heaven, while the sons of the kingdom will be thrown into the outer darkness" (Matt. 8:11–12). There has been considerable debate about whom Jesus is talking about. Traditionally, Jesus has been understood as speaking about the prophetic expectation of a great pilgrimage of Gentiles. By contrast, the Jewish "sons of the kingdom" face exclusion. Dale Allison has argued that the "many who come from east and west" are not Gentiles but "unprivileged Jews"—that is, the Jews of the Diaspora who do not have access to the blessings poured out through the ministry of Jesus.[9] To be sure, the prophets often speak of the return of scattered Jews at the time of Israel's restoration. But, as Allison acknowledges, that cannot be *Matthew's* understanding of the saying, prompted as it is by an encounter with a Gentile.

9   W. D. Davies and Dale C. Allison, *A Critical and Exegetical Commentary on the Gospel According to Saint Matthew*, International Critical Commentary (London: T&T Clark, 1991), 2:28.

And yet, Allison is not without a point. The language of the saying seems to draw on Psalm 107, which speaks of the Lord's "redeemed" as those he gathers "from the east and from the west" (107:2–3). The psalm may have provided Matthew with a scriptural guide for his compilation of miracle stories in these two chapters. The collection echoes the psalm's depiction of Israel in its various experiences of affliction and distress. For instance, the psalm speaks of Israel in its need for healing from sickness and saving from death. Just as Matthew describes those who come to Jesus as crying out to him for mercy, the psalmist follows each new description of trouble with a repeated refrain: "Then they cried to the LORD in their trouble, / and he delivered them from their distress" (107:6, 13, 19, 28). The centerpiece of the psalm is the description of Israelites who find themselves afraid for their lives in a storm at sea: "Then they cried out to the LORD in their trouble, / and he brought them out of their distress. / He stilled the storm to a whisper; / the waves of the sea were hushed" (107:28–29 NIV). The verses bear a striking resemblance to Matthew's description of the disciples, who fear for their lives in a storm on the Sea of Galilee and cry out to Jesus to save them (Matt. 8:23–27). In response, Jesus stills the storm, resulting in "a great calm" (8:26).

Allison is right that these are the "unprivileged," but their lack of privilege does not stem from being Diaspora Jews. The point of Psalm 107 is that the Israel restored by God is not Israel in its experience of ethnic identity, whether inside or outside its own land. Rather, it is Israel in its experience of distress, desperation, and forced dispersion—circumstances brought about by God to turn them from their sin. This is Israel with no place to lay its head; Israel at the point of death; Israel imperiled on the sea; Israel harassed by Satan; Israel dispossessed and despairing because of its rebellion.

This is a new way of thinking about Israel and its privilege. Jesus privileges the unprivileged, to be sure, but the unprivileged are all those whom he saves when they cry out to him. Those who will sit down at table with Abraham, Isaac, and Jacob are not the putative heirs, the privileged sons of the kingdom, but the outsiders, the marginal, those considered excluded from Israel. The phrase "many [who] will come from east and west" is, thus, neither a designation of Gentiles, as such, nor of Diaspora Jews. Rather, it designates those whose desperation and affliction under the hand of God mirror the conditions of Israel in its distress—they are the meek, the poor in spirit, and those who mourn (Matt. 5:3–5), and who therefore stand over against the privileged "sons of the kingdom."

If, in Matthew 8, Jesus speaks of sitting at table with Abraham, Isaac, and Jacob, in Matthew 9, he enacts this meal by eating with the tax collectors and sinners. The eschatological scandal of the many who come from east and west to *sit down at table* with Abraham, Isaac, and Jacob parallels the scandal caused when tax collectors and sinners *sit down at table* with Jesus. Commentators regularly overlook the parallel, but it goes to the heart of Matthew's central point in these chapters. They don't so much tell us as show us what it means to be Israel. The table of the patriarchs—*Israel's* table—is a table for the unprivileged, the unincluded, the undeserving. Israel's table is open to those whose faith and righteousness mirror that of Abraham. The excluded "sons of the kingdom" are identified in Matthew 9 as the scribes and Pharisees, who object to Jesus's practice of gathering with tax collectors and sinners over a meal. They object because they know what it means. It is the symbolic enactment of Jesus's vision of restored Israel—an Israel based not on ethnic descent but on a kinship formed through faith and the righteousness it generates. However unexpected, Israel's privileges belong to such as these.

Bread for Dogs

Jesus's encounter with the centurion in Matthew 8 only partly prepares us for a rather more jarring interaction with a woman described as a "Canaanite" in Matthew 15. We can readily see the similarities between the accounts. Both involve non-Jews; both make use of eating as a metaphor for participation in the blessings that the Messiah pours out on Israel; both portray outsiders whose faith in Jesus's authority to heal prompts them to seek blessing on behalf of others; and both culminate in the exercise of Jesus's authority to heal from afar.

However, there are differences as well. The most important of these is Jesus's disposition toward the two figures who come to him. When the centurion approaches Jesus to ask him to help his servant, Jesus welcomes him with a simple reply: "Shall I come and heal him?" (Matt. 8:7 NIV). By contrast, Jesus is anything but welcoming to the woman. Initially he refuses even to acknowledge her presence, much less heal her daughter (15:23). Why the difference? The answer, it seems, lies in the fact that the centurion comes as an outsider who is welcomed at Israel's table. In this respect, he is very much like the individuals in the genealogy who come from outside of Israel but become a part of Israel as those who are more faith-filled and righteous than their Israelite contemporaries. The Canaanite woman, by contrast, comes as a representative of an outside group that Jesus characterizes as "dogs" vying with "the children" (Israel) for the children's bread (15:26). If the encounter with the centurion makes clear that outsiders are welcomed at Israel's table, the encounter with the Canaanite woman raises a challenging question: What about outside *peoples*? Are they also welcome at Israel's table, or can the bread of Israel's table be theirs only by taking it from Israel?

To answer this question, we must consider the relationship between the two feeding miracles in Matthew. If the inclusiveness of Jesus's vision of the messianic banquet is enacted in his practice of eating with "sinners" and his welcome of the centurion to Israel's table, the lavishness of that banquet is anticipated in his feeding of the five thousand (Matt. 14:13–21). That Matthew intends us to see this miracle as a kind of preview of a banquet celebrating God's restoration of Israel is evident both in its recollection of the manna provided to Israel at the time of the exodus and in the collection of twelve baskets of leftovers, corresponding to the twelve tribes of Israel. The abundance of the provision points to the abundance of the table that God lays for his people through the Messiah.

This, however, is not the only feeding miracle in Matthew's Gospel. In the following chapter, Jesus is again surrounded by a crowd that comes to him seeking healing (Matt. 15:29–31). This time, however, the crowd is not from Israel. They come to Jesus bringing the same conditions as the Israelites who came to him in the previous chapter. Jesus heals them, just as he had healed the Israelites. In response, they praise "the God of Israel" (15:31). Then, unwilling to send the crowds away hungry, Jesus declares his compassion for them (15:32), just as he had for the "harassed and helpless" in Israel (9:36; cf. 14:14). As he had in Israel, Jesus provides bread in abundance (15:32–38). This time, there are seven baskets of bread left over, a number that symbolizes the fullness of the Messiah's provision. The point seems clear: the Messiah's provision of bread for Israel is so abundant as to fully provide for Gentile peoples as well.

Between these two feedings, Matthew situates Jesus's encounter with the "Canaanite" woman (Matt. 15:21–28). The woman comes to Jesus with a request that he heal her demonized daughter. Jesus, it seems, ignores her, but the woman refuses to give up. When Jesus finally speaks, he addresses his words not to the woman but to the disciples in the hearing of the woman: "'I was sent only to the lost sheep of the house of Israel'" (15:24). Still, the woman pleads for help. Finally, Jesus speaks to the now-kneeling woman directly: "It is not right to take the children's bread and throw it to the dogs" (15:26). Jesus's words have proven far more challenging to interpreters than to the woman. Her reply to Jesus is immediate and rich with faith-filled insight: "'Yes, Lord, yet even the dogs eat the crumbs that fall from their masters' table'" (15:27).

Several things about the account must be noted. First, the term "Canaanite" was, by the first century, "probably not a current ethnic term (like Mark's 'Syrophoenician') but a part of traditional biblical vocabulary for the most persistent and insidious of Israel's enemies in the OT period."[10] Matthew's inclusion of Canaanites in his genealogical portrait of messianic Israel confirms our suspicion that the unexpected ethnonym carries particular weight in this passage. Matthew, it seems,

---

10   R. T. France, *The Gospel of Matthew*, New International Commentary on the New Testament (Grand Rapids, MI: Eerdmans, 2007), 592.

is characterizing the woman not simply as a Gentile but as a descendant of the nations whose idolatry led to their exclusion from Israel.

Second, the story clearly emphasizes the salvation-historical primacy of Israel. When at last Jesus grants the woman's request, he does so only on the basis of her acknowledgment that the bread given by Israel's Messiah remains ever and always *Israel's* bread. The woman's logic seems to be that the bread she seeks can come to her not as a direct gift, but only as that which falls from the table of the children. The exchange not only highlights the exclusivity of Jesus's mission to Israel but also suggests that the blessings he brings to Israel are so abundant, so lavish as to be more than enough for others as well. The benefits of the now-arriving kingdom are for Israel. However, because of the extraordinary beneficence of the giver, the benefits poured out on Israel are more than enough for all peoples. The nations also will have them, but they will have them derivatively, as blessings given first to Israel.

The basis of this participation in Israel's eschatological blessings is faith. Jesus has been sent to Israel, but it is also true that not all Israel will experience the eschatological blessings he brings. This passage emphasizes the fact that the eschatological blessings flow only indirectly to those outside of ethnic Israel. However, as the narrative develops, it also becomes clear that the experience of messianic blessing defines the boundaries around the people of the Messiah to include not just people from outside but also outside peoples.

In order to draw this out, it might be useful to set Jesus's encounter with the Canaanite woman alongside the contemporary political concept of "privilege," which focuses on differences in power between peoples within a society. In a country with peoples of varying cultural identities, one group is often perceived as having privilege vis-à-vis other groups. Often this is the largest group within the country, though a smaller group with disproportionate power can also be perceived as privileged. It is important to see that discussions of privilege pertain in the first instance to groups. This point is often misunderstood in part because we frequently speak of individual privilege in a way that has nothing to do with group identity. However, as a political concept, privilege "is properly attributed to groups primarily and individuals derivatively."[11] In this sense, privilege is a good, a benefit, or an advantage enjoyed by individuals because they belong to one group rather than another. This does not mean that all individuals who are part of that group will necessarily enjoy that privilege. But all who enjoy the privilege are perceived to do so because they are part of that group.

Some have suggested that the only just response to privilege is to take steps to remove the privilege from the group that possesses it. However, those who study such matters typically distinguish between two types of privilege—"entitlement privilege" and "advantage privilege." Entitlement privilege refers to a good that everyone *should* have regardless of the groups to which they belong.[12] A society might consider, for example, that all children should have access to a quality education. By contrast, advantage privilege refers to a good disproportionately enjoyed by one group only by depriving another of it. This form of privilege arises when one group enjoys some good unfairly. If a good usually goes to members of one particular group, we might suspect that something is giving that group an unfair advantage. So, for example, we might suspect advantage privilege to be at work in a company in which two ethnic groups are equally represented in the workforce as a whole, while senior leadership roles are held primarily by members of one group.

One recent study identifies yet a third kind of privilege, called "benefit privilege."[13] This refers to a good that promotes human flourishing, but to which no one is necessarily entitled. The dynamic of privilege comes into play when that benefit is enjoyed by one group more than by another. An example of this type of privilege would be access to an effective drug for a deadly disease. It would be difficult to say that anyone has a right to such a drug. But if, for any reason, members of one group have access to that drug and those of another group do not,

11 Rachel McKinnon and Adam Sennet, "Survey Article: On the Nature of the Political Concept of Privilege," *Journal of Political Philosophy* 25 (2017): 487.
12 The technical use of "entitlement" privilege as an attribute of groups should not be confused with the colloquial use of the term to refer to individuals who give others the impression that they deserve something in a way that others do not.
13 McKinnon and Sennet, "Survey," 491.

we could say that the first group is privileged, even if their access to that benefit is not obtained unfairly.

The way to address privilege properly varies with the type of privilege. Though the intuition of some is to address privilege in all its forms by removing the privilege from the group that possesses it, that remedy is appropriate only for advantage privilege. The remedy for entitlement privilege is to work to ensure that the good enjoyed by one group is opened up to all groups. A society that depends on everyone having access to a quality education would be ill-advised to remedy privilege by reducing the quality of education enjoyed by a privileged group. Instead, the availability of quality education should be pursued for all children of all groups. In relation to the third kind of privilege—benefit privilege—the usual primary remedy is for the benefit to be shared. For instance, the President's Emergency Program for AIDS Relief (PEPFAR), which began in 2003, made effective treatments for AIDS available in Africa almost overnight. It was a remarkable example of the transformational impact that shared privilege can bring.

In Matthew, the primary privilege in view is participation in the kingdom of God, along with the benefits brought by that participation—forgiveness, salvation, righteousness, a restored community, and the promise of resurrection and life in the age to come. These benefits and many more are anticipated in Jesus's healings and exorcisms. So what kind of privilege is this?

Clearly, the privilege of kingdom participation is not an entitlement privilege. The kingdom and the benefits it brings are divine gifts to which no one and no group is entitled (Matt. 6:33). Still, the category of "privilege" applies because of the strong statements in Matthew's Gospel that the kingdom belongs to one people, Israel, but not to others. The Messiah comes to save "*his* people" (1:21). Jesus sends the twelve (who symbolize the tribes of Israel) with specific instructions to go only to "the lost sheep of the house of Israel" (10:6). At the same time, no one in Matthew's Gospel thinks that Israel's privileged designation as heirs of the kingdom serves as a guarantee that any individual Israelite will inherit the kingdom. The scribes and Pharisees think that

Israelite tax collectors and sinners will be excluded, while Jesus warns that they themselves are at risk of exclusion (21:31–32). The privilege of inheriting the kingdom belongs to Israel, but not all Israelites will enjoy the privilege.

It is also clear that Israel's designation as heirs of the kingdom is not an advantage privilege—a privilege that Israel has gained unfairly or that has come to Israel at the expense of other peoples. The resemblance to advantage privilege is found only in Matthew's depiction of the attitude of some Israelites to the privilege. Those who believe it to be theirs as a kind of ethnic birthright are precisely those to whom Jesus says, "The kingdom of God will be taken away from you and given to a people producing its fruits" (Matt. 21:43). Thus, John the Baptist warns the Pharisees and Sadducees not to rely on putative descent from Abraham as the basis for laying claim to Israel's privilege (3:9). The privilege of inheriting the kingdom will be removed from those who idolatrously understand what it means for Israel to be Israel in ethnic rather than ethical terms.

If neither entitlement privilege nor advantage privilege adequately describes the privilege given to Israel, what about benefit privilege? This is clearly closer to what we see in Matthew's depiction of the blessing of the kingdom, but it differs in crucial ways as well. In Jesus's encounter with the Canaanite woman, he seems to suggest that the bread of the kingdom is only for Israel: "It is not right to take the children's bread and throw it to the dogs" (Matt. 15:26). This sounds worryingly like the zero-sum calculus of advantage privilege—as though it could be given to another people only if it were taken from Israel. The Canaanite woman does not dispute that the privilege belongs to Israel or complain that it is unjust for Israel to possess the privilege when "Canaanites" do not. Neither does she treat it as an entitlement privilege, one that she should rightly possess. In acknowledging that she has no claim to it, she acknowledges that the privilege properly belongs to Israel—this is the children's bread.

At the same time, it not quite the case that she treats the bread as a benefit privilege. Her access to the bread does not depend in the first instance on the willingness of the children to share it. Perhaps we should call Israel's privilege the privilege of *divine* benefit or blessing. It is Israel's bread. But there is no need for "the dogs" to be given their own bread or for the bread be taken from the children to be given to the dogs. Rather, the giver of the bread is so generous and his gift of bread so abundant that there is far more than plenty for the children *and* for the dogs.

The two miraculous feedings that bracket Jesus's encounter with the Canaanite woman coalesce to make the same point. In the feeding of Matthew 14, there is more than enough bread for Israel—the twelve baskets of leftovers give the point visible form. The feeding of Matthew 15 is often called a "Gentile feeding," but this is true only insofar as the ones who eat come from outside of Israel. The bread they eat is Israel's bread—bread so lavishly supplied to Israel by Israel's God through Israel's Messiah that it is more than enough for them as well.

Some commentators have struggled with and even stumbled over Jesus's placement of the woman in the role of a dog, even as a metaphor. It is important to see that she is not called a dog as an individual, still less because she is a woman. Rather, "children" and "dogs" designate groups. In relation to children, dogs are, of course, unprivileged. However, it is precisely the image, and the unprivileged status associated with it, that becomes the faith-filled basis for the woman's claim. As we have seen, those granted the privilege of sitting at the messianic table with Abraham, Isaac, and Jacob in the kingdom of heaven are those who come from east and west. They are the unprivileged who lay claim to the privilege of the kingdom by acknowledging that they have no claim to it. They are the poor in spirit (Matt. 5:3), who have nothing to offer but their need. However, they bring their need to a lavish giver, who gives only to those with need.

If the dogs are the unprivileged who come to Israel's Messiah from among the excluded peoples, the children are the unprivileged who come to Israel's Messiah from within Israel. In that sense, no people receives the gift of the kingdom as a group. Rather, the people of peoples is formed as individuals from every people come to Jesus in faith, acknowledging that they do not belong within the kingdom and have no claim on its blessings. This is as true for Israelites as for individuals of any other people. Though it is not clear from the metaphor of dogs eating from the table of children, the wider story that Matthew tells does assign a particular role to the unprivileged from Israel. They constitute Israel in its messianic form. These individuals form the nation newly constituted under the rule of the Messiah.

As recipients of God's greatest blessing—life under the Messiah's rule and all the benefits that affords—they become agents of that blessing, called to share it with all peoples. We begin to see that messianic Israel has a role to play within the divine economy of the kingdom. We catch a glimpse of it in the so-called mission discourse of Matthew 10. Jesus sends representatives of messianic Israel to all Israel, with careful instructions that they must neither carry money to support their mission nor charge money for their mission. The blessings of the kingdom conferred through their mission are of surpassing worth, and those worthy of it will naturally return blessing, albeit in a different form. As the bread of the kingdom is given and received, a relationship of reciprocity begins and the bread of hospitality is returned. In turn, the disciples are to pronounce the blessing of God's messianic *shalom* (10:6–13). In effect, through the announcement of the good news, Israel has begun to function according to the divine economy envisioned in God's covenantal promise to restore blessing to all peoples through one people (see chap. 4).

The same reciprocity occurs when the representatives of messianic Israel are sent to the nations. In response to Jesus's ministry of healing and exorcism in Gentile lands, the crowds praise the God of Israel (Matt. 15:31). Jesus, in turn, has compassion on the crowds and tells his disciples to act on their calling as representatives of Israel. These Gentiles have come to him, and he has received them. He has blessed them, and they have returned blessing to God. The disciples may be in Gentile lands, but he wants them to play the host. The disciples respond that the bread they have could never be enough. And it is not, until suddenly it is—a divine gift from a divine host, who makes the unprivileged of Israel the privileged host of unprivileged peoples.

Conclusion

Every banquet needs a host. Mission has been described as "one beggar telling another beggar where to find bread."[14] From Matthew's point of view, the same dynamic exists between peoples. When the eleven worshiping disciples gather around the resurrected Jesus, we have a picture of Israel constituted as a messianic people. The Messiah sends the disciples to the nations, but they will not go as eleven but as twelve because he promises to go with them. This is Israel raised from the dead—the nucleus of a new people formed from the unprivileged within Israel for the sake of the unprivileged within every people. Israel in its messianic form becomes a host for all peoples—including ethnic Israel itself.

In making this case, Matthew explores two interrelated dynamics. On the one hand, individuals marked by the faith and righteousness of Abraham take their place at Israel's table. Whatever their ethnic, national, or racial identities, they are heirs of the blessing promised to Abraham and are formed by faith as one holy nation. As individuals, they are constituted as Israel in its promised, messianic form. On the other hand, as members of groups outside of Israel, those who come into Israel in its messianic form must see themselves as those who share in a blessing given to Israel. It is not blessing given directly to them, but blessing given to Israel and shared with them. In bringing these two dynamics together, Matthew shows us the way in which God's promise to renew humanity as one worshiping people made up of all peoples comes to fulfillment in a community of blessing.

In receiving the good news of a crucified and risen Messiah, all peoples are bound together as one people through obedience to the Messiah. Israel's privilege is its reception of the bread of the kingdom

---

14 Source unknown, though often attributed to Martin Luther.

given so lavishly by the divine giver that those who receive it can only see themselves as host to others.

What applies to the greatest privilege must surely apply to any benefit enjoyed by any group—it is not something to be clutched but something to be received as a divine gift properly enjoyed within a community of blessing given and received, received and returned.

Holy to the Lord

The Destruction and Renewal
of Cultural Identities

*The mistake you make, don't you see, is in thinking one can
live in a corrupt society without being corrupt oneself.*

GEORGE ORWELL, IN *KEEP THE ASPIDISTRA FLYING*

Good and evil appear to be joined in every culture at the spine.

FLANNERY O'CONNER, IN "THE CATHOLIC WRITER IN THE
PROTESTANT SOUTH," LECTURE AT SPRING HILL COLLEGE, 1962

EVERY EIGHT-HUNDRED-YEAR-OLD university is bound to have
a few arcane traditions. One of the first I encountered at Cambridge
had me sitting at "high table" for a "matriculation dinner" feeling
slightly out of place in a borrowed college robe. Across from me was
another newly arrived graduate student, who seemed rather less out of
place—self-assured and properly English. He was friendly enough and
soon asked me what I had been doing before coming to Cambridge.

I told him that I had been living and working in Ethiopia. I paused
for a moment to think of how best to explain my work to a secular Brit,
then decided to throw caution to the wind: "I've been working there as

a missionary," I said. The look that crossed his face was a nearly flawless blend of curiosity and reproach. He didn't quite know what to say, so I thought I'd better try to alleviate some of the awkwardness I had caused. "I suppose that's not very politically correct," I ventured. He agreed.

For many, that would have been a conversation killer. But he was intrigued, and it didn't take him long to come to his main question. I had heard it before, though never quite so bluntly: "Wouldn't the peoples of Africa be much better off if missionaries didn't come in and spoil their cultures with outside religion?"

I had been in Ethiopia for a while, so I decided that the best answer to a direct question might be to tell a story: "In the late 1800s, almost no mission work had been done in the African interior. The three founders of our mission (SIM) hoped to change this and traveled up-river from the Nigerian coast. Within months, two of the three died of malaria. The third managed to get back to the coast and returned to Canada. Several years later, he and several new colleagues made another attempt, establishing several stations in the interior of what was then known as 'the Sudan.' They were taken aback by some of the beliefs and practices of the peoples they encountered. Among one people, twins were buried alive at birth because of a belief that they were the work of the devil."[1]

A look of revulsion crossed my friend's face, so I finished my story: "Now those who embraced Christianity don't bury babies alive anymore. So, would it have been good to leave the culture as it was?"

"No," he allowed, "I suppose it wouldn't have."

The story I told was an extreme example, but I could have made my point with respect to any culture. Certainly not all cultures encountered by those early missionaries harbored such beliefs. In hindsight, I should have conceded that my friend was right in at least one sense. If he was wrong in thinking that cultures untouched by outsiders were pristine and uncorrupted, he was correct in assuming that the cultures

1   There is some evidence that the practice continues among a few groups even today. See Orji Sunday, "'They Ensure Each Twin Baby Dies': The Secret Killings in Central Nigeria," *The Guardian*, Jan. 19, 2018, https://www.theguardian.com/.

of the missionaries themselves were not. Missionaries who imagine their own cultures to be without blemish do not typically find a wide audience for that view.

A somewhat different version of the myth of cultural innocence sometimes arises in historical or political accounts of oppressed peoples. In such accounts, the culture of the oppressors is corrupt and wicked, but the cultures of the oppressed are innocent and pure. In such contexts, the oppressed culture's corrupt features are judged to have roots in the oppressing culture. That, of course, is often true. However, the testimony of Scripture is clear: no culture is free from corruption.

When sinful patterns of belief and action become replicated and normalized across a culture, the effects can be far-reaching, shaping and infecting a culture's institutions and interactions across many generations. To speak of systemic racism or systemic ethnocentrism is simply to speak of an enculturated form of sin. These, however, are not the only sins that corrupt a culture. To be part of any culture is to be subject to the myriad of ways in which sin worms its way into the structure of societies and distorts them. While this does not make any individual guilty of the sins to which that culture is prone, it does indicate that in any culture there will be ways in which its individual members *typically* sin both against one another and against those of other cultures.[2]

In order for cultures to find their places in the purposes of God, they must be rid of their corruption. If the peoples of the earth are to find their places in the one holy people of God, they themselves must be holy. Luke develops this theme in a story that he tells in two parts. In Luke's Gospel, we see God's action in Israel's Messiah to form Israel as

---

2   Cornelius Plantinga describes the Christian notion of corruption by referring to Augustine's argument in *The City of God* that "sin despoils persons, groups, and whole societies. Corruption disturbs shalom—twisting, weakening, and snapping the thousands of bonds that give particular beings integrity and that tie them to others. Corruption is thus a *dynamic* motif in the Christian understanding of sin: it is not so much a particular sin as the multiplying power of all sin to spoil a good creation and to breach its defenses against invaders." Cornelius Plantinga Jr., *Not the Way It's Supposed to Be: A Breviary of Sin* (Grand Rapids, MI: Eerdmans, 1995), 33–34, emphasis original.

one holy people. In Acts, we see the way in which God then incorporates all peoples into that people by making them holy. For that to happen, first Israel and then all peoples must undergo the destruction and renewal of their cultures as individual members repent of idolatry and believe the good news that the crucified and risen Jesus is Lord of all.

A Holy Nation

For those accustomed to hearing the Christmas story as the birth of an infant "tender and mild," the fierce, Israel-centric language that permeates Luke's infancy narrative can be jarring. We celebrate the birth of Jesus as an event that brought joy *to the world*, but the cast of characters to whom the birth was first announced heard it as good news that God had kept his promises *to Israel*. Luke affirms that God "has helped his servant Israel" (Luke 1:54); that the child comes to those "waiting for the redemption of Jerusalem" (2:38); and that his birth will bring about "the consolation of Israel" (2:25) and bring to fulfillment the oath that God made to Abraham (1:55, 73).

We do not often think of the keeping of a promise as an act of mercy, but that is precisely what it took for God to fulfill his promise to Abraham. Only by an act of divine mercy would this people become a nation holy to the Lord—a people delivered by the Lord so that they "might serve him . . . in holiness and righteousness" (Luke 1:74–75). Only by becoming God's holy servant could Israel become the sort of people through whom God could fulfill the covenant he had made with Abraham.

Though the promise that God would form such a people had been given to Abraham, premonitions of *how* God would do it were given many centuries later through the prophets. God promised that he would cleanse the nation with water and pour out his Holy Spirit on the people (Ezek. 36:25–27). Thus, when Jesus offers himself for baptism and the Spirit descends on him (Luke 3:21–22), attentive readers will recognize the paired events as the fulfillment of Ezekiel's prophecy and others like it. This, for Jesus, is a public claim that Israel's identity as a nation is concentrated in him. As Max Turner has argued, the Holy Spirit who comes on him is the Spirit of Israel's restoration.[3] Thus, Jesus's baptism is not simply an act of solidarity with Israel, it is a claim to *be* Israel.

Within the context of Jesus's baptism, Luke supports that claim, in part, by reflecting on the ideology of kingship rooted in Israel's Scriptures. Jesus's baptism climaxes in the declaration of a voice from heaven that Jesus is the Son of God (Luke 3:22) and segues immediately into a genealogy that traces Jesus's lineage all the way back to Adam, the son of God (3:23–38). The significance of the connection may not be obvious to readers unfamiliar with the centrality of kingship in the storyline of Scripture. Adam, the original son of God made in God's image to image God's rule (3:38), fails to do so. In due course, that role falls to Israel. Israel will be God's *chosen* son who will mediate God's rule to the world (Ex. 4:22). But for Israel to mediate God's rule to the world, first God's rule has to be mediated to Israel. This is the role of the *anointed* son of God, Israel's king, who is to represent God to the nation and the nation to God.

Perhaps no text distills this ideology of kingship more clearly than Psalm 2—a text that Luke evokes early in his Gospel (Luke 3:22) and then again in Acts (4:26). The psalm was written to celebrate the enthronement of Israel's king. It begins with the depiction of the nations of the earth in rebellion against the rule of God—a rebellion instigated by their kings. Far from surrendering his right to rule, God reasserts it, installing a King in whom he invests the fullness of divine sovereignty. Among all the kings and rulers of the earth, he alone is declared Son of God: "You are my son; / today I have become your father. / Ask me, / and I will make the nations your inheritance, / the ends of the earth your possession" (Ps. 2:7–8 NIV). The kings of the earth are cautioned against further insurrection, but there is an alternative to destruction. Instead of asserting their own right to rule, they may "kiss the Son"

3   On the Spirit as the power of Israel's eschatological restoration in Luke-Acts, see especially Max Turner, *Power from on High: The Spirit in Israel's Restoration and Witness in Luke-Acts,* Journal of Pentecostal Theology Supplement Series (Sheffield: Sheffield Academic, 1996), 172–85.

(2:12), celebrate his rule "with trembling" (2:11b), and "serve the LORD with fear" (2:11a).

The heavenly declaration of divine Sonship in Psalm 2 is widely regarded as the literary precursor to the words of the voice from heaven at Jesus's baptism (Luke 3:22).[4] The words from heaven also echo Isaiah: "Here is my servant, whom I uphold, / my chosen one in whom I delight; / I will put my Spirit on him, / and he will bring justice to the nations" (Isa. 42:1 NIV). Luke has already alluded to this "Servant Song" in the preceding chapter, when the prophet Simeon takes Mary's newborn in his arms and exclaims that his aging eyes have now seen the salvation that the Lord has prepared in the sight of all nations, a light for revelation to the nations and the glory of his people, Israel (Luke 2:30–32; cf. Isa 42:6). Within the Old Testament context, the servant called to be a light to Gentile peoples is identified as Israel. Now, at Jesus's baptism, the Holy Spirit descends on the servant—the one who takes up Israel's identity and vocation—and the voice declares that he is the Son in whom God delights. The Spirit then leads Jesus into the wilderness to be tested for forty days (Luke 4:1–13). Here again, Jesus retraces the steps of Israel, whom the Lord tested in the wilderness for forty years. This time, however, God's Son proves faithful.

What follows from this narrative of Israel restored in the person of Jesus is not a turn away from Israel "according to the flesh" (Rom. 9:3, 5) but a story of Israel "according to the flesh" now raised to life in the crucified and risen flesh of Jesus. Luke narrates the story of Jesus as the climax of God's purposes for Israel. Through the death and resurrection of Jesus, Israel becomes the people through whom God will fulfill his purposes for the world—a people who "serve him . . . in holiness and righteousness" (Luke 1:74–75). This is not to deny Jewish ethnicity to Jews who reject Jesus. Rather, it is to affirm that the

4   James R. Edwards similarly ties the identification of Jesus as "Son of God" to Psalm 2 and aptly states that the baptism portrays Jesus as "the true Son and thus Israel reduced to one. . . . As the Beloved Son in whom God is pleased and on whom God's Holy Spirit rests (1:35; 3:22), Jesus is both the model of Israel's sonship and the means of its fulfillment." *The Gospel according to Luke*, Pillar New Testament Commentary (Grand Rapids, MI: Eerdmans, 2015), 120–21.

restoration and judgment of Israel occur as simultaneous realities. As an idolatrous nation, Israel must be destroyed. Nevertheless, through faith in the resurrected Messiah, Israel is raised to new life as the people over whom the enthroned Messiah rules. At the turning of the ages, the nearness of the kingdom is no longer contingent upon the adequacy of Israel's national repentance. Instead, the identity of the Israel in the age to come is contingent on the repentance of those who turn in faith to Israel's Messiah.

As the infancy narrative asserts, in the coming of the Messiah, God has kept his oath to Abraham. He has made from him a great nation. The restoration of blessing to Israel, however, was never meant to end with Israel. The promise to Abraham had never been to restore blessing to each in isolation from the others, but to restore blessing to all peoples, each in relation to the other and all in relation to one.

The Meaning of Holiness across Lines of Difference

If Luke's understanding of how Israel comes to be God's one holy people takes a surprising turn, his account of what that holiness looks like takes a surprising form. We see this in one of Scripture's best-loved stories. From one perspective, it is also one of the most confusing. The parable of the good Samaritan (Luke 10:30–37) is the story of a man who meets with God's approval, despite being a Samaritan. The parable says nothing about the man's clearly problematic religious status. The problem is not simply that Samaritans and Jews are culturally distinct peoples, but that the Samaritans hold false ideas about God—an assessment shared by Jesus (John 4:22). Why, then, can the Samaritan of the parable garner Jesus's approval?

The same question arises in Jesus's encounter with ten lepers—nine Israelites and one Samaritan (Luke 17:11–19). Upon meeting Jesus, the ten plead for mercy. Jesus sends them to show themselves to the priests—those charged with the responsibility of confirming that a person is free of leprosy. As they are going, all ten discover that they have been cleansed. The nine Israelites proceed to the priests, but the Samaritan returns. Shouting praise to God, "he fell on his face at Jesus' feet, giving him thanks" (17:16). Jesus, in response, not only commends the man's faith, but wonders aloud why only the foreigner returned to give praise to God.

Both in the parable and in the healing, the actions of Samaritans are set in contrast to those of native-born Israelites. Earlier in the Gospel, an angry mob had attempted to throw Jesus off a cliff for recounting how God had shown mercy to a Sidonian widow and a Syrian general rather than Israelites (Luke 4:24–30). In the story of the ten lepers, nine Israelite lepers *are* healed. Now, however, the accent falls not only on the unexpected favor of God toward a non-Israelite but also on the unexpected response. The Samaritan leper returns to give thanks, whereas the native-born Israelites do not. The actions of the Samaritan leper, like the actions of the "good" Samaritan, are deemed worthy of restored Israel. Like Matthew's centurion, these Samaritans act as those who serve the Lord "in holiness and righteousness" (1:75), whereas those who are "holy" as a matter of status and genealogy do not.

This element within the two stories arises in part from the purity issues implicit to both narratives. The wide range of skin conditions known in Scripture as "leprosy" conferred a ritual status that required exclusion from the community for as long as the condition persisted. Those deemed "unclean" for this reason were not regarded as sinful, but their ritual impurity served as a powerful symbol of the threat that sin posed to the nation. In other words, purity was not equivalent to holiness but *represented* the holiness to which Israel was called as God's people because they lived in the land set aside as the dwelling place of God. The exclusion of those with leprosy served as a grave and constant reminder that moral defilement would eventually result in Israel's exclusion from the land.

The nine healed lepers go to have their "cleansing" certified by the priests as a basis for their reintegration into the national life of the people set apart as holy to the Lord. But to be holy as a matter of status is not to be holy as a matter of conduct. Ironically, in the Samaritan, this is reversed. The nine run to the temple to be qualified for reintegration into people whose status is that of "holy" nation; the Samaritan falls at Jesus's feet and "praises God." His faith, Jesus says, has "saved" him

(Luke 17:19 CSB). Though he is not holy as a matter of status, he alone acts in accordance with that status.

A similar motif appears in the parable of the good Samaritan. The purity concern is evident in Luke's comment that robbers had left an Israelite "half dead." Under Levitical law, a dead body was the most potent source of ritual defilement. Corpse impurity acted as a kind of "miasma" that wafted upward from its source and thus posed a threat to anyone or anything consecrated as holy.[5] We may think of impurity and holiness as having opposite magnetic charges. The greater the holiness, the more powerful the attraction of defilement. Thus, according to a rabbinic view that can be traced to the first century, the high priest was not permitted even to come within sight of a dead body. By contrast, ordinary Israelites were obliged to contract corpse impurity if they came across a dead body in an open field. However, the implications of such a situation for an ordinary priest and, even more, for a Levite were ambiguous.[6]

We may presume that Jesus portrays a kind of tragic comedy in describing the priest and the Levite walking past a *possibly* dead man on "the other side" of the road (Luke 10:31, 32) to avoid impurity that might *possibly* be attracted to their holiness. They go to great lengths to avoid impurity in order to symbolize the holiness of their status, even as their actions reveal that holiness is absent from their conduct.

For the Samaritan in the parable, the situation is reversed. Far from possessing a status of holiness, the Samaritans were regarded as a threat to Israel's holiness. In the middle of the second century BC, Judas Maccabaeus was heady with success as leader of Israel's struggle to throw off the oppressive rule of the Greek Seleucids over Israel. The Seleucids were simply the latest in a succession of occupying powers, dating back to the Babylonian incursions of 605 BC. Now,

5 Jacob Milgrom describes the impurity emitted by a corpse "as a gaseous substance, a volatile force, a miasma exuded by the source of impurity." Milgrom, *Leviticus: A Book of Ritual and Ethics* (Minneapolis: Fortress, 2004), 142.
6 On the purity issues implicit within the parable, see Steven M. Bryan, *Jesus and Israel's Traditions of Judgement and Restoration*, Society for New Testament Studies Monograph Series 117 (Cambridge: Cambridge University Press, 2002), 172–85.

as the five hundredth anniversary of the end of Israel's independence approached, the nation was free once more. One of Judas's first actions as leader of the newly independent nation was a campaign to purge Israel's land of the Samaritans. The rhetoric of the period characterized the Samaritans with the ethnic slur "Shechemites." This played on the coincidence that the capital of Samaria was a city called Shechem and the fact that a man named Shechem had raped Dinah, the daughter of Jacob, over a thousand years before. As reprisal, two of Dinah's brothers slaughtered not just Shechem but every male in the city (Gen. 34:1–26). This not only aligned the Shechemites with preconquest inhabitants of Canaan, but provided added justification for the eradication of a people the Israelites regarded as a defiling presence in their land despite the Samaritan practice of circumcision.

It would seem to have been a challenge for first-century Jews to reconcile that understanding of Samaritan origins with the notion that the Samaritans were descended from intermarriage between Jews who had remained in the land at the time of the exile and the non-Jewish peoples whom the Assyrians had settled in the land in the eighth century BC. Whatever the case, both "histories" could be made to serve the twisted logic of genocide that justified Judas's campaign of ethnic cleansing against the Samaritans. According to Judas, their presence was a defilement to the land and the people declared holy to the Lord. If Israel was to achieve its eschatological destiny, both its land and its people had to be cleansed of Samaritans.

This history explains the profound antipathy between Jews and Samaritans when Jesus tells the parable of the good Samaritan. It is important to recall that Jesus tells the parable in response to an exchange that results from a question posed by an expert in the law: "What shall I do to inherit eternal life?" (Luke 10:25). Jesus turns the question back on the expert: "What is written in the Law? How do you read it?" (10:26). The answer is on point: "You shall love the Lord your God with all your heart and with all your soul and with all your strength and with all your mind, and your neighbor as yourself" (10:27). Jesus replies, "You have answered correctly; do this, and you will live" (10:28). But the expert will not leave it alone. He seems not to doubt his capacity to keep the commandment to love God, but he has one worry—whether or not he has kept the commandment to love his neighbor. His concern turns on the definition of the word *neighbor*. And so, seeking to satisfy himself (and perhaps others) that he is living in keeping with a correct interpretation of the command, he asks a follow-up question: "And who is my neighbor?" (10:29).

The question arises out of Leviticus 19, the Old Testament text from which the expert takes the second part of the double commandment. Leviticus 19 begins with the call for Israel to "be holy, for I the LORD your God am holy" (Lev. 19:2). What follows is not a series of commandments related to ritual purity, but rather commandments having to do with Israel's ethical life, including the command that they must love their neighbors. The wording of the command seems to have suggested to some a different disposition toward non-Israelites, especially enemies: "'Do not seek revenge or bear a grudge against anyone among your people, but love your neighbor as yourself" (19:18 NIV). Some in Jesus's day seem to have read the first half of the verse to imply that only fellow Israelites counted as neighbors.[7]

Whether or not the expert in Luke 10 read the verse that he quotes in this way, the premise of his question is that not everyone counts as his neighbor. He would certainly have been aware that Leviticus 19 goes on to extend the circle of neighbors who must be loved to the foreigners living in the midst of Israel: "You shall treat the stranger who sojourns with you as the native among you, and you shall love him as yourself, for you were strangers in the land of Egypt" (19:34). But this was not how many—perhaps most—in Israel felt about Samaritans. Knowing this, Jesus tells a parable about a Samaritan.

It is important to remember how parables work. When we hear such a story, our natural tendency is to identify with one of the characters in the story. So it is for the expert, for whom there is but one option.

---

7   Jesus rejects the interpretation of Lev. 19:18 as a command to love neighbors but hate enemies (Matt. 5:43–44).

He is neither priest nor Levite. And he is certainly not a Samaritan. That leaves the man badly beaten and left for dead by bandits. The fact that such a fate was probably a common anxiety among first-century travelers made his identification with the half-dead man easier still. We may imagine that the expert smiled at Jesus's characterization—or, perhaps, caricature—of the priest and the Levite. He probably knew their type—too "holy" to be holy. But the smile may have disappeared in shock as he imagined himself unconscious by the side of the road and having his life saved by a Samaritan.

After finishing the story, Jesus invites the man to stay in character: "Imagining yourself as the man left for dead in the story, think back to your original question, which of the three proved to be your neighbor?" (see Luke 10:36). The expert cannot bring himself to say, "The Samaritan," but his answer goes to the heart of what it means to love a neighbor: "The one who showed him mercy" (10:37). His answer is the answer to his question. The Samaritan is his neighbor, and if that realization leads him to "go, and do likewise" (10:37), he, in turn, will be a neighbor to the Samaritan.

Luke sets before his readers two Samaritans who observe the fundamental precepts of Israel's call to holiness—one who demonstrates love for God and the other who demonstrates love for neighbor. In the Israel being formed by God, the Israelite need not stop being Jewish, and neither must the Samaritan stop being a Samaritan. In the Israel being formed by God, the ancient command for Israel to "be holy, for I . . . am holy" (Lev. 19:2) is a command for God's people to be holy in the way that God himself is holy—not simply as a matter of status but as a matter of conduct. Ultimately, the Israel being formed by God comes to fulfillment as the peoples of the world are united in love for God and love for neighbor, no matter the group to which that neighbor belongs.

Incorporation without Assimilation: A Holy Nation and the Kindness of Strangers

Within the holy people being formed by God, love for neighbors characterizes not only individuals but also groups. At the end of his two-part work, Luke introduces us to the island people of Malta. Bound for Rome as a prisoner, Paul finds himself shipwrecked there. Cold and wet, he becomes the beneficiary of unexpected hospitality. The Maltese build a fire for the shivering missionary and his shipmates. As Paul helps gather wood for the fire, a bad situation made better by the "unusual kindness" (Acts 28:2) of the Maltese takes a firm turn for the worse. A viper coiled in the wood bites the apostle. Paul, however, calmly shakes the viper into the fire and carries on unharmed. This persuades the islanders that Paul must be a god (28:3–6).

Remarkably Luke does not pause to recount Paul's response, but continues to praise the extraordinary generosity and hospitality of the Maltese. A Maltese official named Publius welcomes Paul and the others into his home, where he hosts them for three days. Through Paul's prayers, the power of the Lord is present to heal, and all the sick on the island are cured. When they are again ready to sail, the islanders shower the castaways with many honors and supply them for their trip (Acts 28:7–10).[8]

Commentators have long wondered why Luke neglects to tell us whether Paul shared the good news with the Maltese or, if he did, how the Maltese responded. Perhaps Luke simply expects readers to surmise that Paul did so. But Luke's primary focus is clearly elsewhere. It seems that he wishes not simply to narrate the response of individuals to the gospel but to paint a picture of ethnic differences working as they should in the world that God intends. Luke does not conceal the fact that the pagan beliefs of the Maltese had distorted their understanding of God. In this respect, they are like the Samaritans who appear as models of holiness in Luke's Gospel. As Paul had affirmed in Lystra, God had "allowed all the nations to walk in their own ways," but he had not left "himself without witness." He had showered them with gifts—rain from

---

8 Joshua Jipp demonstrates that the giving of honors forms part of the "enactment of ritualized friendship that functions to bind the two ethnic groups into a perpetual kinship/family-like relationship. . . . Luke uses ritualized friendship as a means to establish a new social order for the Christian movement that results in surprising forms of communion and hospitality between distinct ethnicities." Jipp, "Hospitable Barbarians: Luke's Ethnic Reasoning in Acts 28:1–10," *Journal of Theological Studies* 68 (2017): 38–39.

heaven, crops in their seasons, plentiful food, and glad hearts (Acts 14:16–17). In short, God had shown the nations hospitality. And to the extent that the peoples of the world have incorporated hospitality into their cultures—albeit in a host of culturally specific ways—they have been taught to do so by God. When the Maltese shower Paul and his companions with kindness and gifts, they are imitating God's own hospitality and love in a culturally specific way.

Luke portrays Samaritans and Maltese as those who imitate God by demonstrating a capacity to act in loving, grateful, generous, and hospitable ways across lines of ethnic difference, *even before they experience the transforming work of God's Spirit*. In doing so, Luke does not want us to think that the incorporation of the peoples of the world into the one people of God requires them to renounce their cultures. Instead, through his narration of the cultural expressions of God-honoring hospitality practiced by those who are not or not yet clearly Christian, Luke invites us to see these cultures as valuable in their own right. The Jerusalem Council of Acts 15 affirms God's welcome of Gentile peoples into restored Israel, but their incorporation does not—indeed, must not—result in cultural assimilation. Similarly, the interaction on Malta takes place "between two distinct ethnic groups and preserves their ethnic identities," creating an expectation of "both social parity and ethnic differentiation" between distinct peoples within the one people of God.[9] The people of peoples that God has promised to form from Abraham does not come into existence by obliterating or obscuring the cultural identities of those who form this people.

Some years ago, I was part of a small group that flew by helicopter to a remote area in southwestern Ethiopia. En route, we encountered a heavy storm, and the pilot wisely sought an open space to set down until the storm had passed. As the clouds lowered, the helicopter settled to the ground. When the whirr of the rotors stopped, all was quiet but for the rain slapping the windows. We could see very little, but soon first one person and then another appeared out of the grey. Within a

9   Jipp, "Hospitable Barbarians," 39.

few minutes, a crowd gathered, despite the heavy rain. We decided to step out and greet them. The language of the area was not one any of our group spoke, though enough of them spoke enough of the national language for us to exchange greetings. And, then, from out of the crowd, came an invitation: "Come to my home."

Before long, we found ourselves in a *tukul*—a round mud hut with a dirt floor and a grass roof. It was a coffee-growing region, and soon water was boiling in a clay jug over a small charcoal stove—the beginning of the traditional Ethiopian coffee ceremony. Though sugar was plentiful in the area, their custom was to dose the coffee with salt and butter. This may never become my favorite way to drink coffee, but they were showing us "no small kindness" (Acts 28:2 AT). Bread was passed around, then roasted grain and yogurt, infused with flavor from a smoked gourd. We had come as outsiders, arriving in the most unexpected way possible. Despite the vast differences between us, they welcomed us. When the rain finally stopped, they sent us on our way.

Within Luke and Acts, such demonstrations of kindness, generosity, and hospitality across lines of ethnic difference do not simply mark the transformed lives of individuals who share in the holiness of the crucified and risen Messiah. They also mark the restoration of blessing to all peoples in the Messiah, each in relation to the other, all in relation to one.

The Gospel and Cultural Destruction

Though the gospel incorporates the peoples of the world into the people of Israel without requiring them to renounce their cultures, this does not mean that it leaves those cultures alone. Luke narrates the story of the gospel's movement from Judea into the Greco-Roman world as a story of extraordinary cultural disruption. Several recent studies have highlighted the extent to which the early Christian movement tore at the social fabric of ancient pagan cultures. Throughout Acts, early Christian missionaries were brought before the authorities on the charge that their message had "turned the world upside down" (Acts 17:6). This was neither overwrought histrionics nor the hyperbole of a few change-aversive traditionalists who found the early Christian message upsetting. Rather, it was a very serious charge of sedition arising from the very real threat that the gospel posed to the social order.[10]

Why this was the case may not be immediately obvious to contemporary readers of Acts, particularly those who read it through the lens of a Western secular worldview. Such a lens inclines readers to think of ancient polytheistic paganism as the god-ridden equivalent of postmodern pluralism. Read in this way, the early Christian missionaries were merely adding one more religious dish to the ancient religious smorgasbord. If so, the burden of Acts would simply be to show that Christianity could be easily accommodated within the pagan Greco-Roman world. Indeed, this way of reading Acts has a long legacy. But it is mistaken.

As C. Kavin Rowe shows in his groundbreaking study of Acts, the wholesale rejection of the pagan conceptual framework implied by the Christian message meant that people encountered the gospel as a powerful "force for cultural destabilization."[11] This was true because the radically different perception of God carried with it an entirely different way of life—a life in which idolatry and the vast range of cultural commitments it generated were necessarily renounced. In city after city, the Christian message sparked economic and cultural upheaval. Not only were the early Christian missionaries charged with turning the world upside down everywhere they went (Acts 17:6), the iconoclastic implications of their message struck at the foundations of the economic and political order. In Thessalonica, they were charged with acting against Caesar's decrees (17:7). In Corinth, they were accused of encouraging people to worship God in ways contrary to the law (18:13).

The impact of the call to renounce idolatry at Ephesus led to the burning of sorcery books worth fifty thousand pieces of silver (Acts 19:19) and the evisceration of the trade in images of Artemis

---

10   See especially C. Kavin Rowe, *World Upside Down: Reading Acts in the Graeco-Roman Age* (Oxford: Oxford University Press, 2010), 95–96.

11   Rowe, *World Upside Down*, 40–41.

(19:24–25). This was not a Taliban-like act of cultural destruction, but the spontaneous response of a people who realized that key elements of their culture were deeply enmeshed in the enslaving power of pagan faith.

The pagan response to the threat of cultural demise was immediate and violent. The confrontation with Rome arose out of the inseparability of pagan religion from Greco-Roman culture. The Christian message represented a frontal assault on the pagan construction of reality that served as the foundation of Greco-Roman society. As a result, Christians were left dangerously exposed to the charge that they opposed Caesar. If the early Christians were repeatedly exonerated before Roman officials in Acts, it was because their accusers overreached with the charge of sedition. As Rowe puts it, "New culture, yes—coup, no."[12] Against this, the Christians in both the first and subsequent centuries could display "a readiness to respect pagan rulers, pay taxes, and in other ways be good citizens," while at the same time facing the repeated charge that they "refused to honor the gods on which Roman rulers claimed to base their political authority."[13]

The Gospel and Cultural Renewal

If the renunciation of idolatry necessarily wrought cultural destruction for members of various ethnic groups, we must hasten to add that some of this cultural change took the form of cultural revitalization and renewal, as those who believed adopted a new way of life. This was so central and obvious that those who received the message of the risen Messiah simply called themselves followers of "the Way" (Acts 9:2; 19:9, 23; 24:14, 22). But we should not think of this way of life as entirely discontinuous with their previous way of life. Instead, Luke highlights the way in which cultural norms practiced as part of the Way took on a renewed form in drawing people into koinonia across lines of cultural difference.

12 Rowe, World Upside Down, 5, 91.
13 Larry W. Hurtado, Destroyer of the Gods: Early Christian Distinctiveness in the Roman World (Waco, TX: Baylor University Press, 2016), 103.

1. *Cultural Renewal within the Diverse House of Israel.* One common way of summarizing Acts is to see it as a story of mission to the Jewish world followed by mission to the Gentile world. On this account, it is easy to see the Jewish world depicted in the opening chapters as culturally monolithic, with the primary fissure within this world arising from varied responses to the gospel. But this view must be qualified in an important way. To understand what Luke is doing in the opening chapters of Acts, we must see the way he portrays the house of Israel as culturally plural even before the gospel moves outward from Judea.[14]

The annual festival of Pentecost brought Jews and Jewish proselytes to Jerusalem from all over the world. In his description of Pentecost, Luke states that "God-fearing Jews from every nation under heaven" were staying in Jerusalem (Acts 2:5 NIV). As though to prove the point, he includes a lengthy list of nations from which they come, but his real interest is in the linguistic diversity among them.

As the ascended Christ pours out his Spirit, the Galilean disciples begin to speak in the diverse languages gathered there. Those who do not know these tongues understandably mistake the disciples' use of unfamiliar languages as drunken speech. But it was not.

Many have understood Pentecost as the reversal of Babel, but that does not reflect what actually happens. At Babel, everyone spoke a single language, but not at Pentecost. There is no move here toward God-defying cultural uniformity. Rather, Luke suggests that everyone was hearing the praises of God *in their own languages*, as the Spirit enabled the disciples to speak languages they had never learned. It would be difficult to imagine a more radical affirmation of the cultural diversity present on that day. If Babel represented human resistance to the divine purpose of an earth filled with diverse peoples unified in the worship of God, Pentecost represents the fulfillment of that purpose.

---

14 "Certain scholarly descriptions, then, of the peoples of Israel as particular do not do justice to the way in which the author of Acts uses the multi-ethnic diversity of Israel as a precedent and anticipation for the incorporation of non-Jewish peoples into the already multi-ethnic people of Israel." Jipp, "Hospitable Barbarians," 24.

Doubtless, much of that cultural diversity dispersed following the feast. It has long been speculated that churches such as the one in Rome had their origin in the conversions that took place at Pentecost. Still, many who came to faith that day were either from Jerusalem or remained there following Pentecost. The significant diversity between Greek-speaking Jews and Hebraic-speaking Jews already present in Jerusalem flowed naturally into the band of Christ followers in Jerusalem. Luke does not hide the tension that this created. With notable exceptions, the Spirit's work results in an extraordinary experience of community marked by generosity, prayer, devotion to the teaching of the apostles, and the joyful sharing of food and life together. Even so, "a complaint arose on the part of the Greek-speaking Jews against the native Hebraic Jews, because their widows were being overlooked in the daily distribution of food" (Acts 6:1 NET).

The incident is fascinating for the fleeting glimpse it provides of the linguistic and cultural diversity that marked the early Christian community even when it was still concentrated in Jerusalem and still composed only of those who identified as Jews. But the incident also shows us how easily differences in cultural identity can lead to disparities. This is not to suggest that these disparities were intended—Luke indicates that it was simply a matter of oversight—but it is not difficult to see how such disparities arose. The nature of cultural identity is that we naturally think of our own group first. We naturally feel empathy and affinity toward those most like ourselves. It is easier to love our neighbors as ourselves when we see ourselves in our neighbors.

As soon as the inequality between the two groups comes to light, the apostles move to redress it. Neither their apostleship nor their reception of the Spirit prevented them from having a blind spot in the matter. Though the text is often understood to imply that the provision for the widows was a lower-order task and that, in selecting a group of men to lead the effort, the apostles were choosing to focus on more important spiritual tasks, two features of the text point us in a different direction. First, the apostles declare that "it is not good for us to be in charge of the distribution of food while leaving to the side the ministry of the word" (Acts 6:2 AT).[15] This seems to serve as an explanation of why the Greek widows had been overlooked in the distribution of food. In attempting to do both, the apostles were making a hash of both.

Second, if the Greek-speaking widows are being overlooked, it is probably significant that the names of those chosen by the whole congregation for the task of managing the food distribution all have Greek names.[16] To be sure, they are not chosen simply because they are Greek. Above all, they were to be full of the Spirit and wisdom (Acts 6:3). Nevertheless, their "Greekness" was not irrelevant to their task, not least because the disparity may have shaken the confidence of the Greek-speaking part of the congregation. The disparity had led to disunity, and what better way to restore unity than for the whole congregation to entrust the task to a group of godly, Greek-speaking Jews?

The early community does not seem to seek ethnic representation within the recognized leadership. At the same time, they tacitly acknowledge that the preponderance of those identified as linguistically and culturally "Hebraic" (including all the apostles) had developed a kind of blind spot in the administration of benevolence within the community. The solution they sought did not prioritize cultural identity over godliness, but cultural identity does seem to have played a role. Of particular interest is the fact that the solution does not give the culturally Hellenistic group chosen to lead the work responsibility only for the Hellenistic part of the congregation, but for the whole congregation.[17] Perhaps we should say that the cultural majority entrusted the work to the cultural minority. By displaying trust, they restored

---

15 I have attempted to translate the Greek in a way that avoids the value judgment implied by translations like that of the NET: "It is not right for us to neglect the word of God to wait on tables."

16 By contrast, only three of the names in the list of apostles in Acts 1:13 are Greek—Peter, Philip, and Andrew. "Peter," of course, is a nickname for Simon, the Greek equivalent of the Hebrew name Simeon.

17 James D. G. Dunn argues that since the seven have only Greek names, their responsibility must be limited to the Hellenist widows. Dunn, *Christianity in the Making: Volume 2: Beginning from Jerusalem* (Grand Rapids, MI: Eerdmans, 2009), 255. However, the fact that they are chosen by the whole congregation weighs against this.

trust. "Because the new leaders are full of the Spirit and wisdom (6:3), members of both subcultures could trust them to pursue equity rather than factional interests."[18] More than that, Luke portrays the gift of the Spirit as crucial to Israel's eschatological renewal and highlights the wisdom imparted by the Spirit as essential to its functioning as a vibrant multicultural community.[19]

2. *Cultural Renewal in the Common Life of Jews and Greeks.* If the task given to the seven seems limited in scope, these culturally Greek Jews immediately take on an outsized role as the gospel suddenly bursts out of the Jewish context. One of the seven, Stephen, is stoned for his bold message before the Sanhedrin (Acts 7), but his message and martyrdom spark an explosion of cultural diversity among the early followers of Jesus. In Acts 8, another of the seven, Philip, takes the good news first to the Samaritans and then to an Ethiopian. In Acts 11, Luke indicates that the persecution that began with the stoning of Stephen results in a scattering of believers from Jerusalem into Judea, Samaria, and even farther afield:

Now those who had been scattered by the persecution that broke out when Stephen was killed traveled as far as Phoenicia, Cyprus and Antioch, spreading the word only among Jews. Some of them, however, men from Cyprus and Cyrene, went to Antioch and began to speak to Greeks also, telling them the good news about the Lord Jesus. (Acts 11:19–20 NIV)

As with the Greek-speaking Jews of Acts 6, Luke uses the term "Hellenists" (Acts 11:20) to designate these new believers in Antioch,

18 Craig S. Keener, *Acts*, New Cambridge Bible Commentary (Cambridge: Cambridge University Press, 2020), 225.
19 David Peterson rightly argues that this wisdom is "a particular manifestation of the Spirit" rather than a natural gift and is mentioned here because it was "especially necessary in dealing with the complexity" of the cultural tensions they would have to navigate. Peterson, *The Acts of the Apostles*, Pillar New Testament Commentary (Grand Rapids, MI: Eerdmans, 2009), 233.

but in this case, those who believe are not Jewish.[20] By noting that the good news was shared with Greeks in Antioch by men from Cyprus and Cyrene, Luke seems to indicate that the gospel passes from the Jewish world into the Gentile world in a way that was mediated by shared Greek language and culture.

Like the assembly in Jerusalem, the assembly that emerges in Antioch is also culturally mixed, but in a different way. Most members of the congregation may have had cultural sensibilities shaped in part by their Hellenistic milieu. However, the fact that some came from Jewish backgrounds while others came from pagan backgrounds meant that they perceived themselves and were perceived by others as ethnically distinct.[21] But when the two groups began to come together for public worship, outsiders—Roman officials, in particular—regarded this gathering of Jews and Greeks as something so unexpected and new that they coined a novel term for the group: "Christians" (Acts 11:26).[22]

Though some later church fathers spoke of "Christians" as a "third kind" of human,[23] Luke seems to suggest that the term was coined to

---

20 The ESV uses the term "Hellenists" instead of "Greeks," as in the NIV. This tends to suggest that the good news was being shared with Hellenistic Jews in Phoenicia, Cyrene, and Antioch.

21 It would not have occurred to any of the Christ followers in Jerusalem to say that they were no longer Jews, even if some, like Paul, would have spoken of their "former life in Judaism" (Gal. 1:13). They might have left behind a particular understanding of what Jewishness meant, but they had not abandoned Jewishness itself. "Paul remained Jewish ethnically, but he no longer considered himself to be part of Judaism." Thomas R. Schreiner, *Galatians*, Zondervan Exegetical Commentary on the New Testament (Grand Rapids, MI: Zondervan, 2010), 98. By contrast, the Christians whom Paul identifies as "Judaizers" did seem to consider themselves to be still within "Judaism." The term *Judaism* was coined at the time of the Maccabean revolt (167 BC) to distinguish between those whose way of life remained self-consciously faithful to the Torah, in contrast to a way of life characterized as "Hellenism," regardless of whether those who adopted that way of life were Jews or Greeks.

22 "The 'Christians' were so named in the sphere of Roman administration." Rowe, *World Upside Down*, 129.

23 See, for example, the opening section of the anonymous second- or third-century *Letter to Diognetus* or, from the same period, Clement of Alexandria, *Stromata* 6.41.6. Most translations use the expression new or third "race" to translate the Greek term *genos*, but the term *race* in such contexts is anachronistic. Rather, *genos* in this context refers to a broad grouping of humanity along primarily religious lines. Erich S. Gruen argues that

designate a group whose beliefs and practices distinguished it from both Judaism and Hellenism. This group's way of life was the product of a belief that a crucified Jewish Christ, whom they claimed to be bodily raised, was now Lord of both Jews and Greeks—that is to say, Lord of *all*. Their non-Christian Jewish and Greek counterparts made universal claims of their own, but did so in a way that kept the two groups in separate communities. Among the Christians, however, that was no longer the case. This is not to brand the Christians as uniquely inclusive. As Rowe puts it, "in a crucial way, the vision of Acts is profoundly intolerant."[24] The Christian message included the insistence that pagans turn from idolatry and undermined a whole host of cultural beliefs and practices associated with idolatry. The same is true of any truth claim, including the claim in our own day that all such claims are intolerant. But the fact remains that the term "Christian" came to be used first and foremost because the claim that Christ was Lord of all gave rise to a community in which Jews and Greeks worshiped together as one people.

As a result, many of the cultural ideals held by Jews as Jews and by Greeks as Greeks come to shocking, public expression in a single community of Jews and Greeks. This mixed community of culturally distinct peoples overflows with generosity toward the impoverished believers in Judea (Acts 11:27–30) and supports the mission of Paul and Barnabas to proclaim the good news among Gentile peoples in the province of Galatia (13:1–3).[25] The depiction of the common life shared by the Jewish believers in Jerusalem in the early chapters of Acts had a decidedly Jewish cast, reflecting Luke's perception that the outpouring of the Holy Spirit at Pentecost had sparked a renewal of Israel's communal life. If the ideal of Torah was that there should be no poor among the people of God (Deut. 15:4), that ideal is realized in

the use of such expressions in early Christianity did not carry the sense of a distinct ethnicity or cultural identity. Gruen, *Ethnicity in the Ancient World: Did It Matter?* (Berlin: de Gruyter, 2020), 201–14.

24 Rowe, *World Upside Down*, 170.

25 Luke notes that the congregation in Antioch "sent them off" (Acts 13:3), and that sending probably included a measure of financial support for the task.

the community formed by the Spirit (Acts 2:45). But as the narrative progresses, we also gain a sense of the way in which Greek ideals of hospitality, friendship, and fraternity get taken up in a revitalized way in the culturally mixed congregations established during the missionary journeys of Paul.[26]

Conclusion

Luke frames both his Gospel and its sequel with the conviction that the crucifixion, resurrection, and exaltation of Jesus have inaugurated Israel's restoration as God's one holy people. In these events, God has fulfilled his oath to Abraham to form a renewed humanity that serves him in righteousness and holiness. Luke's Gospel gives us an unexpected glimpse of this new humanity through the actions of two Samaritans who fulfill the fundamental precepts of Israel's holiness: one who loves an Israelite neighbor in need (even though "holy" Israelites do not) and another who loves God (even though his Israelite companions do not). In Acts, Luke describes this people as followers of "the Way." We may think of this as a newly constructed identity—a common culture—shared by all who repent and believe. It is formed within Israel, but those who share in it need not become Jewish. To be sure, there is assimilation to norms renewed and revitalized within Israel's own multiethnic identity. However, once exposed to the culture-destroying and culture-renewing power of the gospel, the cultural endowments and identity of any people find their proper place within the people of the Way. The cultural distinctions remain, preserved and realized in the culturally specific ways that each group practices its common life as a single worshiping people.

26 Rowe, *World Upside Down*, 171.

8

The Open Temple

Worship and the Unity of All Peoples

When early Greek Christians spoke of perichoresis *in God, they
meant that each divine person harbors the others at the center
of his being . . . each person envelops and encircles the others.
Supposing that hospitality means to make room for others and
then to help them flourish in the room you have made, I think we
could say that hospitality thrives within the triune life of God.*

CORNELIUS PLANTINGA, IN *ENGAGING GOD'S WORLD:
A CHRISTIAN VISION OF FAITH, LEARNING, AND LIVING*

*On this mountain the LORD of hosts will make for all peoples
a feast of rich food, a feast of well-aged wine.*

ISAIAH 25:6

MY WIFE'S WORK in Ethiopia brought her into a remarkable network of
relationships with women from around the world. She extends friendship
with uncommon ease, so she was often one of the first to welcome women
newly arrived in Addis Ababa. Inevitably, she would soon be meeting
them in one of the hundreds of cafés that account for the unmistakable
aroma of roasting coffee that often wafts through the streets of the city.

One evening, she described a woman who had made a strong impression: "She must have been the warmest, most loving person I've ever met!" (At that point, I'm sure I objected, "No, that would be you, Love.") My wife has the uncanny ability to remember the details of a day, replete with a range of astute observations on a myriad of interactions. That day was no different. She recounted a half dozen or more ways this new friend had impressed her, finishing with a description of how they had parted. "It was not just any hug," she explained. "It was more like a long, lingering embrace. I felt like I had been immersed in a sea of calm. I could feel her smiling into the back of my hair!"

When she finished her description, I wondered what could make a person able to communicate such warmth and love. "So, do you think she is a Christian?" I asked. "No," she replied, "Buddhist, I think."

I wasn't surprised, even though her new friend was not from Asia or from a Buddhist background. I had read recently that Asians comprised 85 percent of Yale University's Campus Crusade for Christ chapter, while "the university's Buddhist meditation meetings are almost exclusively attended by whites."[1] What is it that many in the West find so compelling about Eastern religion? Perhaps it is not just one thing, but in an age of social fragmentation, political polarization, and cultural tribalism, the vision of the oneness of all things in Eastern religions has proved to be deeply compelling. The lingering embrace of my wife's friend tangibly expressed the belief that we are all deeply connected— that everyone, together with everything, is or will be one.

The Gospel of John also has a vision of unity—though, as we shall see, it is a vision that differs profoundly from that found in Buddhism. Within Eastern religions, the ultimate aim is the *dissolution* of difference. All living things experience an ongoing cycle of rebirth until they become so detached from the stuff of earth that their identities meld into one universal consciousness. The goal is, as it were, to stop being born again. Only when individuals stop being individual do they

---

1   Timothy C. Tennent, *Theology in the Context of World Christianity: How the Global Church Is Influencing the Way We Think About and Discuss Theology* (Grand Rapids, MI: Zondervan, 2007), 53.

become one.[2] John, however, envisions a very different kind of rebirth with a very different outcome. For John, the new birth is a singular event that imparts eternal life to individuals. But that gift of eternal life does not merely underwrite the promise that the individual will never die (John 11:26). Because that life originates in the one who "has life in himself" (5:26), we are drawn into the life of God, who is one.

The Gospel articulates the divine will that Jesus's people "may be one" (John 17:11, 21, 22) and models that unity on the oneness of God himself—a oneness in which the distinctions between God as Father, Son, and Spirit are necessary to an eternal relational unity. For John, the saving work of God as Father, Son, and Spirit draws people into the life of the one God, where not just individuals but *peoples* experience the unity of God himself.

In chapter 2, we saw that humanity was placed in a temple—a garden dwelling of God that they were to expand by filling the earth with diverse peoples. John portrays the resurrected Jesus as the temple of the new age, the dwelling place of the Father, out of which the life-giving Spirit flows for the healing of the nations. This temple has many "rooms," prepared as the habitation for all peoples through Jesus's death and resurrection. Though this new people comes into being as individuals believe in Christ and receive new birth, this new birth does not strip them of their cultural identities. Rather, with cultural identities renewed, they come to live in the temple. They are drawn into the Trinitarian life of God and granted an identity as a people of many peoples, characterized by their relational participation in the loving unity of the one God.

Ethnic Discourse in John's Gospel

In John's Gospel, the collective identity of the people of God is carefully negotiated, often but not exclusively through the use of ethnic

2   "Buddhism shares with Hinduism the doctrine of Samsara, whereby all beings pass through an unceasing cycle of birth, death and rebirth until they find a means of liberation from the cycle." Kevin Trainor, *Buddhism: The Illustrated Guide* (Oxford: Oxford University Press), 58.

discourse. This people is designated in a variety of ways, most of them religious. They are "children of God" (John 1:12) and the sheep who hear his voice (10:27). This group emerges through faith in Jesus as Savior of the world (4:42), yet its members are distinguished from "the world" (15:19). At the same time, the group is distinguished from "the Jews," even though within John's Gospel it comprises only Jews. Even so, it is not ethnicity as such that identifies the members of this group. Rather, it is their love for one another—a distinctive way of life that distinguishes them in the eyes of outsiders. This way of life is worked out not simply in the relation of one individual to another, but of one group to another. The Gospel of John specifies only three ethnicities—Jews, Samaritans, and Greeks. All three play a key role in John's conception of this new people, which, in John's view, will comprise all peoples.

1. *Jews and "the Jews" in John.* We must immediately qualify the identification of "Jews" as an ethnic group within John. Although it occasionally describes a group made up of *all* who share Jewish ethnic heritage (John 4:22), this is not how John usually uses the term. Rather, "the Jews" frequently functions as an ethno-religious designation of a particular group of Jews who based their claim to be the children of God, at least in part, on ethnic descent from Abraham. In John, they emerge as a discrete group to which most ethnic Jews—including Jesus and his disciples—did not belong. For this group, the claim to be the children of God began with an ethnic claim. However, it also required adherence to the religious perspectives and commitments of that particular group. This requirement entailed a religious conviction about the significance of ethnicity for determining one's relationship to God. This is profoundly different from the way the term "Jew" functions in contexts today, where it applies equally to all who share Jewish ethnic identity regardless of religious commitments.

In John, most references to "the Jews" designate a group whose commitments to the religious significance of their ethnicity make them hostile to Jesus.[3] Used in this way, "the Jews" are a group to which Jesus and the other Jews who follow him do not belong. Indeed, Jews who follow Jesus risk expulsion from the religious community controlled by "the Jews." Jesus and those who follow him are Jews opposed by the group that John refers to as "the Jews."[4] This fact alone undermines the still-frequent claim that John is anti-Semitic.

Others have claimed that even if John is not anti-Semitic, he is certainly anti-Jewish.[5] But the allegation makes the questionable assumption that John writes as someone who is not or no longer identifies as Jewish. It also fails to account for Jesus's claim to the Samaritan woman that "salvation is from the Jews" (John 4:22). Further, when John refers to "the Jews" in a negative way, he manifestly does not designate a group to which every Jew belongs. John is not anti-Jewish; he is anti-"the Jews." We must tease out the nuances of John's varied use of the term, but clearly it does not function as a broad racial type, conveying a negative assessment of all who share Jewish ethnicity. Rather, he refers to a subgroup that held Jewish ethnicity at the core of their religious claims to be God's people.

We see this in John 8:33, where "the Jews" reject Jesus's insistence that acceptance of his message would set them free. They recoil when Jesus says that they need manumission: "We are Abraham's descendants," they reply, "and have never been slaves of anyone" (NIV). The latter statement is often understood as an expression of fierce national

3   The faith commitments that render those labeled as "the Jews" hostile to Jesus are not always the same. Thus, in John 9, "the Jews" are primarily Pharisees whose hostility to Jesus is prompted by a perception that he has violated the Sabbath. In John 11, however, "the Jews" include both Pharisees and the chief priests, who are more likely Sadducees. The two groups hold quite different views on many issues, but John portrays them as united in their zealous protection of the temple in opposition to Jesus.

4   These complexities make the term difficult to translate. Some simply transliterate the Greek—*Ioudaioi*. Others prefer a geographical designation—"Judeans." While John does mean a group primarily based in Judea with a power base in Jerusalem and the temple, the term no more embraces every Judean than every Jew. I will adopt the convention of putting the term in quotation marks when it refers to a particular group of Jews marked by opposition to Jesus and the central place they give to ethnicity in their religious identity.

5   D. Moody Smith, *The Theology of the Gospel of John*, New Testament Theology (Cambridge: Cambridge University Press, 1995), 171–3.

pride.[6] On this reading, "the Jews" deny the political reality of Roman domination and cling to Abrahamic descent as evidence of their freedom. However, it is not clear how Abrahamic descent alone justifies a claim to an uninterrupted history of national freedom.

In the wider context of John 8, the exchange almost certainly relates to a running debate over parentage and the charge that Jesus's own parentage was ambiguous. The point of such a charge was to undermine Jesus's Jewish heritage. However, recent work has marshalled evidence that enslavement in the ancient world rendered a person ethnically ambiguous.[7] "The Jews" seem to have understood Jesus's assertion that they needed to be set free as an attack on their claim to be unambiguously Jewish. In short, this is but one of many instances of misunderstanding that pepper John's Gospel. "The Jews" take Jesus to mean that they are physical slaves whose enslavement has clouded their physical ethnicity. In fact, Jesus is saying that they are spiritual slaves to sin, and that enslavement has clarified their true line of descent—their father is Satan, the original liar (8:44). Their enslavement to sin *has* distorted their ethnicity. Even if their claim to unambiguous physical descent from Abraham were correct (8:37, 56), their ethical conduct calls their spiritual descent from Abraham into question (8:39).

Because their father is Satan, Jesus pronounces them deceived. In their deception, "the Jews" stand in marked contrast to Nathanael, a "true Israelite," in whom there is no deceit (John 1:47 NET). Nathanael confesses Jesus to be the Son of God, the King of Israel—a confession that brings to light his identity as a "true Israelite."

At the end of the book, the reverse is also true, tragically. If Nathanael's confession identifies him as a "true Israelite," those called "the

---

6   J. Ramsey Michaels, *The Gospel of John*, New International Commentary on the New Testament (Grand Rapids, MI: Eerdmans, 2010), 506.

7   Wally V. Cirafesi, "Jewishness as Genealogy in the Fourth Gospel: Situating John's *Ioudaioi* within Debates over Ancestry and Merit in Ancient Judaism," paper read at the November 2018 meeting of the Institute for Biblical Research, 10–11. The paper will be included in Wally V. Cirafesi, *John within Judaism: Religion, Ethnicity, and the Shaping of Jesus-Oriented Jewishness in the Fourth Gospel*, Ancient Judaism and Early Christianity (Leiden: Brill, forthcoming).

Jews" repudiate that identity in rejecting Pilate's depiction of Jesus as "the King of the Jews." Their efforts to persuade Pilate to alter his charge to read that Jesus "claimed to be king of the Jews" fail (John 19:21 NIV). However, it is here that Johannine irony slashes the ties of "the Jews" to Israel. The crucified Jesus is in fact the King of the Jews. But he is not their King. He is the King of the Jews, but he is not welcomed as King by "the Jews."

The discussion highlights three important points. First, labels matter, but their meanings are unstable. They depend wholly on context. Who is using the label and why? For John (who is a Jew) to use an expression like "the Jews" to describe an intra-Jewish conflict over what it means to be the children of God is one thing. But it is quite another for a non-Jew to refer to "the Jews" in a way that links Jewishness to particular types of negative behavior.[8] Certain kinds of ethnic discourse are available only to insiders. John's use of "the Jews" is one of them. As a Jew, John's negative use of "the Jews" for a group of fellow Jews is very different from the negative use of the term by an outsider to describe all Jews.

Not only does it matter that John uses the phrase "the Jews" as a Jew describing a group that is part of an intra-Jewish debate, it also matters that John uses the expression to describe a particular group of Jews that occupies a position of cultural dominance. Black comedians can, with little fear of giving offense, readily poke fun at the "whiteness" of "white girls" or at certain ways of doing things as "so white" without raising cultural alarms. This is because power dynamics matter. In this case, the "whiteness" in question refers to the cultural idiosyncrasies of a dominant group.

Second, when John uses the term "the Jews" negatively, he refers to a group defined by a religious stance generated in part by a sense of ethnic priority. Far from being anti-Semitic or anti-Jewish, John speaks as a Jew opposing a historically specific and toxic form of racial exclusivity

8   Examples of this stereotype may be seen in Shakespeare's portrayal of a conniving Jewish moneylender, Shylock, in *The Merchant of Venice*; the similar portrait of a Jewish jeweler, Hosea, in James Fenimore Cooper's *The Bravo*; in several early poems of T. S. Eliot (e.g., "Gerontion"); and in the anti-Semitism found at both ends of the political spectrum.

that had gained a following among some Jews. It is rather like a person who, in speaking against white nationalists, not only identifies himself as "white" but also refers to white nationalists as "the whites."[9] Within a single work, the same racial descriptor can be both innocuous and menacing. This helps us understand why "the Jews" in John can refer both to the ethnic group to which Jesus belongs and to a subgroup to which he does not.

Third, John uses the language of ethnic identity to develop a notion of "spiritual ethnicity" as a way of assessing the racial exclusivity of Jesus's opponents. At the heart of Jesus's conflict with "the Jews" in John lies a dispute about three of the features of cultural identity identified in chapter four—a shared ancestry, a shared way of life, and a shared language. John's use of the phrase "the Jews" arises from the central place this group gave to ancestry in defining the people of God. The surprising thing is that Jesus agrees—with one major caveat. For Jesus, the crucial issue was divine, not ethnic, ancestry. Jesus believed that the ancestry that binds people together in one family with God as Father is birth from above. Jesus meets "the Jews'" ethnically exclusive claim with his own: only those born of God are children of God (John 1:12–13). This identity is depicted as a spiritual ethnicity and embraces people from a variety of physical ethnicities, including, of course, people of Jewish ethnicity. To be sure, John largely concedes the ethnonym "Jew" to "the Jews." But not entirely (4:22; cf. 12:11), and at the end of the Gospel, he reclaims it. "The Jews" reject Jesus as King and swear loyalty to a non-Jewish king (19:15). But for his Jewish followers, Jesus remains "King of the Jews" (19:19).

Like Jesus, the Jews who follow him have a dual origin story and hence dual identities. Jesus is both from Bethlehem and from above, and they have been born both from Abraham and from above. The first birth

---

9   See, for example, an essay by Ashley Jardina, assistant professor of political science at Duke University, "White Identity Politics Isn't Just about White Supremacy. It's Much Bigger," *Washington Post*, August 16, 2017, https://www.washingtonpost.com/. Within the essay, she uses the term *whites* in three distinct ways: 1) as a general descriptor, including "whites who do not identify with whites as a group"; 2) as a designation of those who do identify with "whites" as a group; and 3) as a term for a small group of white nationalists.

gives rise to a distinctively Jewish way of life, including, for instance, the practice of circumcision, participation in the Jewish festivals, and worship at the temple in Jerusalem. The second birth also gives rise to a way of life—a common culture, as it were—shared by all whose nature is determined by the second birth. This way of life is characterized above all by obedience to Jesus's commands, most especially the command that they love one another (John 13:34).

Ironically, "the Jews" also have dual ancestry and dual identity. This is why Jesus both allows that Abraham is their father (John 8:37, 56) and denies it (8:39). In the latter case, Jesus associates Abrahamic ancestry with Abrahamic actions: "If you were Abraham's children . . . , then you would do what Abraham did. . . . You are looking for a way to kill me. . . . Abraham did not do such things. You are doing the works of your own father [the devil]" (8:39–41 NIV). Jesus's words are sharp, but they grow sharper still as he draws out another feature of the identity of this second ancestry—their common language: "When [the devil] lies, he speaks his native language" (8:44 NIV). This is a language "the Jews" understand perfectly well. Their fluency in the language of deceit sets "the Jews" in striking contrast to Nathanael, a "true Israelite" (1:47 NET), who speaks truth by confessing Jesus to be the King of the Jews. They claim physical descent from Abraham, but their ethnic exclusivity betrays another, altogether darker ancestry. *In the starkest terms possible, Jesus insists that ethnic or racial supremacy is of the devil.*

2. Samaritans, the Bridegroom, and Sacred Space. While "the Jews" renounce identification with "the King of the Jews," a very different picture emerges in John's portrayal of Samaritans. Here we gain our first glimpse of ethnic differentiation in the portrayal of restored Israel and a corresponding way of thinking about sacred space in the temple of the age to come.

From a first-century Jewish perspective, the Samaritans were neither near-Jews nor Gentiles. They were idolatrous apostates—a status that many believed to be incompatible with their presence within a land deemed holy to the Lord. Earlier we saw that such a view led the

Maccabeans to adopt a policy of ethnic cleansing toward the Samaritans. That policy resulted in the destruction of the Samaritan temple on Mount Gerazim in 128 BC. For many Jews, the Samaritan presence in Israel's land was defiling; their historical claims, provoking; their practice of circumcision, galling. This animosity created immense practical problems for social relations, trade, and travel. For instance, in traveling between Judea and Galilee—the two Jewish population centers of first-century Palestine—many Jews chose the inconvenience of traveling through the Jordan Valley on the east side of the Jordan River in order to avoid taking the direct route through Samaria, where assault and ritual contamination were possible.

For this reason, it is surprising that when Jesus decides to go to Galilee, he chooses the route through Samaria. John does not explain why Jesus makes this choice, only that he "had to" go this way (John 4:4). Whatever the reason, Jesus found himself sitting beside a well at midday, thirsty and lacking means to draw water. But this was not just any well. This was *Jacob's* well, and John surely expected that at least some of his readers would notice the connection back to the story of Jacob meeting his future wife, Rachel, at a well (Gen. 29:1–12). In John 2:1–12, Jesus had been placed in the role of a bridegroom in the story of the wedding at Cana and then explicitly identified as the bridegroom in John 3:27–30. Now, here in John 4, we find out who the bride will be. Against the backdrop of Jacob's encounter with Rachel at this well, Jesus's "encounter with the woman at the well would seem to portend some sort of 'marriage.'"[10] The unexpected nature of this marriage is mirrored in the Samaritan woman's astonishment when Jesus engages her in a conversation. The marriage takes place, or is at least anticipated, as a woman, apostate through willful sin, leads her people, apostate through idolatry, to confess Jesus as the Messiah, the Savior of the world.

As Jesus turns the conversation from his need for water to the woman's need for living water, we gain our first glimpse of the people God

10   Richard B. Hays, *Echoes of Scripture in the Gospels* (Waco, TX: Baylor University Press, 2016), 291.

had promised to betroth to himself as his bride in prophetic tradition. This purified people will be formed not by purging Samaritans
from Israel's midst, but by sharing with them the "living water" (John
4:10–14), which Ezekiel said would flow out from the temple to be the
life-giving source of healing and fruitfulness (Ezek. 47:1–12).

This in no way obviates the particular role of ethnic Israel in mediat-
ing God's salvation to the world. As Jesus insists, "salvation is from the
Jews" (John 4:22). At this point in the Gospel, John has not yet spelled
out the relationship between the identity of the Jews from whom salvation comes and the identity of "the Jews" so implacably opposed to
Jesus throughout John. But if such ambiguities attend the group *from*
whom salvation comes, the identity of the people *to* whom salvation
comes now begins to take shape. The Israel betrothed to God in the
time that "is coming, and is now here" (4:23) will embrace Samaritans.

John's conception of how this transformation takes places emerges
from Jesus's interaction with the woman over the proper place of worship. The woman raises the question in response to Jesus's exposure of
the fact that she has had five husbands and is now living with a man
to whom she is not married. It is an odd response, given the deeply
personal nature of Jesus's prophetic insight into her tragic history.
Indeed, commentators often treat the woman's comment about the
proper place of worship as an attempt to divert the conversation from
the uncomfortable focus on her personal life to the safer ground of
esoteric theological debate. But the issue of her marital status and the
question of Samaritan worship are not as disconnected as they first
appear. In fact, John would have us see the woman's apostate status as
a window to the apostasy of the Samaritans and her marital status as a
window to the need of her people for the true bridegroom.

Whether or not the woman perceives a connection between her marital status and the religious status of the Samaritans, the topic she raises is
not the stuff of stodgy debate. It is explosive. And she does not frame the
issue any more diplomatically than Jesus had framed his comments about
her marital status. She could have simply raised the issue of competing
claims about the proper place of worship. Instead, she evokes a grievance:

"Our ancestors worshiped on this mountain" (John 4:20 NIV). Almost certainly she means that her Samaritan forebears *used* to worship on this mountain, until the Jews destroyed the temple there. "What," she seems to say, "does this Jewish prophet have to say about *that*?"

Perhaps the woman believes that the attempted ethnic cleansing two centuries before had undermined exclusive Jewish claims about Jerusalem as the proper locus of worship. Few things delegitimize a religious claim as much as an injustice perpetrated by those who make the claim. But if the woman's framing of the question invites this prophet's assessment of a historic grievance, Jesus's response points instead to a future that "is coming, and is now here" (4:23)—a future in which worship will take place wherever those who worship the Father do so by the Spirit and in the truth. Jesus's response, however, should not be understood as simply sidestepping the question of ethnic grievance and priority.

The point that Jesus is making is neither that the arriving new age will make the concept of sacred space obsolete nor that it will render all space sacred—two common ways of understanding Jesus's words. Rather, his point is that the pervasive notion of sacred space—holy land, holy city, holy temple—is but an anticipation of Jesus himself and of the worship focused on him that the Spirit will enable. This marks a cataclysm in both time and space. The Jerusalem temple had been the linchpin of Jewish ethnic and national identity. Competing claims about a temple on Mount Gerazim or any other temple implicitly assert the sacral primacy of that place and the people who worship there. Jesus undercuts all such claims by identifying the temple of the new era with himself. So the worshipers who worship his Father in this temple are no longer identified by their ethnic or national attachment to a specific place, but by their dwelling within the one in whom God dwells. If "the Jews'" vision of an ethnically pure people in an ethnically purified land centers on the inviolable purity of the Jerusalem temple, Jesus's vision of Israel takes a very different direction.

3. *Greeks.* The Gospel of John makes just two further references to non-Jews. There are peculiarities around both. To understand the scope

and the means of Jesus's multiethnic vision, we must unravel the ethnic discourse that surrounds both.

The first comes in John 7:35. Jesus is again in Jerusalem, this time for the Feast of Tabernacles. Jesus had initially declined his brothers' sarcastic cajolement to go up to Jerusalem as any aspiring "public figure" would do (7:3–9). Meanwhile, in Jerusalem, John tells us that "the Jews" were watching for him and kept asking, "Where is he?" (7:11). Eventually, without fanfare, Jesus goes (7:10).

This question of Jesus's location then fuels the ensuing exchange about his origins, driven in part by an expectation that when the Messiah comes, "no one will know where he comes from" (John 7:27). The crowds think they know where Jesus is from—Nazareth—leading some to conclude that he cannot be the Messiah. Others arrive at the same conclusion on the basis of another expectation—that Messiah would be born in Bethlehem (7:42). Though the expectations differ, the conclusion is the same: Jesus cannot be the Messiah because they know where he is from.

There is irony and tragedy on both counts. He *was* born in Bethlehem, but Bethlehem only begins to describe Jesus's true origins. Jesus comes "from above" (John 3:31). So, in Jesus, the apparently incompatible expectations that no one will know where the Messiah is from and that he will be born in Bethlehem are both true. Though both appear to be untrue of Jesus, this does not dissuade many in the crowd from believing that he might nevertheless be the Messiah. If this man is not the Messiah, he is surely his equal (7:31)!

That galling conclusion, along with Jesus's claim to come from God, prompts the Pharisees and chief priests to send temple guards to arrest Jesus. But if his claim to come from God is infuriating, Jesus's response to the plots against his life is baffling: "I am with you for only a short time, and then I am going to the one who sent me. You will look for me, but you will not find me; and where I am, you cannot come" (John 7:33–34 NIV). Having declared his opponents ignorant about where he is from, he now insists that they are similarly ignorant about where he is going.

With this, "the Jews" speculate that Jesus might leave for foreign lands to "teach the Greeks" (John 7:35 NIV). Only in this way can they imagine Jesus becoming inaccessible. Of particular note is the way they describe these foreign lands: "Will he go where our people live scattered among the Greeks, and teach the Greeks?" (7:35 NIV). The designation of non-Jewish people as "Greeks" reflects the pervasive influence of Greek language and culture that has endured long after the Latin-speaking Romans came to power. From a Jewish perspective, the division of humanity into two categories—Jews and Greeks—is basic and broadly equivalent in a first-century context to the categorization of all people as either Jews or Gentiles.

The speculation that Jesus might be going to foreign lands to teach the Greeks is another instance of Johannine irony. Jesus is not going to the Greeks but to the Father, and only those who believe can come to the Father. But if he is not going to the Greeks, his going will make possible the coming of the Greeks to him. This reading is confirmed in John 12:20–22, where Andrew and Philip tell Jesus that some Greeks who have come to Jerusalem to worship at the time of the Passover want to see him. In response, Jesus declares, "The hour has come for the Son of Man to be glorified" (12:23). As is well known, the hour of Jesus's glorification in John's Gospel is the hour of his death, as John 12:27 immediately confirms. An oblique reference to impending death seems an odd response to a request for a brief chat!

Adding to the oddity, the text never indicates whether Jesus met with the Greeks or responded in any way to their request to see him. The interpretive framework for understanding this text almost certainly lies in the Isaianic expectation that the Gentile nations will come in pilgrimage to Jerusalem when God brings about the restoration of Israel. That will be the moment when Israel will be lifted up, exalted by God, as a banner to which all the nations will rally to worship the God of Israel. That will be the moment at which the nations will join in the assembly of Israel (e.g., Isa. 49:22). For John, the ultimate irony is that this exaltation of Israel is fulfilled in the crucifixion of Israel's representative. The coming of the Greeks signals that the hour for the lifting up of the Son of Man as a banner for the nations has also come (John 12:23–33).

4. *All Nations.* The ingathering of the nations becomes a subtle focus of the epilogue in John 21. Though John is not the only evangelist to record an extraordinary catch of 153 fish (cf. Luke 5:1–11) or to depict the disciples as "fishers of people" (Matt. 4:19; Mark 1:17 NET), he alone sets a commissioning of the disciples to gather the nations within a narrative about an extraordinary ingathering of fish made possible by the resurrected Jesus (John 21:1–14). The episode is widely interpreted as a symbol-laden equivalent to Matthew's Great Commission. Once more, the symbolism arises out of John's reading of the Old Testament prophets—in this case, Ezekiel 47 and its extraordinary vision of a life-giving river flowing out of the eschatological temple.

John made use of Ezekiel 47 back in John 7:37–39, where Jesus declares, "If anyone thirsts, let him come to me and drink." He then adds, "Just as the scripture says, 'From within him [i.e., Jesus] will flow rivers of living water.' (Now he said this about the Spirit, whom those who believed in him were going to receive, for the Spirit had not yet been given, because Jesus was not yet glorified)" (NET).[11] The reference to "the Scripture" is an allusion to the imagery of the life-giving river in Ezekiel 47:1. John's earlier identification of Jesus not only as the eschatological fulfillment of the temple (John 2:13–22) but also as the source of living water (John 4:1–15) prepares us to see Jesus as the new temple from which the life-giving Spirit flows to those who believe.

John may also have Ezekiel 47:1 in mind when he recalls the flow of water from Jesus's side when it is pierced by the soldier's spear (John 19:34). The language of Ezekiel 47:1 anticipates a flow of water "from below the shoulder/side of the temple."[12] Thus, John may understand

---

11   The NET translation, unlike many English translations, allows for the possibility that the one out of whom the living waters flow is Jesus rather than the believer.

12   Richard Bauckham, *The Testimony of the Beloved Disciple: Narrative, History, and Theology in the Gospel of John* (Grand Rapids, MI: Baker, 2007), 280.

the flow of water from the side of the crucified Jesus as a symbol of the fulfillment of the eschatological temple.

It would not be surprising, then, if John is thinking of Ezekiel 47 in recalling the extraordinary catch of fish as a way of reflecting on the commission of the disciples to the nations. Elsewhere in the Johannine literature, Ezekiel 47 serves as the source of the expectation that the trees watered by the stream flowing from the temple will provide "healing [for] the nations" (Rev. 22:2; cf. Ezek. 47:12). In the Gospel's epilogue, however, the focus is not on the trees watered by the temple-river but on the fish that swim in it. The river finds its way into the Dead Sea, which, like the river itself, soon teems with fish of "many kinds" (Ezek. 47:10). Fishermen spread their nets to catch fish of every kind. The church father, Justin Martyr, cites a Greek poet who claimed that there were 153 different kinds of fish known at that time, representing the various nations and peoples of the earth. Whether or not we are to think of the number of fish as a symbol for all the nations, it is not at all unlikely that the abundance of fish represents the extraordinary ingathering of the children of God scattered in every nation through the mission of these fishermen turned fishers of men.[13]

The Open Temple

In John 10:16, Jesus uses the striking metaphor of bringing sheep from another pen to join the flock. The result is that there will be "one flock [under] one shepherd." John does not directly speak, here or elsewhere, about the diversity of the flock formed as the sheep from the other pen are brought into the flock of Israel. Rather, using a rich variety of images, he puts the focus repeatedly and powerfully on the unity of this people formed by the ingathering of "other sheep" from another fold. Among the images John employs, perhaps none is as important as that of the temple for depicting the unity of the people of God within the life of God. I want to consider three often-overlooked ways in which John

---

13 For the argument that the number of fish is significant because the Hebrew equivalent of "children of God" has the numerical value of 153, see Bauckham, *Testimony*, 178–79.

explores temple motifs to foster a vision of the unity of all peoples in the risen Messiah—a unity that depends on ongoing ethnic differentiation within the one people of God.

1. *Prophecy and Prediction.* Israel's preexilic prophets dreaded the destruction of the temple but also dreamed of a new temple—a temple built by God himself. It would be difficult to overstate the importance of the temple to Israel's national identity or the sense of desolation when the Babylonians razed it. For many, the temple served as a guarantee of God's presence and protection, so its decimation had one clear meaning: God had abandoned them.

This national trauma was made worse by errant understandings of Israel's sacred traditions that seemed to guarantee that even if Israel was removed from the land as punishment for disobedience, the temple would remain. After building the temple, had not Solomon implied as much in his prayer of dedication?

> When they sin against you . . . and you become angry with them and give them over to their enemies, who take them captive to their own lands . . . if they turn back to you with all their heart and soul . . . and pray to you toward the land you gave their ancestors, toward the city you have chosen and the temple I have built for your Name; then from heaven, your dwelling place, hear their prayer and their plea, and uphold their cause. (1 Kings 8:46–49 NIV)

This, however, did not appear to be a prayer that God had answered. The people had indeed been taken from the land, but there was no temple toward which to pray. Not only had God's presence departed from the temple, the temple had been destroyed. Israel had been taken from the divine presence, and the divine presence had been taken from them.

Nevertheless, the prophets sustained an expectation that God would lead his people back to the land and gather them into a new temple—a temple even more glorious than the first one. In the expectation of many, that temple would be capable of accommodating the whole of Israel. But it would not accommodate just Israel.[14] The house of the Lord was to be "for all nations" (Isa. 56:7 NIV; cf. Isa. 2:2; 27:13). In the Synoptic Gospels, this prophecy is cited as part of Jesus's protest in the temple—an action that leads directly to his trial and the accusation that he made threats against the temple, promising to "build" a new one.

That Jesus does in fact make such a prediction in relation to his action in the temple is confirmed by John, but he places it near the beginning of his Gospel: "Destroy this temple, and in three days I will raise it up" (John 2:19). It is sometimes supposed that John's placement of the incident early in his Gospel distances it from the crucifixion. The effect, rather, is to characterize the whole of Jesus's mission as God's act to raise a temple that will be a house for all nations. From the beginning of the Gospel, John wants his readers to see the resurrected Jesus as the dwelling place of God for all peoples.

2. *Preparation.* In John 14:2–3, Jesus tells his disciples, "In my Father's house are many rooms.... I go to prepare a place for you ... that where I am you may be also." The passage has been misunderstood in multiple ways. Under the influence of older translations, many have understood Jesus's words as a promise of a luxurious palace for every individual believer. Those influenced by more recent translations have tended to think of a heavenly hotel or of a place with many rooms, and the postascension work of Christ as principally occupied with the preparation of those rooms for occupation.

However, there is good reason to think that the house in view is not heaven but the temple, which Jesus has promised to raise in three days. In John's Gospel, "my Father's house" (John 2:16) and "place" (11:48) function as temple language.[15] On this understanding, the preparation takes place through Jesus's death and resurrection.

---

14 For a discussion of the relevant biblical and Second Temple Jewish texts, see Steven M. Bryan, "The Eschatological Temple in John 14," *Bulletin for Biblical Research* 15 (2005): 187–92.

15 On this point, see Bryan, "Eschatological Temple," 193–94.

The image of the temple as the place where God's people were granted access to his presence runs throughout the Old Testament. The sacrificial system provided a constant reminder that the privilege of worshiping in God's presence carried with it the threat posed by the absolute holiness of that presence. For this reason, entrance into the temple required preparation of the worshipers (e.g., Lev. 15:31). But the temple itself also had to be prepared. At the original temple dedication, Solomon slaughtered innumerable sheep and goats in preparation for the entrance of the divine presence into the temple. Hezekiah replicated this preparation when he rededicated the temple in 2 Chronicles 29.

In John, the preparation of the temple and the preparation of people for entrance into the temple come together in the death and resurrection of Jesus. As Jesus goes to the Father through death and resurrection, the new temple is prepared for worship even as the worshipers are prepared for the new temple. Thus, through his death and resurrection, the temple of the resurrected Jesus is prepared to serve as the new creation dwelling of God with his people.[16]

3. Perichoresis *and a People of Peoples.* The notion that Jesus's death and resurrection prepare him to serve as the permanent cohabitation of God and his people opens up a new way to think about the unity of all peoples within the life of the triune God. John arrives at this way of thinking as a development of the temple-centric language of John 14:1–3.

In John 15, John moves from the image of "rooms," or "dwellings," within the temple to the image of branches that "dwell" in a vine and thus bear fruit.[17] However, before this shift, John explores

---

16 The image of many "dwellings" within the temple may evoke descriptions of the eschatological temple, which was said to have many rooms (Ezek. 40:44–46; 41:6, 10–11; 42:1–14). If so, John's innovation is that these rooms are not for materials and money, but for the people or, perhaps, peoples who dwell in the eschatological temple as their eternal dwelling. Bryan, "Eschatological Temple," 191.

17 John 15 makes frequent use of the verbal form of the Greek noun that is typically translated as "rooms" or "dwellings" in John 14:2. In John 15, it is usually translated as "abide" or "remain."

the possibilities produced by the identification of Jesus as the temple. Though Jesus insists that they know the way into this "place" (John 14:4), Thomas struggles to understand: "Lord, we don't know where you are going, so how can we know the way?" (14:5 NIV). Jesus replies that he is not only the place but also the way into the place (14:6a). To enter this place is to come to the Father (14:6b), since Jesus is not only in the Father, but "the Father is in me" (14:10a). More particularly, to see the Son is to see the Father, Jesus claims, because "the Father . . . dwells in me" (14:10b).

Though John affirms that the Son is in the Father, the language of "dwelling" is used only of the Father's dwelling within the Son. In keeping with the metaphor of the temple, it highlights John's conviction that believers enter the presence of the Father by dwelling in the Son even as the Father also dwells within the Son. This gathering of God's people into the temple of the resurrected Jesus is anticipated in John 11, where the chief priests and the Pharisees finalize their determination that Jesus must die. They decide this on the pragmatic grounds that if Jesus is allowed to continue unchecked, Roman disquiet over his rising popularity will prompt them to "take away . . . our place"—that is, to destroy the temple (11:48). The irony is that in putting Jesus to death, they themselves will destroy the temple and set the stage for the raising of a new temple and the gathering of multiethnic people into it. Caiaphas declares "that it is better for you that one man die for the people [laos] than that the whole nation [ethnos] perish" (11:50 NIV). Though the two Greek terms are often interchangeable, John invests high significance in Caiaphas's use of two different words: "He did not say this of his own accord, but being high priest that year he prophesied that Jesus would die for the nation [ethnos], and not for the nation only, but also to gather into one the children of God who are scattered abroad" (11:51–52).

The union of these scattered children with the Jewish ethnos into one people through the death of Jesus is then taken up at the climax of Jesus's prayer in John 17. He offers the bulk of the prayer for his Jewish disciples. He prays, "Holy Father, keep them in your name, which you have given me, that they may be one, even as we are one" (17:11). Then, having prayed for their unity, joy, and sanctification, he asks for the Father's same work among those who will believe as a result of the disciples' proclamation:

> I do not ask for these only, but also for those who will believe in me through their word, that they may all be one, just as you, Father, are in me, and I in you, that they also may be in us, so that the world may believe that you have sent me. The glory that you have given me I have given to them, that they may be one even as we are one, I in them and you in me, that they may become perfectly one, so that the world may know that you sent me and loved them even as you loved me. Father, I desire that they also, whom you have given me, may be with me where I am, to see my glory that you have given me because you loved me before the foundation of the world. (John 17:20–24)

At one level, this is simply a prayer for unity. Four times Jesus prays for the oneness of believers, connecting it each time to the oneness he shares with the Father. However, the interpretation of this unity often assumes that the unity envisioned by Jesus focuses on the gathering of individuals into a community of those who believe in the revelation of the Word made flesh. Certainly that is one dimension of the text, as the focus is on the unity of those who believe. But there is also a clear movement in John 17:20—not just "these" but "those"—that casts the focus not simply on the unity of individual believers but also of groups. It is at this point that the prayer's theology is most profound. The revelation of the glory of God—the transcendent presence of the one God—comes to visible manifestation in a unity of peoples. In that unity, we see the glory of God as the love of God that flows between the Father and Son as each opens up to the other, one within the other. This unity is what the church fathers called *perichoresis*—an "eternal embrace."[18]

---

18 The memorable phrase is that of Miroslav Volf, *Exclusion and Embrace: A Theological Exploration of Identity, Otherness and Reconciliation* (Nashville: Abingdon, 1996), 126.

Jesus's prayer is that this people of peoples may be one, just as the Father is in the Son and the Son is in the Father. That is to say, it is a prayer that they may dwell within the mutual indwelling of the Father and the Son that constitutes the unity of the two persons. The loving unity between the Father and the Son is the *origin* of the gospel; it is this love that leads to the divine initiative toward the world. The most striking *outcome* of the gospel is the loving unity that exists between the people *and peoples* who make up the one people, unified by their participation in the loving unity of God himself. John roots his vision of human community as a loving embrace between peoples in a profound understanding of the "eternal embrace" of the triune God. The differentiation of persons within the one being of God not only makes the claim that "God is love" (1 John 4:8) sensible but also provides the paradigm for the fullest realization of the divine image in the differentiation of peoples within the one people of God.

Conclusion

A popular, bumper-sticker form of the secular vision of difference encourages people to simply "coexist." John's vision for God's people moves well beyond mere tolerance of difference. John's Gospel also stands over against Eastern eschatologies that offer up a unitarian vision of ultimate reality in which all differences dissolve into pure consciousness. When difference disappears, so also does the possibility of love.

For John, God is one. Some have suggested that monotheism necessarily leads to ethnic or racial exclusivity.[19] However, in John, the God who is one is also love. And because love is inherent to who God is, it goes to the heart of what it means for God to be God—each person of the Trinity within the others in an eternal, loving embrace. John's theological vision for the unity of all peoples is rooted in this way of thinking about what it means for God to be God. For John, the God who promised to form from Abraham a people made up of all peoples

---

19 This is the premise of Regina M. Schwartz, *The Curse of Cain: The Violent Legacy of Monotheism* (Chicago: University of Chicago Press, 1997).

did so as an expression of his own identity as one God in three persons. As individuals come to faith in Christ, they enter into the relational unity of God himself, but they do not do so merely as individuals. For John, Jesus's death and resurrection constitutes the fulfillment of God's promise to build a temple not made with hands to serve as the permanent dwelling of all peoples as one worshiping people in the presence of God.

9

Paul and the Practices of Belief

The Gospel and Cultural Diversity

When two cultures clash, the loser is obliterated.

DAN BROWN, IN *THE DA VINCI CODE*

I have always felt that the action most worth watching is not at the center of things but where edges meet.

ANNE FADIMAN, IN *THE SPIRIT CATCHES YOU AND YOU FALL DOWN: A HMONG CHILD, HER AMERICAN DOCTORS, AND THE COLLISION OF TWO CULTURES*

I WRITE THESE WORDS on the one hundredth anniversary of the "Tulsa Race Massacre." I went to a high school an hour's drive from the site of the massacre and took a course in Oklahoma history. But the massacre was not a part of the course. In 1997, when the state of Oklahoma finally acted to recover the memory of the tragedy more than seventy-five years after the fact, it established the "1921 Tulsa Race Riot Commission," framing the event not as a massacre but as an episode of racial unrest. Only in 2018 was the name of the group changed to the "1921 Tulsa Race Massacre Commission," reflecting the brutal reality of the event.[1]

Joe Carter, "9 Things You Should Know About the Tulsa Race Massacre," The Gospel Coalition, May 29, 2021, https://www.thegospelcoalition.org/.

At the time, the massacre was blamed on Blacks, though the vast majority of those who died in the violence—as many as three hundred—were Black. Thousands of Black-owned homes and businesses were destroyed, along with dozens of Black churches and schools. In total, thirty-five city blocks were burned to the ground, destroying the lives and livelihoods of those who lived and worked in the prosperous neighborhood known by locals as Black Wall Street. The natural result of the violence was that much of the Black community was driven out. Without question, that was the intent of the estimated five to ten thousand whites who participated in the violence. The term did not exist at the time, but the massacre could properly be called "ethnic cleansing."

The names of the men, women, and children who have been "ethnically cleansed" in the one hundred years since would fill many books. Though we remember the worst ethnic cleansings—the Holocaust, Rwanda, Srebrenica—many (like the massacre in Tulsa) have been quickly forgotten. But is memory alone enough to stem the deep-seated and very human impulse to see difference and act with malice? Is there anything *practical* to be done to cultivate and nurture the form of human community anticipated within God's covenant with Abraham and announced as an arriving reality by Jesus and the early Christians?

Our search for an answer will take us on a back-to-front tour of a theological tour de force—Paul's letter to the Romans.

The Reasons for Romans

When Paul sat down to write a letter to the Christians in Rome, he didn't come straight to the point. Instead, he dipped his pen into a well of biblical history that stretched back to the early chapters of Genesis. Missionaries can be a pragmatic lot, quick with strategies and plans to solve problems. If Paul had been that sort of missionary, one of history's most important theological documents might never have been written. Only toward the end of the book do we realize that Paul *was* writing to solve a problem—two actually. The first was a money problem.

1. *The Money Problem.* Paul was a missionary; he was also a fund-raiser. Or perhaps we should say that he was a fundraiser *because* he was a missionary. That, it seems, is how Paul saw it. Some of the money he raised was for a project to alleviate poverty among the believers in Jerusalem. As Paul wrote Romans, it was time to bring the decade-long project to an end by taking the money to Jerusalem. Though he was not writing to ask the believers in Rome to add to the gift, he explained at the end of the letter (Rom. 15:25–29) that the money would serve an important purpose. In addition to alleviating poverty, the gift was to be a practical demonstration that God's purpose to unify all peoples in a relationship of reciprocal blessing was finally coming to fulfillment. Rich spiritual blessings had been poured out on Israel—the blessings of the gospel itself—and now the generosity created by the gospel among the Gentiles was flowing back to the believers in Jerusalem. This purpose was closely related to a second fundraising objective. If all went according to plan (which it did not), Paul would come to Rome after delivering the gift to Jerusalem. The church in Rome would then send him on his way (Rom. 15:24)—Paul's wonderful euphemism for the financial support he needed for onward mission to Spain. His time in Rome not only would be marked by a rich reciprocity of blessing received and blessing returned between Paul and the believers there (1:11–12), but also would facilitate the westward expansion of the community of blessing being formed by the gospel.

2. *The Ethnicity Problem.* The money problem was tightly tied to a second problem—one arising from ethnic and cultural differences within the church at Rome. Unlike many of the churches to which Paul wrote, he had not planted the church in Rome. One likely scenario is that Jews living in Rome had come to messianic faith while visiting Jerusalem for Pentecost. Over time, non-Jews living in Rome had also heard the gospel and believed, but in its earliest stages the church in Rome was predominantly Jewish. Circumstances soon changed that. The Roman historian Suetonius tells us that a dispute broke out among Jews in Rome over someone named "Chrestus." Many suppose that

the lightly informed Suetonius mistook the title "Christ" for a proper name and that the dispute was actually between Jews who had come to faith in Christ and those who had not. The Emperor Claudius had never been known for mental stability or personal forbearance. So in AD 49, he ordered the expulsion of *all* Jews from Rome. Overnight, a church that had been predominantly Jewish in flavor and feel became dramatically less so.

By the time Paul wrote his letter to the Romans (around AD 56–57), Claudius had died (AD 54) and his successor, Nero, had rescinded the edict. As a result, Jews who had been expelled had begun filtering back into the city, including Priscilla and Aquila (Acts 18:1–3), whom Paul greets by name at the end of his letter (Rom. 16:3), along with several others whom he identifies as his "fellow Jews" (NIV). The ethnic identifier appears twice (16:7, 11) in the list of those Paul greets, and then again in a list of those whose greeting Paul sends with his own (16:21).[2]

With Paul's third use of the ethnic identifier, he has our attention and (we may assume) that of his non-Jewish readers. Paul evidently had a particular interest in emphasizing not only his own Jewish ethnicity but also that of other Jewish believers whose labors for the gospel had brought great blessing to Gentile believers.[3] The individuals whom Paul names are made the face of a foundational idea, deeply embedded in Israel's Scriptures, that God had endowed the Jewish people with extraordinary spiritual blessings. He enumerates these blessings in a stirring passage at the beginning of Romans 9, where he had earlier spoken of his "fellow Jews" (9:3 AT) and of the gifts that had shaped their history and identity as a people (9:4–5). Although it was true that many Israelites, both present and past, had not received these gifts in faith, this does not negate the fact that through the Messiah the blessings that had come to Israel were now bringing great blessing to the world.

---

2 Paul's "fellow Jews" include another husband-wife missionary team named Andronicus and Junia (Rom. 16:7), as well as a man named Herodion (16:11). The ESV renders the Greek term *syngeneis* as "kinsman" in all three instances, though this could be mistaken to mean that they are Paul's biological relatives.

3 Cf. Peter Lampe, "The Roman Christians of Romans 16," in *The Romans Debate*, rev. and exp. ed., ed. Karl P. Donfried (Grand Rapids, MI: Baker Academic, 2011), 224–25.

The good news of God's salvation had not simply come to all peoples; it had come to all peoples by way of one people. Paul wants these gifts to be named and known as gifts that God had uniquely given to *Jews*, even if God's ultimate purpose in doing so was universal in scope.

But why was this important? The answer lies in the strong indications that the return of Jews, including Jewish Christians, to Rome had stirred an unmistakable antagonism among Gentile believers toward their Jewish counterparts. In part, this may have mirrored anti-Semitic sentiment that arose episodically across the empire. But the antipathy toward Jewish Christians also had a theological rationale. To many, it seemed that widespread Jewish rejection of the gospel indicated that God had turned away from the Jews and toward the Gentiles. Such a view threatened to marginalize Jewish believers within the church, especially those who remained culturally Jewish in their sensibilities and practices.

Compounding matters, the two cultural groups had begun identifying themselves by their differences over certain practices.[4] Those from a Jewish background avoided meat and wine on offer in the market, while those from a Gentile background did not. As a simple matter of practice, Paul has no problem saying that a person could honor God both in eating meat and in determining not to. The same goes for drinking wine. The practice per se was not the problem. But if the members of one group did things one way, they did so because they thought that their way of doing things was better. Unfortunately, then as now, it proved all too easy to go from thinking that the way one's group *does* things is better to thinking that one's group must *be* better. And that, for Paul, was the problem.

In one sense, the issue wasn't what we typically think of as a cultural difference, inasmuch as Jews generally had no qualms about eating meat

---

4   It is not necessary to presume that *all* those who came from a Jewish background did one thing and that *all* those from Gentile backgrounds did another. Individuals often act in ways that differ from the norms of the cultural groups with which they identify. Paul, for instance, shares the viewpoint of those he characterizes as the "strong" (Rom. 15:1) even though he is Jewish and the cultural identity of the "strong" is not.

or drinking wine. But abstention from both had also become a part of Jewish culture *in certain circumstances*. Jews living in the Diaspora suspected that meat and wine had been offered as sacrifices to pagan gods before being offered for sale in the market. The link between pagan temple and table seemed wholly incompatible with the command to worship God alone. As is often the case even today, culture and religion were so enmeshed with one another that it was difficult to separate them.

By contrast, Christians from non-Jewish backgrounds could see no reason to stop eating and drinking as they had always done. For them, to buy and eat meat from the market felt entirely normal. So, it probably took little to persuade them that a cultural practice with which they were already comfortable could be grounded in good theology. They were no longer polytheistic pagans but monotheistic Christians. As such, they knew that all created things, including the meat and wine for sale in the market, were divine gifts and could be received with gratitude. Thus, the two groups drew different conclusions from the same reality, resulting in opposing practices. There can be little doubt that Paul believed that the Christians from non-Jewish backgrounds had the better argument over against those whose "faith is weak" (Rom. 14:1).

Paul had similarly described the pagan-background believers in Corinth as weak in faith because they feared they might be led back into pagan worship if they ate meat that had been sacrificed to an idol. Given the threat to Corinthian believers who had not yet internalized the implications of their new monotheistic faith, Paul had strong words for the strong; they may have been theologically savvy, but they were pastorally obtuse (1 Cor. 8–10). In Rome, however, there was relatively little risk that Jewish Christians were going to stumble into paganism. Still, Paul describes them as weak in faith because they had not properly thought through the implications of their monotheism and were thus unable to consume meat and wine purchased in the market as "to the Lord" (Rom. 14:6 NIV). Nevertheless, Paul perceives the "weak" of faith in Rome, like the "weak" in Corinth, as potentially vulnerable, and warns the "strong" that the practice of their freedoms might result in the *destruction* of the "weak"—perhaps because they were "grieved" (14:15) enough by the behavior of the "strong" to abandon the Christian community and return to the synagogue.

Though the core of the matter is the same in the two churches, in Rome, the issue had taken on an ethnic dimension. Though the issue was not inherently a matter of cultural difference, it had effectively become one. The difference in practice had enhanced the awareness of the members of each group that they belonged to one group and not the other.

Earlier we noted that cultural identity is formed at the boundaries between groups—at the point at which we say, "My group does this and not that" (see chap. 1). But if the perception of difference is not only unavoidable but also necessary for the formation of group identity, the danger is that the perception of opposed practices easily leads to opposition between groups. Each group sees its way of doing things as better. In some cases, the members of a group may not know why they do what they do. In other cases, they may have reasons for what they do—reasons that become sharper and clearer when they encounter a group that does things differently. When that happens, the reasons for a practice simply reinforce the sense that their way is the right way.

The ethnic dimension to the conflict in Rome is reinforced by another difference—one that had not been a part of the division in Corinth. Though abstaining from meat and wine is not inherently Jewish, it has become tied to other practices that are much more uniformly perceived as Jewish. Unlike those in Corinth whose faith Paul describes as "weak," the Jewish Christians in Rome feel obliged to observe various days marked as holy to the Lord in the Mosaic Law. Jewish Christians in Rome tend to do one thing, while Gentile Christians do another. Though it might seem to some that treating certain days as sacred is more Jewish than abstaining from meat and wine, the role that the two practices play in distinguishing one group from another is essentially the same. As such, Paul treats both issues as practices in which two ethnically distinct groups differ and over which they have divided.

If these are the problems on Paul's mind when he sits down to write Romans, we might well ask why they don't come fully into view until the end of the letter? The answer, it seems, lies in the way Paul approaches most things. He begins with the gospel.

First, the Gospel

1. *A New Perspective?* Some might suppose that the obvious tack in the face of such discord would be to downplay the importance given to theology in order to foster more inclusive attitudes between Jews and non-Jews. This, however, misses the mind of Paul by a wide margin, as the deep and extended theological exposition of Romans 1–11 demonstrates. But how does the theology work within a letter prompted, in part, by the ethnic tensions we have seen?

Over the past several decades, a number of scholars associated with the so-called "New Perspective on Paul" have drawn attention to the ethnic tensions I have just outlined and argued that Paul's primary aim in Romans and elsewhere is to undermine the sense of ethnic superiority and exclusivity that he believes is fueling the tensions. Properly understood, Paul's concern is to show that in Christ the Gentiles have been included within Israel as a demonstration of God's faithfulness to the covenant with Abraham. Indeed, one leading proponent argues that "the righteousness of God" in Romans *is* God's faithfulness to that covenant.[5] Closely related to this view, proponents of the New Perspective regard the inclusion of Gentiles within God's covenant people as the heart of what Paul means by "justification by faith." On this account, when Paul insists that no one is justified by "works of the law" (Rom. 3:20), he refers to specific elements within the Mosaic Law that serve as marks of Jewish identity and affirms that no one is included within God's covenant people (i.e., justified) by becoming Jewish. Rather, they are included simply by trusting in the Messiah. In this way, "faith," not "Jewish identity markers," becomes the sole indication of identity as the

---

5   This is reflected in both the title and overall thrust of N. T. Wright, *Paul and the Faithfulness of God* (Minneapolis: Fortress, 2013).

people of the Messiah. By faith in the Messiah, believers are united to the Messiah—they are "in Christ" and so participate in *his* faithfulness.[6] Critics of the New Perspective have acknowledged the importance of the attention paid by the New Perspective to the question of ethnicity. It is an important point, especially when we consider that Martin Luther, whose engagement with Romans restored the centrality of justification by faith to our understanding of the gospel, became increasingly anti-Semitic over the course of his life. That fact alone should alert us to the possibility of focusing so exclusively on the individual that bias toward groups remains untouched. In other words, if Paul's concern is simply to set forth the way in which God declares sinful individuals to be righteous through faith in Christ, then one can easily miss the way in which he constantly comes back to the significance of God's justification of individuals for achieving his purposes for peoples. This is not to suggest that Paul's focus is solely on groups and not individuals. Rather, it is to halt the swing of the pendulum away from the traditional Reformation focus on the individual toward the New Perspective's focus on the group. God's purposes, now fully displayed in the gospel and through the gospel, have always been about both.

2. *Apostle to the* Ethnē: *Individuals and Peoples in the Practice of Paul.* We get a sense of Paul's approach from the opening lines of the letter, in which Paul claims that a distinctively Jewish Messiah has commissioned him to be an apostle to the non-Jewish nations of the world. Paul begins by highlighting the ethnic particularity of the Messiah by identifying him as "descended from David according

6   Many advocates of the New Perspective, including N. T. Wright, have followed Richard Hays in understanding the expression *pistis tou Christou* in texts such as Rom. 3:22 and Gal. 2:16 as a designation not of "faith in Christ"—as the phrase is usually translated—but of "the faithfulness of Christ." See especially Richard B. Hays, *The Faith of Jesus Christ: The Narrative Substructure of Galatians 3:1–4:11*, 2nd ed. (Grand Rapids, MI: Eerdmans, 2002). Other proponents of the New Perspective opt for the traditional understanding. The significance of the debate is not so much that a decision on the matter determines where scholars land on the question of the New Perspective as that it reinforces the notion that union with Christ or inclusion within the Messiah's faithfulness is central to key texts that focus on justification by faith, including Rom. 3:21–26 and Gal. 2:15–21.

to the flesh" (Rom. 1:3).[7] However, he immediately moves to assert the universality of the Messiah's reign over all peoples. By virtue of his resurrection, Israel's Messiah has been enthroned as "the Son of God" (1:4)—an expression that has its origins in texts, such as Psalm 2, that highlight the universal sovereignty of the ideal King of Israel. As the world's one, true Lord, Israel's Messiah has appointed Paul as an apostle and given him the task of bringing the non-Jewish peoples of the world to the obedience of Israel's King (Rom. 1:5). Paul will return to this description of his task in the closing lines of the book (16:25–26), where he speaks of the gospel as the disclosure of a "mystery" that God has revealed to bring about the obedience of the non-Jewish nations. If God's purpose *in* the gospel is to bring about the salvation of individuals, God's purpose *through* the gospel is to accomplish the divine vision for a people of peoples.

To this point, we have suggested that Paul thinks of himself as an apostle to "the non-Jewish nations." This translation of the term *ethnē* reflects Paul's conception of his missionary task and seeks to avoid certain misconceptions created by both "Gentiles" and "nations"—the two most common translations of the term. On the one hand, "Gentiles" suggests individuals of non-Jewish ethnicity. On the other hand, "nations" points to groups of any ethnicity. However, as Paul's argument develops, it will become clear that he does not think only of mission to non-Jewish individuals, but to all individuals in non-Jewish lands. In other words, in describing himself as an apostle to the *ethnē*, Paul seems to be thinking of his mission in *geographic* terms and himself as a messenger sent from Israel to the nations outside of Israel.

Paul's description of his mission both past and planned confirms that he conceptualizes it as a geographic movement from one Roman province to the next in a generally westward direction. Paul writes that

---

7   The designation "according to the flesh" is sometimes taken as a reference to the human nature of the Messiah. Although this is true, the connection to David is rare in Paul's letters, occurring elsewhere only in Rom. 15:12 and 2 Tim. 2:8. The ethnic particularity of the designation in the latter text plays an important role in Paul's call for mutual acceptance between ethnic groups in Romans 14–15.

he has "fulfilled" the gospel from Jerusalem—the center of what Luke calls "the Jewish nation" (Acts 10:22)—all the way round to Illyricum (Rom. 15:19), a Roman province opposite Italy across the Adriatic Sea. As he writes, he has plans for further westward movement to Spain—a geographic designation of a territory comprising a cluster of Roman provinces at what was regarded at the time as the western "end of the earth."[8]

Though Paul evangelizes the *ethnē* by moving province by province from Jerusalem to Spain, it is unlikely that he thinks of each Roman province as an *ethnos* ("nation"). Rather, in moving from province to province, he is "fulfilling the gospel" among the *ethnē* ("non-Jewish nations"). Although we may be surprised that specific ethnic labels for the *ethnē* are rare in Paul's letters,[9] he seems to think that the Roman provinces comprise the *ethnē* to which he has been sent. These *ethnē* consist of peoples who, depending on the situation, may identify themselves with a variety of cultural designations. Phrygians, for instance, are associated with territory within the Roman province of Asia. Many speak Greek in addition to their native tongue. So, depending on the context, they may identify as Phrygian, Greek, and perhaps also Roman or even Asian. But their sense of peoplehood comes from a sense of common history, customs, and descent, as well as a shared sense of connection to the territory of the Phrygians.

The close connection between peoples and lands helps us understand another feature of Paul's mission—the fact that the self-described apostle to the *ethnē* always begins his ministry with the Jews who live in those lands. As he carries out his task of taking the good news to

8 "Thus with reference to the general scheme of Paul's mission, both the letters and Acts place Paul in the same area of the Mediterranean world and in the same provinces, and take him through these provinces in the same general sequence." W. Paul Bowers, "Mission," in *Dictionary of Paul and His Letters*, ed. Gerald F. Hawthorne, Ralph P. Martin, and Daniel G. Reid (Downers Grove, IL: InterVarsity Press, 1993), 609.

9 There was a rich variety of ethnic designations for the native populations of Roman provinces, but these are rare in Paul. Only one is certain—the reference to "Scythians" in Colossians 3:11. The reference to the "Macedonians" in 2 Corinthians 9:4 and to the "Galatians" in Galatians 3:1 may be provincial designations—an uncertainty born of the fact that ethnic designations sometimes doubled as provincial names.

the nations outside of Israel, his practice reflects a principle referenced frequently in the early chapters of Romans: "to the Jew first and also to the Greek."[10] To be sent to the *ethnē* is to be sent to the lands of the *ethnē* in order to announce the good news to both the Jews and the non-Jews who live there. Thus, although it is not a complete misnomer to refer to Paul as an "apostle to the Gentiles," the reality is that Paul's mission to the *ethnē* always includes Jews within its scope and always aims to plant churches that include a nucleus of believing Jews and the non-Jews in the area who come to faith. This is what Paul means when he tells a congregation that includes Jews that he desires to minister among them as he has among other Gentile peoples (Rom. 1:13, using *ethnē*).

Although Paul understands that he has been sent to the non-Jewish nations, he pursues his task by sharing the gospel with *individuals* regardless of ethnicity. In setting out his understanding of the gospel in Romans, Paul's focus falls primarily on the significance of what God has done for individuals as the key to understanding how God is accomplishing his purposes for the nations in fulfillment of his promise to Abraham. He wants the congregation not only to grow in their understanding of the gospel, but in their understanding of what it does: it places individuals in a right relation to God, thereby reconfiguring the relationships between peoples.

10   The term *Greek* is typically used of non-Jewish individuals and thus rendered as "Gentile" in some translations. Because Greek language and culture predominated throughout the Roman Empire, Paul often describes non-Jews as "Greeks" when the focus is on their non-Jewishness. In Romans 1:14, he divides non-Jews into two categories—Greeks and barbarians. The latter term was used to describe the non-Greek-speaking peoples who lived primarily beyond the reach of Roman rule. It "is an onomatopoeic word (i.e., a word that sounds like what it means) that plays on the repetition of the sounds *bar . . . bar . . . bar*, which was all that Greek-speaking people could comprehend when first coming into contact with foreigners." Richard N. Longenecker, *The Epistle to the Romans: A Commentary on the Greek Text*, New International Greek Testament Commentary (Grand Rapids, MI: Eerdmans, 2016), 138. The Greek-barbarian polarity was also used to distinguish between those peoples whose cultural outlook had been shaped by Greek culture, as opposed to those who, from a Greek cultural point of view, lacked the learning and sophistication conferred by Greek culture. Thus, the second pair in 1:14—"wise" and "foolish"—mirrors the second cultural dimension of the Greek-barbarian polarity.

3. *The Truth about All Peoples*. Paul begins his exposition of the good news by pointing to something that everyone has in common, regardless of cultural identity—the fact that *all* have sinned and fallen short of the glory of God (Rom. 3:23). Paul's point is not simply that every individual has rebelled against the Creator, but that while Jews may differ from non-Jews in the fact that they sin against the law, they differ not at all in the fact that they have sinned.

In depicting the sins of the *ethnē* in Romans 1:18–32, Paul deploys language "typical of Jewish censure of Gentiles."[11] Nevertheless, there is little in the description that could not also be found somewhere in the Old Testament narratives about Israel.[12] After the exile, Israel largely succeeded in bringing an end to the worship of foreign gods and the use of idols to represent them. However, the end of Israel's exile did not bring an end to Israel's rebellion. As Paul turns his attention to the particular case of Israel's rebellion, he cautions those who endorse his characterization of rebellion among the *ethnē* while failing to see that they themselves "do the same things" (2:1 NIV). By "the same things," Paul probably does not mean that Jews are *characteristically* guilty of the sorts of sins he highlights in 1:18–32. Rather, he means that they, too, are guilty of violating what they know to be the righteous requirements of God (1:32). The only difference is that they know more. Jewish rebellion not only rejects the consciousness of the "good" that God has built into the moral order of creation (2:10), it also turns away from the "good" expressed in the commandments that God has given to Israel (7:12). This imbues Jewish rebellion against God with a specifically transgressive character (4:15).

4. *The Role of Culture in the Way We Sin*. Though there is something unique about the nature of Israel's Torah-mediated relationship with God and the Torah-rejecting nature of its rebellion against God, Paul

---

11   Colin G. Kruse, *Paul's Letter to the Romans*, Pillar New Testament Commentary (Grand Rapids, MI: Eerdmans, 2012), 83.

12   Cf. Stephen Westerholm, *Perspectives Old and New on Paul: The "Lutheran" Paul and His Critics* (Grand Rapids, MI: Eerdmans, 2004), 386.

at times seems to speak about the culturally characteristic way in which various cultural groups rebel against God. Here in Romans, he reflects an awareness of Jewish stereotypes about the characteristic sins of the *ethnē*. Elsewhere, he seems to adopt a generalization about a specific cultural group. In Titus 1:12, he quotes a Cretan "prophet" who claimed that Cretans are "always liars, evil beasts, lazy gluttons." Paul credits the claim. A number of commentators have pointed out the implicit paradox of a Cretan asserting that Cretans always lie. If Cretans always lie, was the Cretan who said it lying? Perhaps the more salient point is that the saying reflects an insider's perspective on his own culture's unsavory tendencies. Such cultural generalizations find their mark when they originate within the culture itself. "Social generalizations can be pernicious," but they can also "shed light on what is happening in a particular setting."[13] "Paul is not making an ethnic slur, but is merely accurately observing . . . how the sin that affects the whole human race comes to particular expression in this group,"[14] even if it is not true or true to the same extent of every member of the group.

Though Paul can speak of culturally specific tendencies toward certain forms of sin, sin itself is universal. For Paul, that fact binds all groups together to such an extent that it is quite pointless to ask whether one group is worse than any other. In indicting those who rely on the law as lawbreakers, Paul cites Isaiah 52:5: "The name of God is blasphemed among the non-Jewish peoples [*ethnē*] because of you" (Rom. 2:24 AT). It is pointless to ask whether blaspheming God's name is worse than causing others to blaspheme. Both Jews and Gentiles are responsible for profaning the divine name. More generally, both groups are obliged to the good—the one, through the imprint of God's righteous decrees on the human conscience; the other, through the imprint of God's righteousness in the Torah. Neither has fulfilled its obligation. To have God's law is better than not (3:1–2), but having

13   Robert W. Yarbrough, *The Letters to Timothy and Titus*, Pillar New Testament Commentary (Grand Rapids, MI: Eerdmans, 2018), 495.
14   George W. Knight, *The Pastoral Epistles: A Commentary on the Greek Text*, New International Greek Testament Commentary (Grand Rapids, MI: Eerdmans, 1992), 299.

it has left Jews no better off (3:9a). Greek claims of cultural superiority do not confer superiority before God. Before an impartial God, "all, both Jews and Greeks, are under sin" (3:9b).

In one sense, the point that Paul is making is about group identity, but more fundamentally, it is about individuals. Our cultures influence *how* we sin as individuals but do not determine *whether* we sin. We are sinners because human nature is corrupted by sin—a fact that Paul drives home by asserting the universality of sin's power in relation to Adam (Rom. 5:12). As a result, no one is exempt from sin, no matter what group he or she may belong to. Paul's "indictment of fallen humanity, Jews and Gentiles . . . builds, like a fireworks display, toward a climactic explosion of scriptural condemnations in Rom. 3:10–18"[15] that leaves in ruin all human pretense to righteousness before God.

The significance of this for cultural identity is twofold. On the one hand, the essence of ethnocentrism, racism, and nationalism is the belief that my ethnicity, race, or nation is superior to others. Thus, if my group is dominant, it deserves to be. If it is not, it should be. Often this is rooted in an extraordinary sense of clarity about the failings of other groups. But even if I can demonstrate that my culture is better than another in this way or that, it does not establish my righteousness before God.

On the other hand, the belief that my group is superior to others is typically paired with blindness to the tendencies of my group to sin in particular ways. In part, this is the nature of culture itself. We do not realize what we are like as a group except when we encounter people from other groups. Until I lived outside of America, I did not know that people in other countries often regard Americans as loud, brash, overconfident, arrogant, and self-focused. At the same time, I could rehearse a long list of stereotypes about the peoples of other places. We are quick to take umbrage when someone from another group points out the God-dishonoring proclivities of our culture. At the same time, we

---

15 Richard B. Hays, *Echoes of Scripture in the Letters of Paul* (New Haven, CT: Yale University Press, 1993), 41.

are also slow to recognize the degree to which our actions and attitudes have been shaped by the cultural group or groups to which we belong. As Paul says, we judge those who belong to other groups, even as we fail to recognize and repent of our own shortcomings (Rom. 2:1–4).

In short, culture prevents us from seeing our unrighteousness as individuals in two ways: (1) by situating our sense of self within a group of people who rebel against God in similar ways; and (2) by causing us to focus on the characteristic ways in which members of other groups fail rather than on the ways in which we, as individuals, fall short of the glory of God (Rom. 3:23).

5. *The Heart of the Gospel.* The remedy for this, of course, is the saving action of God in Christ. Paul comes to this in Romans 3:21–25. If no one is righteous, we must be made righteous. This is what Stephen Westerholm refers to as the "extraordinary righteousness" of God.[16] Ordinary righteousness is the righteousness that is attributable to a person who does righteousness—the sort of righteousness that no one has. Paul, however, speaks of the *extraordinary* righteousness that originates in God's character and by which righteousness is attributed to the ungodly. The declaration of the unrighteous to be righteous is possible only because God in Christ has borne the penalty of God's just wrath toward rebellious human beings. This righteousness is thus imputed to us by grace through faith.

The reception of this gift comes through individual faith, but Paul does not leave behind his concern for peoples. This becomes clear through a succession of "all's," beginning in Romans 3:22. The importance of this section is evident in the mass of recent scholarship on every verse in the sequence. A number of scholars have charged either Paul or his traditional interpreters with an intolerable redundancy in 3:22—the notion that the righteousness of God comes "through faith in Jesus Christ for all who have faith" (AT).[17] But the redundancy is

16 Westerholm, *Perspectives*, 273–84.

17 On the debate about whether the first reference to "faith" (*pistis*) should be taken as a reference to the faithfulness of Jesus, see note 6 above.

actually an emphasis that picks up the preceding focus on the universal sinfulness of *all*, regardless of ethnic identity. Now Paul argues that the righteousness of God has come to *all*, regardless of ethnic identity, provided they believe. That this is Paul's point is underscored by the last clause of the verse: "For there is no distinction"—that is, no distinction between Jew and Greek. "This righteousness from God is available not simply to Jews . . . or to those who become Jews . . . ; it comes to *all* who have faith. It is open in principle to all human beings without ethnic distinction . . . on condition of faith."[18]

The contrast between the universality of sin and the universality of the divine gift is recapitulated in Romans 3:23–24. But there is a shift in the referent of "all." In 3:23, "all" clearly refers to all individuals regardless of group: "All have sinned and fall short of the glory of God." However, in 3:24, "all" cannot refer to all individuals: "and all are justified freely by his grace" (NIV). To suggest otherwise would require us to conclude that God freely justifies "all" who fall short of his glory—that is, every individual. This would conflict with 3:22, which states not that God justifies all individuals, regardless of faith, but that he justifies all individuals who believe, regardless of *ethnicity*. Thus, "all" in 3:24 must refer not to all individuals whatever their ethnicity, as in 3:23, but to individuals who believe from *all* ethnicities.

Paul grounds God's indiscriminate justification of sinful individuals from all groups in the fact that God is one. Thus, in Romans 3:29–30 he asks, "Or is God the God of Jews only? Is he not the God of Gentiles also? Yes, of Gentiles also, since God is one—who will justify the circumcised by faith and the uncircumcised through faith." With this, the reader is fully prepared for Paul's exposition of God's covenant with Abraham. Since God is one, his purpose expressed in the promise to Abraham was to form one obedient people. In Christ, God has brought that promise to fulfillment by constituting a people who share Abraham's faith, even if they do not all share his blood.

---

18 D. A. Carson, *Scandalous: The Cross and Resurrection of Jesus* (Wheaton, IL: Crossway, 2010), 55.

Picking up the "all" of Romans 3, Paul writes that the promise is fulfilled not only to his physical descendants, whose identity as a people was established, in part, through the giving of the law. The promises are also fulfilled "to the one who shares the faith of Abraham, who is the father of us *all*, as it is written, 'I have made you the father of many nations'" (4:16–17).

We see, then, that the traditional Reformation emphasis on God's justification of individual sinners is entirely in keeping with Paul's focus in Romans 1–3. However, as Romans 4 demonstrates, the significance of God's saving act does not end with individual human beings. Rather, God's intention, manifest first in creation and then in redemption, has always been to form a people of peoples. He accomplishes this purpose by giving his own righteousness to individuals—that is, to believing sinners of every ethnicity.

6. *The Implications of the Gospel.* Having laid down the gospel foundation of Romans 1–4, Paul builds a theology of the life created for this newly formed people of peoples in Romans 5–8, before turning his attention to the relationship between the peoples who form this people in Romans 9–11. The questions that Paul must address on the way to forming an understanding of the relationships between Israel and the *ethnē* are too numerous for us to consider here. We must content ourselves with two comments.

First, in much popular and some scholarly thought on these chapters, there has been an assumption that God deals with ethnic Israel under the terms of one covenant and with the *ethnē* under the terms of a different covenant. Though there are numerous problems with such a reading, perhaps the most important criticism is that it undermines the centrality of Christ's death and resurrection for ethnic Israel. On this view, ethnic Jews will be "saved" not by believing the gospel but through animal sacrifice and observance of the law—an idea that is foreign to the argument of Romans and to the rest of Scripture. Not only does it undercut the relevance of the gospel for ethnic Israel, it also effectively reconstructs "the dividing wall of hostility" between

Israel and the *ethnē* that Paul insists has been torn down by the work of Christ (Eph. 2:11–21).

Second, central to Paul's argument in Romans 9–11 is the idea that in the crucifixion and resurrection of Jesus the exclusion of the *ethnē* from Israel has come to an end. If God's purpose has always been to constitute Israel as his one holy and righteous people *in order* to include within that people every other people, Paul argues that this is what God has done in the death and resurrection of the Messiah. If, formerly, the *ethnē* were excluded from Israel (Eph. 2:12), that had as much to do with Israel as with the *ethnē*. But the Messiah has taken up the role of Israel and opened up access to Israel to "all who believe" (Rom. 3:22). In these chapters, Paul mounts a powerful scriptural case for the idea that "through Messiah and the preaching which heralds him, Israel is transformed from being an ethnic people into a worldwide family."[19] This is entirely in keeping with God's intent to restore humanity as a community of blessing made up of all peoples.

The prophets had set out a pattern by which the unbelief of ethnic Israel would result in divine judgment. But in the wake of that judgment, a remnant of ethnic Israel would turn from their rebellion and receive the good news of restoration and salvation. That good news would then be proclaimed among the *ethnē* and to the scattered Jews living among them. As both the *ethnē* and the Jews among them hear the good news, they are incorporated into the remnant of penitent, believing Israel. "And in this way *all* Israel will be saved" (Rom. 11:26). Thus, "all Israel" becomes a designation of the multiethnic people of peoples formed by the incorporation of believing Gentiles from among the nations into the remnant of believing Jews.[20]

Whether we understand the Jews of the Diaspora who come to faith in the Messiah as part of that remnant or as the scattered from Israel whom God calls into Israel along with believing Gentiles hardly matters. The point is that, through the redemption announced in the

19 N. T. Wright, *Climax of the Covenant: Christ and the Law in Pauline Theology* (London: Bloomsbury, 1993), 240.

20 For this reading of Romans 11, see especially Wright, *Climax*, 246–51.

gospel, God accomplishes his purpose in creation—the formation of one holy people made up of all peoples, a people united in the worship of God but immeasurably varied in the culturally specific ways they worship him. Here, in short, is the divine purpose that Paul refers to as a long-hidden "mystery" (Rom. 11:25) that is now "made known to all nations [*ethnē*] . . . to bring about the obedience of faith " (16:26).

Gospel Practices across Lines of Difference

Having traced the broad contours of the gospel and the way in which it transforms individual lives and, in doing so, forms this new people of peoples, Paul turns (and we return) to the questions that prompted his extended discussion of the gospel. Sometimes the shift that takes place at Romans 12:1 is described as a shift from the theological to the practical, but the new section is better understood as Paul's description of practices shaped by the gospel he has just set forth. He begins with worship.

1. *Worship.* Romans 12:1–2 is a succinct and powerful depiction of the only fit response to the revelation of the goodness of God in the gospel: our whole lives must be devoted to God as worship. That Paul speaks specifically of the presentation of our "bodies" to God places the focus on the individual. This should not surprise us given the fact that the individual's relationship to God lies at the core of what God has done in the gospel. In 12:2, Paul focuses on one particular aspect of the individual's worship of God—resistance to the world's way of thinking and renewal to the pattern of thinking that comes from the gospel. Only then will believers be able to discern God's will.

Much of what Paul says in Romans 12–13 focuses on what those whose lives are fully devoted to God will do as individuals both in Christian community and in the wider society. But in Romans 14–15, the focus shifts to the relationship between groups within the Christian community. This, too, must be seen in relation to the exhortation of Romans 12:1–2 to present our whole selves to God. If we are to do so, it will require resistance to the world's way of thinking and renewal of our own thinking about cultural identity.

The connection between Paul's instructions regarding the relationship between the two groups in Romans 14–15 and the whole-life conception of worship introduced in 12:1–2 is evident in the way that he conceptualizes the conflicting practices of both groups as worship. This is more obviously the case in relation to those from non-Jewish backgrounds. In their determination that no day should be regarded as more sacred than another, they mirror Paul's own view that the only fit response to the gospel is to give our lives as living sacrifices in continual worship. The clear implication of such a view is that every day is sacred. In treating meat and wine as gifts given by the Lord to be received with thanks, regardless of prior use, they again have the better argument.

Why, then, does Paul not urge those from Jewish backgrounds to adopt the position of the "strong" (Rom. 15:1)? Some have suggested that even if Paul does not state it plainly, the unavoidable effect of his position would be to undermine the cultural integrity of Jewish identity within the church at Rome.[21] But need this be the case? It is not Jewish practices per se but the theological rationale for them that Paul depicts as a manifestation of "weak" faith. To be sure, Paul's position does undermine the religious *obligation* to continue with the practices. At the same time, he seems quite happy for those from Jewish backgrounds to continue a range of practices associated with Jewish identity as part of their *Christian* worship. This would be rather like believers from Muslim backgrounds who continue to abstain from alcohol as part of their Christian devotion long after they come to understand that abstention is not an obligation of Christian faith.

In order to understand Paul's approach, we must see that he does not proscribe the practices of those he describes as "weak in faith"

---

21 John Barclay, "'Do We Undermine the Law?' A Study of Romans 14:1–15:6," in *Paul and the Mosaic Law*, ed. J. D. G. Dunn (Tubingen: Mohr Siebeck, 1996), 287–308, cited in David G. Horrell, "Solidarity and Difference: Pauline Morality in Romans 14:1–15:13," *Studies in Christian Ethics* 15 (2002): 273. Barclay's view is not uncommon but effectively places Paul in the same camp as the Judaizers he condemns in Galatians. If the message of the Judaizers was that Gentiles must become Jewish to be fully accepted as God's people, an approach that pressured Jewish Christians to become like Gentiles for the sake of unity would have had the same effect.

(Rom. 14:1) even as he questions the theological basis for them. The key point is that both groups regard their practices as an expression of devotion to God. Even if the form of their devotion differs to the point of being expressed in contradictory ways, the thing that matters most to Paul is that ethnically Jewish Christians and Christians from non-Jewish peoples are worshiping God together. We know this because, after setting out his thoughts on the matter, he unleashes a litany of Old Testament texts that evoke the expectation that one day the *ethnē* will worship the Lord in the midst of Israel under the rule of Israel's Messiah (15:8–12).

Paul's point is not that the two groups should forget their differences in the interests of harmony. No, the point is that even though the two groups have adopted practices that differ and that mark them as different, the practices on both sides have been undertaken as worship. He wants them to see this fact as evidence for the fulfillment of the expectation that one day the *ethnē* would take their place within the assembly of Israel. For this reason, Paul is clearly unwilling to insist that the practices be abandoned, even when the obligation to continue has been abandoned. Indeed, he seems hopeful that the differences in practice will continue as a palpable demonstration that God's promise to Abraham has come to fulfillment in culturally diverse communities formed by the gospel.

2. *Mutual Acceptance.* Earlier we noted the similarities between the situations in Rome and Corinth. But there was also a crucial difference. In Corinth, the division between the groups that differed over "idol meat" did not fall along ethnic lines. Instead, the division was yet another manifestation of the party spirit that had taken root in the Corinthian church. In his first letter to the Corinthians, Paul moves to break up the parties, whereas in the epistle to the Romans, he urges the groups to accept one another.

The intended effect of Paul's words to the Corinthians is to pull the two parties to common ground. "The strong" have the better theological case for their decision to buy and eat meat from the market regardless of its prior use in pagan worship (1 Cor. 8). Yet the concern of "the weak" (8:9) about the dangers of idolatry is not without point. To eat "idol meat" in the home of a non-Christian might well suggest that Christianity is, like pagan religion, open to the worship of many gods. Worse, to eat "idol meat" in a pagan temple, as some of "the strong" are wont to do, risks not just giving the wrong impression about Christian openness to the worship of other gods but actually joining in that worship (1 Cor. 10). There is thus a middle ground between the positions of "the strong" and "the weak," and Paul urges the two parties to find it.

But the effect of Paul's words to the Romans is different. He certainly prods the "weak in faith" (Rom. 14:1) to come around to the "strong" (15:1) way of thinking about the matter. But he seems more than happy for them to carry on with practices that identify them as Jewish as part of their worship of Christ. It is this difference that helps explain the particular exhortation of Romans for the two groups to accept one another. In Romans, Paul may move the two groups toward one another in terms of their *beliefs*, but he does so in a way that leaves the differences in *practice* intact. Both groups are simply continuing the practice they had before they were Christians, and both groups have come to see the continuation of the practice as an appropriate expression of Christian devotion. And it is on that basis that Paul urges them to accept one another. The point is not simply that individuals should accept one another despite theological differences. The point is that groups should accept one another despite and even *because* of the differences of practice that identify them as members of different groups.

What this means for Jewish Christians is slightly different from what it means for those from non-Jewish backgrounds. To the former, Paul says, "Stop judging" (see Rom. 14:10). To the latter, he says, "Stop despising" (see 14:3). In the matter of meat and wine, those who abstain are not to condemn those who imbibe; those who imbibe are not to belittle those who abstain. The first attitude condemns the other as worthy of exclusion. The second attitude looks down on the other as inferior. Neither attitude is appropriate toward those whom God has accepted. Whether they will stand or fall in the judgment is a decision that belongs to God alone, and their faith in Christ marks them as those whom God will cause to stand. In positive terms, to stop judging means to treat the other inclusively; to stop despising means to treat the other as an equal.

3. *Love.* Attitudes of judgment and superiority indicate that a person is "no longer walking in love" (Rom. 14:15). The comment picks up Paul's earlier statements about love as the quintessential mark of the believer (13:8–10). Whereas every other debt should be paid, love, Paul says, is a debt we owe to one another that can never be marked "paid." The metaphor of an unpayable debt does not imply that the obligation is onerous but that it is ongoing. Paul's use of a different metaphor in Romans 14:15—"walking in love"—points in the same direction. This is the way that followers of Christ live their lives, most especially where the edges of cultural difference meet.

This, sadly, is not a natural first instinct. As we saw in the early chapters of this book, sin always seeks to eradicate difference, giving birth to the sins of either violence or co-opted sameness. Love, however, "does no wrong to a neighbor" (13:10). Instead, it seeks the welfare and well-being of the other, particularly when the other belongs to a group other than one's own. Paul's claim that such love "is the fulfilling of the law" is striking because the words of Jesus identify love for neighbor as the distillation and true direction of the law that governed the life of one people, Israel (cf. Matt. 7:12; 22:40). Now that one people has been constituted as a people of peoples. As a result, the expression of God's will in the law finds its proper end when it governs the life of this people of peoples in love that extends across lines of cultural difference.

4. *Missions.* It has become common in some circles to speak of *mission* rather than *missions*. In part, the shift has come as an attempt to broaden the scope of Christian engagement with the world. By contrast, the older term *missions* tended to focus more particularly on efforts to take the gospel to places and peoples where Christ was not yet known.

This is what Paul has in mind in Romans 15 as he sets out his hope for the church in Rome to send him to Spain.

As we have seen, Paul is also planning a trip to Jerusalem to deliver a collection of funds gathered from the churches he has planted among the *ethnē*. While Paul does not seem to regard gospel proclamation as part of the purpose for his trip to Jerusalem, in one respect, at least, both trips will serve a similar aim. He asks the church in Rome to pray that his effort to collect funds from the churches among the *ethnē* will find acceptance among the Jewish Christians in Jerusalem (Rom. 15:31). In Paul's mind, the acceptance of the gift will be an indication of their acceptance of the *ethnē* as coheirs through the gospel of God's promise to Abraham. This, of course, is also precisely the thing that he hopes his lengthy exposition of the gospel will bring about within the ethnically divided church in Rome.

If the gospel is to renew the Romans' minds, as Paul hopes, it will alter their thinking about the significance of cultural identity within their church. But it will also serve as a major motivation to throw their support behind Paul's planned mission to Spain. The proclamation of the gospel in Spain will accomplish the very thing that Paul hopes the gospel set forth in Romans will do in Rome and that the collection will demonstrate in Jerusalem. It will show the power of the gospel to transform individual lives and, through that transformation, to create a worldwide people of peoples living in obedience to Israel's Messiah.

Conclusion

Paul regards himself as an apostle to the nations outside of Israel— a commission he carries out by preaching the gospel and gathering believers into churches. For Paul, each community represents the whole of a new humanity that God has formed in Christ, consisting of individuals whose faith in the Messiah constitutes them as the one people of God. His missionary practice of preaching to Jews first and then to non-Jews reflects his understanding that this one people has been formed from a "remnant" of Israel—a group of ethnically Jewish believers—into which non-Jewish believers have been grafted to form a new whole, as branches into an olive tree. The result, however, is not the assimilation of individuals into a culturally singular community, but a culturally plural community of peoples in which the restoration of blessing to one people has resulted in the restoration of blessing to all. This, for Paul, is the unexpected form that the fulfillment of God's promise to Abraham has taken. Paul refers to this people of peoples using the Danielic language of "mystery" (Rom. 16:25)—the divine plan to form one people from all peoples.

If this people of peoples is to function as a true picture of a renewed humanity, they will have to adopt practices appropriate for such a people. Above all, each community must make space for culturally plural worship. Paul's concern is not that they contrive culturally plural worship services, as important as that might sometimes be. Rather, his concern is that they regard culturally varied ways of life as appropriate expressions of worship. For that to happen, members of various cultural groups must practice mutual acceptance and love. Their capacity to do so will be greatly enhanced through their support for initiatives such as Paul's mission to Spain because such missions serve as an ongoing reminder of God's purpose to unite all peoples in Christ (cf. Eph. 1:10).

The Unity of All Peoples

Parody, Reality, and the Wealth of Nations

Humanity is constantly struggling with two contradictions.
One of these tends to promote unification while the other
aims at maintaining or re-establishing diversification.

CLAUDE LÉVI-STRAUSS, IN *STRUCTURAL ANTHROPOLOGY*

THE FIRST TIME I traveled to Ethiopia, I arrived after curfew. The streets of Addis Ababa were still as we drove from the airport. The curfew was just one of many reasons why the communist government had lost its shine in the eyes of most Ethiopians. Still, as we made our way through the city, I could see that the government excelled at one thing at least: it was very good at erecting monuments. Imposing statues, massive arches, and Soviet-style murals and banners lined the streets and filled the squares. Many of these symbolized the imported ideology of the communist regime. They portrayed the people of Ethiopia as workers, united in the struggle against economic oppression and marching as one toward a glorious and prosperous future.

The propaganda made quite an impression. But what I didn't see was what it didn't say. The message of a united Ethiopia not only glossed over the grim reality of a decades-long civil war between the government and ethnic groups in the country's northernmost regions but also obscured an extraordinary diversity of peoples and cultures. The communist government had made it a priority to suppress ethnic identities in pursuit of a vision of one Ethiopia. To that end, the authorities ruthlessly quashed difference of every kind. Communism is an ideology of economic sameness, and the imposition of cultural and irreligious sameness served that end.

The communists' vision for one Ethiopia had replaced the very different vision of one Ethiopia promoted by the imperial government they had overthrown. Ethiopia's emperors had long promoted the priority of national rather than ethnic identity. The reality, however, centered on the emperor's ethnicity and represented his culture as the culture of the nation.[1]

When the communist government fell in 1991, the government that took its place was again dominated by a single ethnic group, though not that of the emperor. The new government did not want other groups to think that it was representing its own group's culture as the culture of the nation. It also rejected the communist suppression of ethnic difference. Instead, the new government gave maximal salience to each group's ethnic identity. However, amid all the emphasis on diversity, many were left wondering whether a sense of national unity could be sustained. If previous regimes had purchased unity at the cost of diversity, was diversity now being pursued at the cost of unity?

---

1   Some will regard this description of the imperial regime that persisted until the communist revolution of 1974–1975 as an oversimplification. See, for example, Donald N. Levine's influential thesis that the sharing of cultural values by many of Ethiopia's major ethnic groups was a natural evolution of a shared identity. Levine, *Greater Ethiopia: The Evolution of a Multiethnic Society*, 2nd ed. (Chicago: University of Chicago Press, 2000). Perhaps it was, in part, especially among highland peoples who shared the emperor's Orthodox faith and Semitic linguistic heritage. But, as others have noted, this interpretation does not fully account for the aggressive program of "Amharization" that followed the imperial conquests and territorial expansion undertaken by Amhara emperors. See, for example, Simon D. Messing, "Review of *Greater Ethiopia: The Evolution of a Multiethnic Society*," *ASA Review of Books* 2 (1976): 76–78. Levine partially acknowledges the point in the preface to the 2nd edition of *Greater Ethiopia*, but still emphasizes the theme of unity and unification in his interpretation of Ethiopian society.

A similar tension between unity and diversity plays out in countless ways in most countries. The tension takes a vivid geographic form in Indonesia, where seventeen thousand islands form a single nation with a motto, "Many, yet one,"[2] that makes the archipelago a model for the society. Pick up any coin in the United States, and you will find the Latin phrase *E Pluribus Unum*. The translation is straightforward—"Out of many, one"—but what exactly does it mean? I once had an academic supervisor who joked that people use Latin phrases when the claim they are making doesn't actually make sense. Can nations be both one and many? If we do not say (as some do) that the answer to the question is a flat no, we must nevertheless admit that the political philosophies surveyed in chapter 1 only manage the problem. None resolves it.

In the book of Revelation, we meet a different kind of politics— a politics based not on one group's power over another or the sharing of power between groups, but on the forfeiture of power. Revelation depicts the climax of God's purposes for the world not simply as a conflict between God and Satan, but as a conflict of ideas about what it means to be one people comprising diverse nations, races, and peoples of the world. The writer imagines a world—a new creation—in which the tension between unity and diversity is finally resolved. However, the resolution comes not in the domination of one cultural identity over all others. The unity of all peoples does not come at the cost of diversity, but at the cost of a life. It is achieved as a Jewish Messiah takes the identity of a particular people—Israel—into himself and, through the self-surrender of crucifixion, opens up that identity to all peoples. Through his resurrection, a new creation comes into being and, with it, the possibility that one people might also be many.

Parody and Peoples

At the heart of the book of Revelation lies a cosmic struggle often described as a conflict of kingdoms, a clash between the rule of God and the rule of Satan. Although that is true, it is important to see that

---

2   In Javanese, *Bhinneka Tunggal Ika*.

this conflict is portrayed, in part, as a clash of two visions of what it means for humanity to be united as one. In many ways, the two visions resemble one another. Both claim to unite the peoples of the world under one benevolent rule in common worship. But the unity of one kingdom is secured by exploitation, oppression, and violence that subjugates peoples and leaves diverse cultures in ruins. The unity of the other, by contrast, is purchased with self-forfeiture, self-sacrifice, and subjection to violence. The result is a true unity of the diverse peoples of the world, whose cultural particularity comes to full expression in the worship of the crucified and risen Messiah.

If the two visions for the unity of all peoples resemble one another, they do so because one representation of reality is a parody of the other. But if one version of reality so closely mirrors and mimics the other, how can we know which one is true? John must have seen that question as having particular urgency for his first readers. His pastoral assessment of the situation faced by Christians in Asia Minor toward the end of the first century suggests that for some, the lines between two competing representations of reality had blurred. In fact, some seem oblivious to the fact that their lives have been shaped by a worldview that John regards as false in both whole and part. Thus, above all, Revelation is a call to see; it is an unveiling of reality that gives the lie to Rome's lofty claims to be the unifier of the world's peoples. John's opening exhortations to the seven churches encourage them to see their struggle as part of a wider contest between the world's true King and a satanic pretender. Only by seeing the reality of Christ's kingdom alongside its parody in an earthly regime propped up by Satan's power can Christians remain faithful to the one who is "faithful and true" (Rev. 3:14; 19:11).

Beginning in Revelation 17, the contest is depicted as a struggle between two cities—Babylon and Jerusalem, the holy city that comes down from heaven (cf. Rev. 3:12; 21:2, 10). Babylon is widely and correctly understood as a cipher for Rome, but why represent Rome as Babylon? The choice of "Babylon" may have seemed odd even to the first readers. At the time John writes, Babylon had long ceased to exist as a city, much less as the power center of a vast empire. But John's activation of scriptural memories of Babylon provides a powerful tool for undercutting Roman propaganda, with its promises of prosperity for all, its pretensions of permanence, and its claims to be the greater unifier of nations and peoples.

1. *From Babel to Babylon: A Brief History of Empires.* We have seen how the early chapters of Genesis set forth a divine vision of an earth filled with nations and peoples, creating an extraordinary diversity of cultures united in the worship of God. The human experiment at Babel was a parody of the divine vision. Humanity succeeded in creating a false unity in rebellion against the divine command to fill the earth with peoples. This was uniformity, not unity; *in the absence of difference, there is nothing to unite.* God refused to accept the parody. Instead, he set about to achieve true unity among the peoples of the earth through a covenant with Abraham.

In the aftermath of Babel, the Old Testament describes the scattering of nations. The earth filled with peoples, but antagonism, oppression, and violence marred the relationships between them. The early history of the people descended from Abraham unfolded in Egypt, but it was not long before early intimations of reciprocal blessing between Israel and Egypt gave way to subjugation. The collective life of one people unfolded inside another, but not for their good.

For several centuries following the exodus and conquest, Scripture gives the impression that the nations and peoples of the earth existed in a state of ongoing rivalry and shifting alliances. Though certain nations projected power beyond their traditional territories, most lacked the means to do so very far or for very long. However, all of this changed with the rise of empires. The first that comes into view in Scripture is the Assyrian Empire. Although the Assyrian hegemony over other peoples had existed in various forms previously, the militaristic expansion that began in the late tenth century BC left it astride much of the known world for the next three hundred years. In the late seventh century BC, however, the Assyrian Empire gave way to the Babylonian Empire, followed in the fifth century BC by the Medo-Persian Empire, followed in turn by the sprawling empire of the Greeks. Though these empires differed from one another in important ways, all alike asserted their power and authority over other peoples.

From the perspective of the Old Testament, at least, Babylon was the greatest of these empires or, perhaps one should say, the worst. This was the empire responsible for the destruction of the temple of Jerusalem and the depopulation of Judea. Much more than with other empires, the power of Babylon emanated from a single urban center. Moreover, the Babylonians claimed sovereignty not just over neighboring peoples but over *all* peoples (Dan. 4:22). Worse, although Babylon represented its authority as a positive good for the peoples under its sway, participation in its prosperity and beneficence came at a cost. The book of Daniel depicts Babylon's uncompromising insistence that conquered peoples assimilate to its culture. Readers struck by the similarity between Babylon's monocultural vision of unity and the cultural uniformity pursued at Babel understand Daniel correctly. Thus, as the book of Daniel opens, we find ourselves once more in "Shinar," the location of the Tower of Babel (Gen. 11:2) and the seat of Babylonian power (Dan. 1:2).[3] Daniel and his friends are taken from their homeland, given the king's food to eat, and educated in Babylon's language and culture. But the Babylonian king also insists that they worship the Babylonian high god, Bel. On the assumption that Babylon's conquest of other nations reflects Bel's conquest of their gods, the Babylonian ruler's claim to be king of kings corresponds to Bel's claim to be lord of lords. Thus, in Daniel 3, King Nebuchadnezzar erects an idol of gold—probably an image of Bel—and compels all "peoples, nations, and languages" to bow the knee to it (3:4, 7). It is an

3   The Hebrew term "Shinar" in Daniel 1:2 is sometimes translated "Babylonia" (e.g., NIV) because it is an older name for the area. See, for example, John Joseph Collins and Adela Yarbro Collins, *Daniel: A Commentary on the Book of Daniel*, Hermeneia (Minneapolis: Fortress, 1993), 134. For other parallels between Babel and Babylon in Daniel, see Michael Hilton, "Babel Reversed—Daniel Chapter 5," *Journal for the Study of the Old Testament* 20 (1995): 99–112.

impressive display of the unity of all peoples. It is also idolatrous and false—a parody of the coming kingdom of Israel's God.

2. *Rome as Babylon (and Babel)*. As we open the pages of the New Testament, a new empire has already cast its shadow not only over Europe but over the whole of the Mediterranean basin. In the propaganda of Rome, its rule was personified in the goddess Roma and embodied in the emperors who often claimed divine honors for themselves. Like Babylon, Rome promoted itself as beneficent with the promise of boundless prosperity and lasting peace. The vaunted *pax Romana* was not simply a contemporary label for a lengthy period of calm that began during the reign of Caesar Augustus. The Romans themselves "felt that their domination was entirely right, divinely ordained and a good thing for the wider world. Emperors boasted that their rule brought peace to the provinces, benefiting the entire population."[4]

However, those who felt the hard heel of Rome's military might did not always share this view. The Roman historian Tacitus records the words of a Caledonian leader named Calgacus just before his attempt to rebuff Roman aggression failed: "To robbery, slaughter, plunder, they give the lying name of empire; they create a wasteland and call it peace."[5] His perspective on Rome is not far from the apostle John's.

In Revelation 17, we are introduced to a vision of a woman. Richard Bauckham explains:

At first glance, she might seem to be the goddess Roma, in all her glory, a stunning personification of the civilization of Rome, as she was worshipped in many temples in the cities of Asia. But as John sees her, she is a Roman prostitute, a seductive whore and a scheming witch, and her wealth and splendor represent the profits of her disreputable trade.[6]

4 Adrian K. Goldsworthy, *Pax Romana: War, Peace and Conquest in the Roman World*, (New Haven, CT: Yale University Press, 2016), 2.
5 Tacitus, *Agricola*, 30, cited in Shane J. Wood, *The Alter-Imperial Paradigm: Empire Studies & the Book of Revelation* (Leiden: Brill, 2015), 109n173.
6 Richard Bauckham, *The Theology of the Book of Revelation* (Cambridge: Cambridge University Press, 1993), 17–18.

John never directly identifies this woman as Rome, though his note that she sits on seven hills leaves little room for doubt (Rev. 17:9).[7] Instead, he identifies her by the mystery name written on her forehead—"Babylon" (17:5). This whoring goddess who sits on seven hills also sits by "many waters" (17:1), corresponding to ancient Babylon's location at the juncture of two great rivers. However, unlike the seven hills, this literal description of Babylon is given a figurative meaning: the many waters "where the prostitute sits, are peoples, multitudes, nations and languages" (17:15 NIV).[8] Though John has added a term, we readily recognize the precursor to John's fourfold reference to the peoples of the earth in the threefold reference to the "peoples, nations, and languages" that bowed to Bel in Babylon (Dan. 3:4, 7). Like Babylon before her, Rome "rules over the kings of the earth" (Rev. 17:18 NIV). Though separated in time, Rome mirrors Babylon's idolatrous ambition to subsume all peoples under one rule by force. If the towering idol in Babylon replicates the diversity-defying Tower of Babel, Rome's version of the tower takes an even more odious form. The people of Babel displayed their defiance of God's purpose by piling up stones that reached to the heavens, but Rome piles up *sins* that reach to heaven (18:5). In both cases, a kind of unity is achieved, but it is idolatrous and false.

"Babylon" achieves its vaunted unity through violence and subjugation. Following the lavish description of the harlot in Revelation 17:4, we learn that she is drunk with the blood of God's people (17:6). The following chapter repeats that charge but adds another—she is guilty of the blood not only of the prophetic witnesses and saints but also of "*all* who have been slaughtered on the earth" (18:24 NIV). Though this statement has been interpreted as a reference to Christian martyrs, this understanding misses the climactic force of the whole chapter. "Rome

7   The "seven hills" of Rome are a geographical feature for which the city was (and remains) well known.
8   G. K. Beale notes a number of texts that use this imagery, including Isa. 17:12–13. Beale, *The Book of Revelation: A Commentary on the Greek Text*, New International Greek Testament Commentary (Grand Rapids, MI: Eerdmans, 1999), 882.

is indicted not only for the martyrdom of Christians, but also for the slaughter of all the innocent victims of its murderous policies. The verse expresses a sense of solidarity between the Christian martyrs and all whose lives were the price of Rome's acquisition and maintenance of power."[9]

Those murderous policies only partially account for the "peace" that unifies the nations and peoples of the earth (Rev. 17:15). The harlot's golden chalice may be filled with abominations and "the filth of her adulteries" (17:4 NIV), but the nations have all drunk her wine and the kings of the earth have all indulged her adulterous favors (18:3). We should not miss here John's use of the common biblical image of adultery for idolatry. If the people of the Lamb are unified in their worship of him, the nations of the earth are also unified in worship. But they do not worship the Lamb. Instead, their parody of unified worship is offered to the parody of deity—the unholy trinity depicted as the dragon (Satan), the beast from the sea (the emperor), and the beast from the earth (promoters of the imperial cult) (Rev. 13:4, 8, 11, 15).

John further explains the participation of the nations and kings of the earth in this parody of true unity and true worship by describing the extravagant wealth and luxury secured through their complicity. Only those who receive the mark of the beast are free to engage in the lucrative trade between nations made possible within Rome's dominion and international reach (Rev. 13:16–17). Those who have the mark grow rich from "her excessive luxuries" (18:3 NIV). That extravagance, however, has been purchased with human lives. Among the commodities listed on the bill of lading in Revelation 18:12–13 are many of the luxury items with which the harlot adorns herself (17:4). However, the cargo also includes human beings, commodified lives sold into bondage as part of a lucrative slave trade. Tragically, the nations and kings of the earth willingly

9   Richard Bauckham, *The Climax of Prophecy: Studies on the Book of Revelation* (Edinburgh: T&T Clark, 1993), 349.

join in Babylon's parody of unity out of lust for the opulent lifestyle afforded to the prostitute's consorts. The extravagance they seek in the harlot's embrace stains them with the exploitation of those she deems expendable.

3. *The One and the Many in the New Jerusalem.* John, however, has his own vision of all peoples within one people. Our first glimpse of this people comes in Revelation 5, in John's vision of the heavenly throne room. An angel appears with a scroll that has writing on both sides (5:1). It has been sealed with seven seals. As the ensuing chapters make plain, this scroll contains the divine decrees for final judgment and salvation. John weeps because no one in all creation has been found worthy to break the seals and open the scroll (5:3–4). But suddenly someone is found. John is told to look, but, at least initially, we are not told what he sees but what he hears—the voice of the angel announcing the identity of the one worthy: "Weep no more; behold, the Lion of the tribe of Judah, the Root of David, has conquered, so that he can open the scroll and its seven seals" (5:5). When John lifts his eyes, however, he does not see a Lion but rather a Lamb, looking as though it has been slain and receiving worship from a myriad of heavenly creatures (5:6–14).

The song they sing explains the paradoxical identity of the one who is worthy. He is a conquering Lion *because* he is the sacrificial Lamb, whose blood has ransomed a people for God "from every tribe and language and people and nation" (Rev. 5:9). We must not miss the curious correspondence between this people and the Lamb:

> The word "Lamb", referring to Christ, occurs 28 (7 x 4) times. . . . As seven is the number of completeness, four is the number of the world with its four corners (7:1; 20:8) or four divisions (5:13; 14:7). . . . The 7 x 4 occurrences of "Lamb" therefore indicate the worldwide scope of his complete victory. This corresponds to the fact that the phrase by which John designates all the nations of the world is fourfold ("peoples and tribes and languages and nations"): the phrase varies

each time it occurs, but is always fourfold) and occurs seven times (5:9; 7:9; 10:11; 11:9; 13:7; 14:6; 17:15).[10]

This is the triumphant people of the triumphant Lamb. Like the triumph of the Lamb, the triumph of the Lamb's people is won through suffering.

John applies the triumph-through-suffering motif to God's people in the double image of Revelation 7, which mirrors the double image of the Lion of Judah/sacrificial Lamb of Revelation 5. In the first image, the people is portrayed as the army of Israel arrayed for battle, led by the tribe of Judah. They number 144,000 (12 x 12 x 1,000)—a number derived by considering Israel's initial form of twelve tribes alongside its eventual form as a people of twelve apostles brought now to vast, messianic fullness (1,000, symbolizing a large, even uncountable number). As with the image of the lion in chapter 5, John does not see this conquering army, but only hears an angel announce it (7:4). When he looks, he sees not an army but the people of the Lamb—"a great multitude that no one could number, from every nation, from all tribes and peoples and languages, standing before the throne and before the Lamb, clothed in white robes" (7:9). Their robes are white because they have been washed in the blood of the Lamb (7:14).

Here we have one of the most striking representations in all of Scripture of the divine purpose for the configuration of all peoples as one people. In the first scene, this people is identified as Israel. In the second, the same people is identified as the innumerable host of nations, languages, tribes, and peoples. This uncountable multitude of peoples and nations is united by their shared experience of redemption by the Lamb and by their common response of worship of the Lamb. But they are also united by their shared participation in the triumph of the Lamb. Most of the military imagery from the first half of the text has disappeared, but not completely. Another Jewish text from the period, part of the Dead Sea Scrolls, portrays a vast messianic army dressed in white who wash the blood of their enemies from their garments

10 Bauckham, *Theology*, 66–67.

following the final battle (1QM 14:2–3). But the army in John's vision is different. Their garments are white not because the blood has been washed from them, but because they have been washed with blood—the blood of the Lamb.[11] The battle they wage in overcoming their enemies is spiritual. They overcome by remaining faithful even to the point of shedding their blood in devotion to the Lion-Lamb, who loved them and gave himself for them.

John's vision for the unity of all peoples comes to climactic expression in the vision of the new Jerusalem at the end of Revelation. If Babylon is a harlot, Jerusalem appears as a radiant bride (21:1–2). But the imagery quickly shifts to the city's architecture. The Jerusalem that descends from heaven is not just a city, it is a garden-city, and not just a garden-city but a garden-temple-city. Like many ancient cities, this one has walls. The images that describe its dimensions cannot be reconciled by any literal reckoning but work together to convey the profound meaning John builds into the architecture of this city. This is a city of one people, inhabited by all peoples. The four walls constitute a square—twelve thousand stadia in both length and width. In each of the four walls are three gates inscribed with the names of the tribes of Israel. At the same time, the city encompasses the whole of the new creation. The dimensions of the walls—12 x 1,000 stadia—together with the inscription of tribal names on each gate suggest that the city encompasses the whole of Israel in its complete and final form. But the walls are also built on twelve foundations, which bear the names of the twelve apostles. This, in turn, suggests another identity for the inhabitants of the city: the multiethnic host that gathers around the throne in the last half of Revelation 7. This intuition is confirmed in 21:24–26 with the depiction of this Israel-encompassing city populated by the nations of the earth.

Remarkably, this perfectly square city is as high as it is wide and long—a perfect cube. This can be understood only as a city modeled after the Most Holy Place of the temple. Thus, we are told that an angel

---

11 Bauckham, *Climax*, 227.

measures the city to ensure its suitability for divine habitation (Rev. 21:15–17). The presence of the Lord fills the city as though it were a temple. As a result, the people dwell in the presence of God and of the Lamb as though they *are* the temple (21:22).

As Revelation 22 opens, the imagery shifts again. The city has become a garden, evoking the memory of Eden (Rev. 22:1–3). Eden was to have been the temple of the first creation, filled with God's presence, with ever-expanding boundaries reflecting the divine command to fill the earth with peoples, nations, tribes, and tongues. Now, the final chapter of Scripture depicts the realization of the divine purpose, as the nations of the earth gather in a city holy to the Lord, drinking from the river of life that flows from God's throne and eating from the tree of life that grows on both sides of the river.

The oddity of a single tree growing on both sides of the river has been the cause of much discussion. Perhaps the detail is of little moment. However, it may be that the image of one life-giving tree yielding twelve different kinds of fruit and leaves that heal the nations supports the dual identity of the city's inhabitants. Viewed as a whole, the city inhabitants form God's one covenant people who enjoy equal access to the fruit of the tree of life. Viewed in its parts, the inhabitants of the city are the nations who enter the city of God's one covenant people through gates that stand open to receive all peoples into God's life-giving presence.

The Judgment and Conversion of the Nations

At the heart of Revelation lies a paradox. On the one hand, John's vision depicts a final judgment of all nations that results in their complete annihilation. Thus, in Revelation 19, we meet a rider on a white horse prepared for battle, and "coming out of his mouth is a sharp sword with which to strike down the nations" (19:15 NIV). Though the final battle is not described, its outcome is clear. Carrion birds are summoned to "eat the flesh of kings . . . and the flesh of all people, free and slave, great and small" (19:18 NIV). On the other hand, John also envisions the conversion and salvation of all nations. In Revelation 21, the nations— all of them, it seems—take their place in the new Jerusalem. Illumined as it is by the glory of the Lord, the city requires no other source of light. The nations all walk by that light and "the kings of the earth . . . bring their splendor into it" (21:24 NIV). "The glory and honor of the nations" (21:26 NIV) are likewise brought into the city, recalling the prophetic expectation of a great migration of nations into the temple of the messianic age.

1. *A Paradox without Resolution?* The paradox has not escaped the attention of scholars, who continue to debate the relationship between these seemingly disparate strands of expectation regarding the fate of nations and peoples. Some commentators posit a subtle shift in focus as a strategy for dealing with the apparent antinomy. Nations *qua* nations are destroyed, but God calls citizens of the new Jerusalem out of every nation. Thus, the nations are not present in the new Jerusalem, but are nevertheless represented there by the individuals who come out of them. These individuals are formed into a kingdom made up of those purchased by the Lamb from every nation.[12] This view correctly notes that John's vision does not lose sight of individuals. Whatever the fate of the nations, it is inextricably bound to the choices made by individuals. And yet, at the climax of both the vision of judgment in Revelation 19 and the vision of the new Jerusalem in Revelation 21–22, it seems clear that God is dealing not just with individuals but also with nations.

A second approach to the paradox suggests that the nations destroyed at the end of Revelation 19 are only the nations aligned with Babylon. The nations that appear in the new Jerusalem of John's final vision must therefore be the nations who resist and reject Babylon's rule. In this approach, it is easy to see how "the nations" can be both judged and converted, but it is hard to account for the apparently universal language that marks both the vision of nations judged and the vision of nations converted.

A third approach recognizes that all nations are both judged and converted, but maintains that ultimately the latter emerges as the domi-

---

12 Beale, *Revelation*, 1097.

nant perspective. Some who take this view argue that the nations that are converted to the worship of the Lamb are identical to the nations destroyed by the Lamb at the end of Revelation 19. Such solutions do not fully explain how the nations can be destroyed and *then* converted. Moreover, the result eviscerates the reality of judgment in favor of universal salvation. A better version of this view maintains the reality of judgment but nevertheless grants "theological priority" to the final vision that situates all nations within the new Jerusalem.[13]

According to the view taken here, it is important to allow the universality of both visions to stand.[14] All nations will be destroyed in judgment; all nations will take their place in the new Jerusalem. The apparent contradiction is resolved when we recognize that in Revelation, every nation assumes two forms. These forms are manifest in the divided response of individuals to the messages that come to them. *Every* nation is implicated in the idolatrous worship of the beast because individuals of every nation, tribe, and tongue fall prey to the deceptions and propaganda of the second beast. At the same time, *every* nation enters the new Jerusalem because individuals of every nation, tribe, and tongue renounce the idolatrous regime and its lies, and wash their garments white in the blood of the Lamb. These divergent responses give rise to divergent forms of humanity—one that portrays all nations as idolatrous and subject to destruction, and another in which all nations are redeemed by the blood of the Lamb.

In the first instance, John draws on the *herem* tradition of the Old Testament, which depicted the complete annihilation of idolatrous nations from land deemed holy to the Lord (see chap. 5). The purpose of the decree was to purge the land of idolatry to make it ready for the dwelling of a holy God in the midst of a holy people. However, in a portion of Isaiah on which John frequently draws, we find an anticipation of a future *herem* against *all* nations. This is the natural consequence of

13 Bauckham, *Climax*, 310.
14 The description of this position and its development below is indebted to Dave Mathewson, "The Destiny of the Nations in Revelation 21:1–22:5: A Reconsideration," *Tyndale Bulletin* 53 (2002): 121–42.

God's action to fill the whole earth with the glory of his holy presence. Thus, in Isaiah 34:2, we read that "the LORD is enraged against all the nations, / and furious against all their host; / he has devoted them to destruction, has given them over for slaughter." Here we have a decree of total destruction not just against one nation or some nations but *all* nations. Given the Babylonian claim to encompass all nations within its idolatrous regime, John may also see the decree of universal *herem* implicit within Old Testament texts that prophesy complete destruction over Babylon.[15] For John, the execution of the *herem* decree against all nations brings about the destruction of all who swear loyalty to Babylon (Rev. 19:19–21). At the same time, he points to the salvation of all nations through their allegiance to the Lamb.

2. *"For the Healing of the Nations."* Ironically, John draws on that same *herem* tradition to cast his vision of a redeemed humanity as one people comprising all peoples. In Zechariah 14:11, the prophet speaks of the new Jerusalem as a city that shall never again be subject to the *herem* decree. This text seems to stand behind the declaration of Revelation 22:3 that "there will no longer be any curse" (NET) over the city. The previous verse states the reason: the life-giving stream that flows from the midst of the city will water trees whose leaves will be "for the healing of the nations" (22:2). The phrase alludes to Ezekiel's vision of a stream that flows from the temple, watering trees whose leaves are for healing (Ezek. 47:12). John's Gospel had drawn on that vision to speak about the life-giving Spirit to be given by the resurrected Jesus (John 7:38). In Revelation, John alludes to the healing properties of the life-giving stream. In specifying that the healing is "for the . . . nations," he suggests that the nations have been healed of their idolatry, making it possible for them to dwell within the new Jerusalem.[16]

This "healing of the nations" takes place as individuals respond in faith to the proclamation of the truth. The identities of these are

---

15 On John's use of Isaiah 34 and Jeremiah 50–51 to speak of the total destruction of the nations and of Babylon, see especially Bauckham, *Climax*, 317–18.

16 Mathewson, "Destiny," 139–40.

reshaped; the name of the Lamb is written on every forehead (Rev. 22:4). This transformation of individuals does not dilute but mediates John's emphasis on the presence of nations in the new Jerusalem. This individual/nation duality comes to the fore at the beginning of the final vision, where John sees the new Jerusalem, prepared as a bride for her wedding (21:1–2). The marriage covenant described in Revelation 21:3 draws on prophetic texts (e.g., Ezek. 37:27–28) that anticipate the formation of a new covenant between God and Israel. Now, however, the marriage covenant is not with Israel alone but with the "peoples" of the world: "Look, God's dwelling is with human beings, and he will live with them. They will be his *peoples*, and God himself will be with them and will be their God" (Rev. 21:3 AT).[17] The plural "peoples" may seem strange, but it is not without Old Testament precursor. Here, John seems to read the promises of a new covenant with Israel in relation to Zechariah 2:10–11, in which God calls forth praise from inhabitants of restored Jerusalem: "Sing and rejoice, O daughter of Zion, for behold, I come and I will dwell in your midst, declares the LORD. And *many nations shall join* themselves to the LORD in that day, and shall be my people. And I will dwell in your midst." The result of John's reading is an image of redeemed humanity comprising all peoples, with God dwelling in their midst.

If we cannot think of "the healing of the nations" apart from the repentance and faith of individuals, the result is nevertheless the healing of *nations*. The significance of this is probably twofold. First, the image is not simply about individual salvation but about "*reconciliation among peoples*."[18] This reconciliation is not assimilation. Rather, the healing of the nations makes their unity possible. This is not empire but kingdom. And this kingdom effects a new configuration of nations that eviscerates both the will and the desire of any single nation to dominate

17 Several translations note a textual problem in 21:3. The strength of the evidence for the plural "peoples" has led to its adoption in the standard editions of the Greek text, though this is reflected only in the NRSV and CSB. For a discussion of the textual issue, see Mathewson, "Destiny," 128.

18 Michael J. Gorman, *Reading Revelation Responsibly: Uncivil Worship and Witness: Following the Lamb into the New Creation* (Eugene, OR: Cascade, 2011), 166, emphasis original.

all others. This new configuration of peoples is constituted by a new covenant within which God binds himself to one holy people whose identity has opened up to include all nations within it.

Second, the healing of the nations not only results in their reconciliation but enables every people to contribute its distinctive "glory" to the glory of God. Following a description of the beauty and purity of the new Jerusalem (Rev. 21:5–21), John returns once more to the image of a future gathering of all peoples into the city that has "no need of sun or moon to shine on it, for the glory of God gives it light, and its lamp is the Lamb. By its light will the nations walk, and the kings of the earth will bring their glory into it. . . . They will bring into it the glory and the honor of the nations" (21:23–26).

Once more, John is indebted to a set of prophetic texts that anticipate a pilgrimage of all peoples to Jerusalem to worship the Lord. Perhaps the most well-known of these texts is Isaiah 56:7—"My house shall be called a house of prayer for all peoples"—a text cited in the Synoptic Gospels to explain Jesus's act of protest in Herod's temple (Matt. 21:13; Mark 11:17; Luke 19:46). In Jesus's view, the time for the temple of the coming age had come, and Herod's temple was not that temple.[19] As a result, Jesus consigned Herod's temple to destruction and hinted that he would build a temple of another kind in three days—a temple not made with hands (John 2:13–22). In Revelation, we see clearly what that temple will be—the Lord and the Lamb—whose presence is coextensive with the whole of the new creation.[20] But what does it mean for the nations to bring their "glory" and "honor" into such a temple?

It is important to see the way in which John's thought both draws on and develops the expectation of Isaiah. In the vision of Isaiah, the good news of Israel's restoration goes out from Jerusalem. When the nations hear of it, they stream toward Jerusalem, bringing their wealth

---

19 On the significance of Jesus's temple action as an indictment of Herod's temple for failing to be the eschatological temple, see Steven M. Bryan, *Jesus and Israel's Traditions of Judgement and Restoration*, Society for New Testament Studies Monograph Series 117 (Cambridge: Cambridge University Press, 2002), 189–235.

20 For a detailed argument that Revelation depicts the temple of the new creation as coextensive with the new creation, see Beale, *Revelation*, 1109–11.

with them—wealth used to adorn the house of the Lord (Isa. 60:11). As an example, Isaiah chooses Lebanon:

> The glory of Lebanon will come to you,
>   the juniper, the fir and the cypress together,
> to adorn my sanctuary;
>   and I will glorify the place for my feet. (60:13 NIV)

Commentators tend to suggest that John has simply spiritualized the language—if Isaiah thought the nations would bring literal wealth to a literal temple, John indicates that the nations will bring their spiritual wealth—praise and worship—into a spiritual temple. To be sure, there is a doxological intent in John's adaptation of Isaiah's language, but if Isaiah was his guide, John may have something more in mind than generalized praise. In Isaiah, the glory of Lebanon—the wealth its people bring—is *particular* to Lebanon, materials that set their nation apart from other nations and for which they were honored by other nations. This is their glory. And they gladly offer it to the Lord as an act of worship. In doing so, their glory becomes the glory of the Lord.

Perhaps, then, what we see in this text from Revelation is not simply the hope that one day every nation, people, tribe, and tongue will gather as one to worship the Lord. Rather, it is the hope that the beauty of each culture in all its uniqueness will fulfill its true purpose in magnifying the glory of the Lord. This is not a vision of tolerance between peoples, but of the cultural abundance of all peoples offered as blessing shared and blessing returned in unified worship of the Lamb who was slain.

In 1776, the Scottish economist and philosopher Adam Smith published *The Wealth of Nations*. Smith did not express himself in simple terms, but one of his most important ideas *was* simple. The prevailing economic theory of his day held that the wealth of the world was finite and fixed. A nation could increase its wealth only by selling its own goods and impeding the purchase of goods from others through the imposition of tariffs. Smith demurred. In a famous passage, he considered the example of Scottish wool and French wine. The Scots were very good at producing wool, and the French were very good at producing wine. The Scots, he supposed, could cultivate grapes. However, the challenges of a cold climate would make the cost of Scottish wine thirty times that of French wine. But what if the Scots enjoyed the benefits of French winemaking in exchange for French enjoyment of fine Scottish wool? Scotland, after all, did not grow more prosperous by producing more wool than it could use. Similarly, the French would not benefit from storing more and more wine in barrels that would never be opened. If abundant Scottish wool were traded for abundant French wine, would not both peoples be the better for it?

Smith, of course, was thinking primarily in economic terms. However, it does not take too much imagination to see that the wealth of nations and peoples is not simply the sort held in banks. French winemaking and Scottish wool production do not just add to the gross domestic product of those nations; they are also part of their material culture. If, in God's design, every human being images the glory of God, so, too, in a way, does every culture. This is the cultural capital of a people—the glory they bring into the one covenant people of God. With this "wealth," they both bless the Lord and bless other peoples. Their presence does not threaten the common culture of the one covenant people, for they are all "his peoples" (Rev. 21:3 CSB). For all the myriad of differences between them, they live as one in holiness and love under the rule of the Messiah.

Conclusion

In the opening chapters of Genesis, we catch a glimpse of the divine purpose to form an ever-expanding garden-temple, filled with the holy presence of God. As we have seen, God's purpose was that humanity would image his glory, in part, by filling the whole of creation with diverse cultures and peoples. This was to be a community of blessing with God, the source of life and blessing, living in the midst of all peoples. In turn, the peoples would live in God's presence, united within the community in which they both blessed one another and returned blessing to God. Revelation depicts the fulfillment of that purpose.

In our divided world, it is hard to see calls for unity as anything more than empty or even dangerous rhetoric. The French anthropologist Claude Lévi-Strauss, whose quote heads this chapter, could not imagine a world in which the impulse to unity and the reality of diversity could ever be anything more than a contradiction. But John could, and God did. Our own aspirations for a unity between and within nations that does not quash the differences between and within them will invariably fall short this side of the Messiah's consummated kingdom. Still, to strive toward that end goes to the heart of what it means to live in hope—a hope nurtured by John's vision of the garden-temple-city of the new creation.

11

A Purpose for Peoples

The Dilemma of Cultural Identity
and the Hope of a New Humanity

Because God has fulfilled his purpose to form one humanity through
the gospel, I worship the Father, who gave a name to every people.

EPHESIANS 3:15 (EXPANDED AT)

OUR STUDY BEGAN with Nebuchadnezzar's dilemma. Can one people contain within itself many peoples or will the mixing of peoples always give that one people feet of clay? It is the dilemma of the one and the many. Virtually all societies face this dilemma in some form. For many, the answer has been to do away with the mixing of peoples. In fashioning an image of unalloyed gold and demanding that all peoples unite in worshiping it, Nebuchadnezzar envisioned an assimilationist form of this solution (Dan. 3). But the judgment of Scripture is firm: both the image of gold and the ideology that produced it were idolatrous and dangerous. Whether in ancient empires or modern states, the imposition of cultural uniformity has brought multiplied horrors to the multiplicity of peoples under their rule. A strong urge to be free of such strictures helped birth the classical liberal focus on the individual that undergirds Western democracies. It provides important protections to individuals mediated through the Western focus on human rights. But this focus also has been used to undercut and undervalue cultural diversity within the whole, opening a back door to the oppression of individuals on the basis of group identity.

Others societies have resolved the dilemma by abandoning the quest for unity between peoples, not least as a response to past oppression. That impulse births ideologies that give maximal salience to group identity with little thought to the importance of shared identity. These ideologies, too, are idolatrous to the extent that groups are conceived in strictly oppositional terms, pitted against one another in a zero-sum contest for power. In contexts shaped by these ideologies, the capacity of a group to maintain or acquire power in relation to other groups becomes the primary measure of the good. Even when the aim is not the dominance of one group but equality between groups, societies struggle to forge agreement on what equality is or what it will look like if achieved.[1] Locked in a perpetual contest for power, the relationships between groups come to be defined by power (i.e., control of resources and influence). The casualties at both ends of the ideological spectrum are individual lives.

Scripture, however, casts a different vision and charts a different course. Perhaps the most significant conclusion of this study is that God's purposes for humanity are realized in the formation of a people of peoples through the restoration of individuals to right relationship with himself and others. In Christ, God has acted to form a new humanity, one whose cultural specificity is underscored by the fact that it is formed within a Jewish Messiah who concentrates in himself the collective identity of a particular people. In the death and resurrection of Jesus, Israel is constituted as the one holy people of God. The death of the Messiah purges idolatry from individuals who repent and believe and sets them in a right relationship with God. The resurrection of the

---

1   See below on the sharp disagreement between those who believe equality should be measured in relation to opportunity and those who focus primarily on equitable outcomes.

Messiah constitutes them as the one holy people of the one holy God. Together with the Messiah, they become the Israel of God (Gal. 6:16). As individuals come into the Israel of God, they take on the cultural identity of a holy nation. Their way of life marks this people as Israel, originating in Israel's covenantal commitment to love God and love neighbors, not least those who live across lines of cultural difference. In this sense, the frequent claim that the identity of this people is one that "transcends ethnic identity" does not do justice to the particularity of this people.[2]

Yet, in coming into Israel, they do not become Jewish. Those who are Jewish remain Jewish and provide the shared history and ancestry that remain central to the identity of the whole. Even so, the nature of this people is such that the culture of the whole does not eviscerate the cultural particularity of the peoples that constitute the whole. Rather, the cultural particularity of each people becomes what God intended as it takes its place within the whole—part of a community of blessing. In this community of peoples, the response of each people to the blessings of the new creation poured out on Israel is to bring the wealth of its own people into the one people of God as a way of returning blessing to God.

The local church is the living expression of hope for a humanity constituted in this way. This people of peoples shares a single identity even as the particular identity of each people becomes a vital source of blessing for the whole. In the local church, the cultural wealth embedded in the way of life of every people is offered to God as an act of worship and is experienced by all peoples as a return of blessing in

---

2   The cited phrase is from Aaron J. Kuecker, *The Spirit and the 'Other': Social Identity, Ethnicity and Intergroup Reconciliation in Luke-Acts* (New York: T&T Clark, 2011), 216. The phrase reflects Kuecker's understanding of the Christian social identity depicted in Acts. In relation to John's Gospel, Stewart Penwell similarly concludes that Christian social identity is "trans-ethnic." Penwell, *Jesus the Samaritan: Ethnic Labeling in the Gospel of John*. Biblical Interpretation (Leiden: Brill, 2019), 5. I have argued that in both texts and in the New Testament generally, the social identity constructed by the early followers of Jesus did not transcend the identity of a particular people. Rather the identity of a particular people opened up to all peoples.

response to blessing received. As God's one holy people, this people of peoples resembles God's own identity—an identity that eternally opens to include the other. Within the identity of the one God, we see the differentiation without which love is neither necessary nor possible. This makes possible a unity of difference between peoples within which the power to love is drawn from the life-giving presence of the triune God that fills the new creation (Eph. 3:14–21).

Individuals within Peoples, Peoples within a People

If these are God's purposes for the humanity of the new creation, what does it mean to live in the hope of its final realization? The possibilities are many, but I want to consider four implications to seed further reflection within the myriad of contexts where people experience cultural difference.

1. *Politics and the Hope of the New Creation.* In the opening chapter, we surveyed the political approaches taken to the dilemma. We noticed the way in which classical Western liberalism elevates the primacy of the individual as the basis of national identity. This emphasis on the unique value and dignity of the individual coheres with the powerful scriptural claim that every person is made in the image of God. That truth provides an important defense against the justification of oppression with a claim about the inherent superiority of one group over all others. Moreover, within Scripture, the whole is formed as individuals come to faith in the Messiah. To be constituted as a community of blessing, God's one holy people must be resurrected in the Messiah through individual faith in the resurrected Messiah.

Although not without strengths when viewed from the perspective of Scripture, in the absence of significant qualifications, classical liberalism leaves little space for the cultural identities of groups within the whole. In focusing on individuals, some may come to identify a majority or dominant culture as the culture of the whole. Some Americans, for instance, don't think of themselves as part of any group based on race, ethnicity, or country of origin. They have rightly rejected "whiteness" as an identity rooted in oppression and simply identify as Americans. However, in doing so, they identify as part of a group—that is, the group of people within America who construct their group identity *in that way*. As sensible as this might seem as a liberal response to a politics of identity that sees only groups, Christians must resist it as an assimilationist form of "soft" nationalism. The claim that the focus must fall only on individuals is untrue both to the way God formed the world and to his purposes for the world. Thus, Christians must resist thinking of themselves simply as individuals who constitute the whole conceived as a normative national identity over against the ethnic or racial identities of groups within the whole.

If Christians must resist this soft nationalism, they must certainly reject harder forms that pursue a singular culture through strategies of separation, segregation, subordination, "reeducation," or "cleansing." All forms of nationalism are idolatrous because they insist that the identity of the group is properly the identity of the whole without remainder. To speak, then, of "Christian nationalism" is a contradiction in terms because it implies that a nation should be free of cultural multiplicity.

Christians must also be wary of political systems and movements that give little room for a meaningful expression of a common and unified national culture. They must be suspicious of a politics that sees people only as members of fixed racial or ethnic groups and never looks beyond group identity to see individuals or to see the whole. A politics of Christian hope will always search for common ground (and thus be nonpartisan) and value cultural difference as essential to the cultivation of a unified whole.

This does not mean that the culture of the whole is the sum of the cultures represented within the whole. Rather, the values and norms of the whole become a source of vitality and renewal for the parts, just as the particularity of the parts provides resources for the ongoing project of constructing the whole. Like the Samaritans in Luke's Gospel whose actions provided a vivid reminder of what God's one holy people must be—a people marked by love for God and neighbor—so, too, voices from outside one's own group can serve as a powerful reminder of what a nation should be when true to its best ideals. This kind of politics requires the recognition that national cultures are not static things. Rather, they take in the past, both good and bad, and embrace the reality and necessity of ongoing change in a nation's common life.

As the anticipation of God's new humanity, the local church's identity as a people of peoples is central to its witness within any political order. In a divided world, the local church makes visible the gospel's achievement of the unified humanity of the new creation. But the church must never forget that this people of peoples comes into existence as individuals hear and believe the gospel of a crucified and risen Messiah. A church that focuses only on the restoration of relationships between peoples without remembering that this is an achievement of the gospel risks the loss of both the gospel and its power to restore peoples to right relationships. Without the gospel, the quest for justice simply becomes a zero-sum dispute about power between groups in which equality is always pursued and never gained.

2. *Multiplicity and Salience.* One important feature of the humanity of the new creation is the fact that individuals who come into it acquire the identity of Israel reconstituted in the resurrection of the Messiah. As we saw in our study of Acts, those who enter this new people necessarily acquire its beliefs and practices, its values and norms. They acquire, in other words, the cultural identity of God's one holy people constructed through the death and resurrection of Israel in the death and resurrection of the Messiah. At the same time, each culture is cleansed of idolatry to make it a fit instrument for worship as part of the one people of God. This means that within the humanity of the new creation, there is an identity associated with the whole and, simultaneously, identities of groups within the whole. Every member experiences at least two identities and sometimes more.

To live in hope is to recognize this dynamic between the identity that comes from the whole and the identity that comes from one or more of the groups that make up the whole. A significant feature of

Christian maturity is to know when to give salience to each of the multiple identities we all possess. Within any church anywhere in the world, one should see God's worshiping people giving expression to the common culture of God's new humanity in the constellation of beliefs and practices, values and norms that flow out of the gospel and into the life of the church. At the same time, we should also expect to see marks of cultural particularity. In many churches, the presence of multiple cultures creates challenges not unlike the ones experienced by the church in Rome. That church had to learn not simply to make space for the expression of cultural difference, but also to value it as part of "true and proper worship" (Rom. 12:1 NIV).

To do so will require both creativity and love. Let us imagine a church in which everyone speaks the language of the majority, but a sizable minority speaks another language as its mother tongue. It would be just as wrong for the minority group to break away from the whole in order to worship in its own language as it would be for the majority group to neglect the culture and language of the minority. It will be a challenge for such a church to give salience both to the whole and to the cultural identities within the whole, but, as Paul reminds the church at Rome, this is what the church was made for (Rom. 15:5–13).

3. *Equality and Power.* Much contemporary debate about equality begins with the assumption that the concept of equality itself is meaningful within a discourse about power. To speak about "equality of opportunity" is to speak about access to resources; to speak about "equality of outcomes" (or "equity") is to speak about the distribution of resources. In both cases, "equality" is a made a matter of control over resources. The fact that such debates take place makes sense in contexts in which group identity has been used by members of one group to assert power over another.

In Scripture, the language of equality is sensible within a discourse not about power but about powerlessness. We see this by observing the way in which equality bears on biblical notions of human dignity, human rebellion, divine wrath, and divine grace. All individuals are made in God's image and are equal in dignity. That truth precedes and, in part, provides the impulse for the formation of groups in the narrative of Genesis. At the same time, all have sinned. As a result, no individual is more worthy of divine benefits than any other, and no individual is less liable to judgment than any other. Those who receive God's gift of grace do so neither on the basis of human merit nor group identity. As Judge and giver, God is impartial.

If God's election of Israel does not arise from the moral or cultural superiority of Israel as a group, the same is true of his reconstitution of Israel in the Messiah. The people formed in the Messiah are marked by the Messiah's gracious, self-sacrificing, others-serving forfeiture of power. The Messiah takes into himself the identity of a people whose rebellion has made them objects of wrath. As we saw in Revelation, in their idolatrous forms—that is, as assertions of power—all nations will be destroyed. Only through the death and resurrection of the Messiah are the cultural identities of all peoples renewed as identities marked by the Messiah's forfeiture of power as individuals repent and believe. The equality that results is thus not an equality of power but an equality of blessing received and blessing shared for the good of all.

To live in this way is to exchange the language of rights for the language of righteousness. To defend the rights of my group is to defend a claim to power, but to pursue righteousness is to give up power or to disadvantage oneself in order to advantage others. This is the nature of God's own righteousness displayed in the Messiah. This, of course, works only when all groups have abandoned power as the basis for constructing relationships between groups. To live this way in our relationships as individuals, especially relationships across lines of difference, goes to the heart of what it means to live in hope for a world where the defense of rights is no longer necessary and the pursuit of righteousness creates an equality of blessing.

4. *Holiness and Hospitality.* Radiant in Scripture and recurrent throughout, the image of an abundant table and a generous host takes us to the heart of what it means to be God's people. The image, of course,

is one of blessing. In our own day, "blessing," as a concept, is troubled because it seems to muddy "the distinction between two very different categories: gift and reward."[3] As such, it has become "the humble brag of the stars," a boast of hard-earned but vaguely embarrassing extravagance made approachable, even endearing, with the language of gratitude.[4]

In Scripture, "blessing" is pure gift. God's initiative to instill living things with the power to flourish in the fulfillment of their purpose stands behind the pronouncement that they are "good" and that they have been blessed by him. Thus, the measure of blessing is not extravagance but fitness for the purpose given to humanity to fill the earth and steward it as the image of God. Divine blessing enables humanity to become a unified community of peoples who form cultures that mediate divine blessing to all others and return blessing to God. Through rebellion, this blessing is lost; through covenant, it is restored, and with it the capacity of humanity to function as a community of blessing comprising all peoples. The nature of the blessing dictates the nature of the restoration—the blessing of properly functioning humanity can be restored only in and through a people fit to receive and return blessing to God and fit to receive and share blessing with all peoples. To be such a people, they must be made holy to the Lord and made a host to others. In forming one holy people, God makes that people a host to all peoples.

God forms this people in the Messiah, in whom he has granted "every spiritual blessing" (Eph. 1:3). The Messiah has taken into himself the identity of one people, and through death and resurrection has opened that identity to all peoples. Thus, the restoration of humanity takes place as the granting of every spiritual blessing in Christ results in the uniting of all peoples in Christ (1:10). As a result, all who belong to this people are simultaneously included and inclusive as a matter of

---

3   Kate Bowler, "Death, the Prosperity Gospel and Me," New York Times, February 13, 2016, https://www.nytimes.com/.

4   Bowler, "Death." Bowler notes that this speech form has been mastered both by prosperity preachers and the secular prophets of self-actualized success.

identity. They are in Christ because they have been included. They are inclusive because they are in Christ.

Each individual who comes to the table takes his or her place as both host and honored guest. As members of the whole, they are Israel, the servant of the Lord, whose guests are the peoples who have turned from their idolatry to serve the Lord. As guests, they are the peoples of the world, who come to the table at the invitation of the Messiah. As a result, inclusion is not what a dominant culture offers to other cultures, but what we all offer to one another in the Messiah.

In a world marred by division and oppression, even the offer of inclusion can seem to be another form of domination. As one Black American put it, "So much of everything we consume is centered around whiteness, and then, maybe they'll have to fill a quota and splash in some so-called diversity and inclusion. . . . We're gonna include ourselves."[5] To be sure, if the whole is conceived as one dominant people, inclusion may indeed turn out to be another form of domination. But if the whole is not Han, Hausa, or Hutu, not Oromo, French, or white, but a whole formed of all who are in Christ, inclusion becomes an act of reciprocity.

That reciprocity is deeply embedded in the cultural rules of hospitality around the world. In America and elsewhere, this often means that guests bring a gift for the hosts or perhaps drinks or a dessert to supplement the meal. In Ethiopia, we found this to be rare; the blessing returned took a different form. If the guest was an Orthodox priest, he would not leave without a pronouncement of blessing. Sometimes when we were guests in someone's home, we would pray for our hosts before we left. But there was something else we brought. We brought our stories.

Several years ago, we visited the Simien Mountains National Park in northern Ethiopia. The park appointed guides to serve as our hosts and to make sure we didn't get lost. The guides knew the area intimately, and

5   Jesse Williams, in Jonathan Capehart, "'We're Gonna Include Ourselves': Actor Jesse Williams on Race, Culture and Cultural Appropriation," *Washington Post*, May 30, 2017, https://www.washingtonpost.com/.

we quickly grew to rely on them for everything. After the day's hike, we shared a meal around a fire and talked about our very different lives. Except for a shortwave radio, this was their access to the peoples and places of the outside world. After a night of swapping stories, one of our hosts looked at the other and commented, "Can you imagine if these foreigners lived here with us? We would never get tired of their stories."

Every culture has its own shape that frames the stories of individual lives. Those stories come together and find their meaning within the story of God's creation of a new humanity in Christ. The unity of this new humanity, depicted in Scripture as a gathering of peoples around an abundant table with a generous host, is not a brittle and fragile solution to an unsolvable dilemma. Rather, it is a unity that comes from the blessing of our shared participation in the unified life of the triune God.

Questions for Study or Discussion

Chapter 1

1. What is Nebuchadnezzar's dilemma? How do you experience it in your country?

2. What forms of cultural identity exist in your country? Which form (or forms) of cultural identity best describes how you think about yourself?

3. Do you think all people should have a national identity in addition to whatever other forms of cultural identity they may have? Why or why not?

4. The author surveys a number of ways in which states have addressed the challenge of cultural multiplicity within their borders. What approach has been taken in your country? How successful has it been? What strengths and weaknesses can you see in other approaches?

Chapter 2

1. What does it mean to say that "God created human beings for, rather than with, cultural identity"? Why is this important?

2. In many countries, there are sharp divisions over how to tell the history of the country. Is this true where you live? Why is this the case?

3. What are the three forms of collective identity discussed in this chapter? What are the differences between them? Can different forms of cultural identity exist together?

4. What role, if any, does skin color play in the formation of cultural identity in your context?

5. What role do the gender differences between men and women play in the formation of cultural identity? Can you give some examples?

Chapter 3

1. The Jewish author Elie Wiesel describes Cain's murder of Abel as "the first genocide." How do the details of the story in Genesis 4 bear out this description, and why is it important?

2. Can you identify ways in which your particular ethnic group shows antipathy toward another ethnic group (or groups)?

3. Some view diverse cultures as a source of conflict and sin, while others see them as a gift and a good. How have you thought about cultural difference in the past? How does this chapter challenge that thinking?

4. In what ways do contemporary depictions of racism or ethnocentrism as "systemic" reflect what we see in Scripture? In what ways do such depictions differ from Scripture?

5. This chapter deals with Genesis 3–11 and describes two different ways in which sinful humanity rejects God's purpose for a world filled with diverse peoples united in the worship of God. How do the chapters leading up to the flood narrative differ from the focus of the chapters following the flood?

6. What are some examples of ways that "unity" has become distorted into uniformity or cultural sameness?

Chapter 4

1. In light of the example of Ethiopia's emperor during the Italian occupation, what do you see as some blind spots of your nation, ethnicity, or race in terms of injustices inflicted against other people? How could the recognition of such injustices aid our relationships?

2. This chapter defines divine blessing as God's enablement of something to function in "robust fulfillment of the divine design." What are some ways that your culture functions in keeping with God's design? How have you seen this as a blessing? How have you benefited from cultures other than your own?

3. If God's purpose is to restore blessing to all peoples, why does he choose to form a covenant with only one people? What does it mean to speak of a divine and human community of reciprocal blessing?

4. In this chapter, we learned of God's initiative to restore "properly functioning peoplehood" within Israel. What are some early examples of this in Genesis? What are some things that your culture does particularly well?

5. Abraham's righteousness is evident when he disadvantages himself in order to advantage others. What does it look like when a people is righteous in this sense? Can you think of some examples?

Chapter 5

1. According to the author, why is it mistaken to describe the account of Israel's conquest of Canaan as "genocide?" What does the language of total destruction mean?

2. How does the author account for the fact that some Canaanite peoples that are said to be totally destroyed nevertheless have survivors that continue to live within Israel? Why is this significant?

3. What were the three key components of ancient conceptions of nationhood? How do they shape the conquest narratives?

4. What are some ways in which your culture of origin is marred by idolatry or unholiness—that is, not just ways in which individuals act sinfully, but patterns of sinful action that are woven into the culture?

Chapter 6

1. Why is Matthew's genealogy important for our understanding of God's purposes for peoples?

2. Matthew refers to the woman who asks Jesus to heal her demonized daughter as a "Canaanite." Given the material in the previous chapter about the conquest of Canaan, why is this important?

3. What are the types of privilege discussed in this chapter? How does Matthew's understanding of privilege differ?

4. What does the author mean in speaking about Israel as host? What are some practical ways for churches to mirror this hospitality? What are some implications for the way we think about church settings in which one culture group predominates?

Chapter 7

1. What did you find illuminating in the two stories about Samaritans in the Gospel of Luke?

2. In Acts, the gospel brings cultural destruction and destabilization. How have you seen this in your community? What might this look like in the future?

3. What practical forms did cultural renewal take in the early Christian community? What does it or could it look like in the Christian community of which you are a part?

4. What are some examples of "incorporation without assimilation" in the book of Acts? What does resistance to this idea look like in your country?

Chapter 8

1. The author introduces the concept of "spiritual ethnicity" to get at an important idea within the Gospel of John. How can this concept shape the way that we think about the meaning of ethnicity?

2. What is important about John's characterization of a group he calls "the Jews" to our understanding of ethnicity?

3. How does Jesus make use of the temple motif to speak about a unity between peoples in God's purposes?

4. Given what we have learned in this chapter about God's desire for unity, why and how does the church often confuse unity with uniformity?

5. The author states that "when difference disappears, so also does the possibility of love." What does he mean by this and how do you see it in John? Why is this important to the way that we think about the cultivation of unity between culturally different peoples?

QUESTIONS FOR STUDY OR DISCUSSION

Chapter 9

1. What was the nature of the ethnic conflict within the church at Rome?

2. What are some ways in which your culture inclines its members to sin in particular ways?

3. Given that the gospel is addressed to individuals, how does it nevertheless serve as a vital source of reconciliation between peoples?

4. How might the gospel practices identified in this chapter promote unity and reconciliation across lines of cultural difference in your community or church?

Chapter 10

1. Many governments claim to unite diverse peoples. How is "Babylon" a parody of genuine unity? To what extent do you think the rhetoric of unity falls short of reality where you live?

2. Revelation claims that every nation will be destroyed and that every nation will take its place in the new Jerusalem. How can these two expectations both be true?

3. According to the author, Revelation shows that "the healing of the nations not only results in their reconciliation but enables every people to contribute its distinctive 'glory' to the glory of God." What forms of cultural "wealth" does your nation and/or people have to contribute?

Chapter 11

1. What are some of your ideas or beliefs about cultural identity within God's purposes for humanity that have changed as a result of reading this book?

2. How does your understanding of God's purpose to form "a people of peoples" change the ways in which you pursue reconciliation and the unity of the church?

3. Human societies typically pursue unity at the cost of diversity or diversity at the cost of unity. Which form of imbalance characterizes your context? What would bring better balance?

4. In many societies, social discourse about cultural difference is framed in the language of equality, power, and rights. To what extent is this true in your context? What are the limits to this approach? Is there an alternative?

General Index

Scripture Index